AF482498

THE LANGUAGE GYM

INDONESIAN SENTENCE BUILDERS

A lexicogrammar approach

Beginner to Pre-intermediate

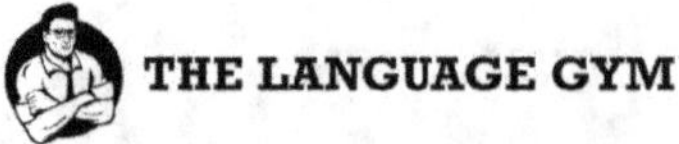

Copyright © G. Conti and D. Viñales

All rights reserved
ISBN: 9783949651502

SECOND EDITION

Imprint: Independently Published
Edited by Cici Lang

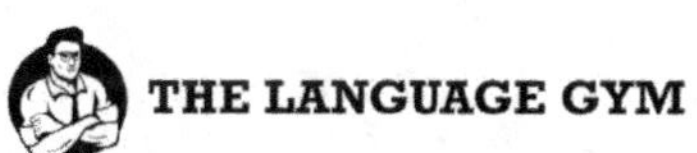

About the authors

Gianfranco Conti taught for 25 years at schools in Italy, the UK and in Kuala Lumpur, Malaysia. He has also been a university lecturer, holds a Master's degree in Applied Linguistics and a PhD in metacognitive strategies as applied to second language writing. He is now an author, a popular independent educational consultant and professional development provider. He has written around 2,000 resources for the TES website, which have awarded him the Best Resources Contributor in 2015. He has co-authored the best-selling and influential book for world languages teachers, "The Language Teacher Toolkit" and "Breaking the sound barrier: Teaching learners how to listen", in which he puts forth his Listening As Modelling methodology. Gianfranco writes an influential blog on second language acquisition called The Language Gym, co-founded the interactive website language-gym.com and the Facebook professional group Global Innovative Language Teachers (GILT). Last but not least, Gianfranco has created the instructional approach known as E.P.I. (Extensive Processing Instruction).

Dylan Viñales has taught for 15 years, in schools in Bath, Beijing and Kuala Lumpur in state, independent and international settings. He lives in Kuala Lumpur. He is fluent in five languages, and gets by in several more. Dylan is, besides a teacher, a professional development provider, specialising in E.P.I., metacognition, teaching languages through music (especially ukulele) and cognitive science. In the last five years, together with Dr Conti, he has driven the implementation of E.P.I. in one of the top international schools in the world: Garden International School. This has allowed him to test, on a daily basis, the sequences and activities included in this book with excellent results (his students have won language competitions both locally and internationally). He has designed an original Spanish curriculum, bespoke instructional materials, based on Reading and Listening as Modelling (RAM and LAM). Dylan co-founded the fastest growing professional development group for modern languages teachers on Facebook, Global Innovative Languages Teachers, which includes over 12,000 teachers from all corners of the globe. He authors an influential blog on modern language pedagogy in which he supports the teaching of languages through E.P.I. Dylan is the lead author of Spanish content on the Language Gym website and oversees the technological development of the site.

Sharon Stoyanoff taught for more than 20 years in Primary and Secondary schools in Adelaide and Melbourne, Australia. She has experience devising and implementing primary and secondary Indonesian programs, and was Head of Languages for the final years of her Secondary teaching career. She attained a Bachelor of Arts majoring in Indonesian, then a Diploma of Education (Primary), followed by a Bachelor of Education In-Service Languages Education. In addition to spending time in Papua during University days, and Java, Sulawesi and Bali for several weeks each in later years, she has completed short language courses in Indonesia at Satya Wacana University, Salatiga and at IEP, Bandung. Currently she provides editing services for the resources created by Teaching Indonesian, an online resource for Primary teachers of Indonesian.

Acknowledgements

Writing a book is a time-consuming yet rewarding endeavour. I would like to thank my husband, Michael and children, Bethany, Natasha, Amy and Jordan for enabling me to indulge my interests and forays into Education and Languages for more than 40 years. This has ultimately prepared me for the task of creating this resource for learners of Indonesian. Their support was especially significant when hosting teachers and students of varying nationalities, including Indonesian, in our family home. Thanks are due also to the numerous Languages teachers and assistants I have worked with during my career, who have demonstrated a passion for language teaching and learning. Together we encouraged our students to connect with not only the language they are learning, but also the people and culture which permeates it. To be a global citizen in these times is challenging and we should be prepared to engage with and be curious about those around us. Participation in learning languages creates connections between people and leads to understanding, tolerance and respect for differences.

Secondly, a huge thanks to our editor, Cici Lang. She is always a pleasure to work with; good humoured, extremely dedicated and with an eagle-eye. Her contributions have gone **far** beyond proofreading for accuracy, into advising on best selection of language content, and offering inter-cultural boosts along the way. Her methodical approach has enabled us to produce a book of high quality and we appreciate her valuable comments and suggestions. She has been a real asset to our team.

Lastly, our thanks to Mimi Thorpe for her valued contributions to the final edit of the book. We are truly grateful to her for lending her time and expertise to the project and for being such a helpful, positive and upbeat person to work with. Mimi's support in proofreading, and editorial comments and suggestions have been of great value in fine-tuning and refining the content of the book.

Kami mengucapkan banyak terima kasih atas dukungannya.

Introduction

Hello and welcome to the first 'text' book designed to be an accompaniment to an Indonesian, Extensive Processing Instruction course. The book has come about out of necessity, because such a resource did not previously exist.

How to use this book if you have bought into our E.P.I. approach

This book was originally designed as a resource to use in conjunction with our E.P.I. approach and teaching strategies. Our course favours flooding comprehensible input, organising content by communicative functions and related constructions, and a big focus on reading and listening as modelling. The aim of this book is to empower the beginner-to-pre-intermediate learner with linguistic tools - high-frequency structures and vocabulary - useful for real-life communication. Since, in a typical E.P.I. unit of work, aural and oral work play a huge role, this book should not be viewed as the ultimate E.P.I. coursebook, but rather as a **useful resource** to **complement** your Listening-As-Modelling and Speaking activities.

Sentence Builders – Online Versions

Please note that all these sentence builders will be available in bilingual versions on the Sentence-Builders.com website (available via subscription).

How to use this book if you don't know or have NOT bought into our approach

Alternatively, you may use this book to dip in and out of as a source of printable material for your lessons. Whilst our curriculum is driven by communicative functions rather than topics, we have deliberately embedded the target constructions in topics which are popular with teachers and commonly found in published coursebooks.

If you would like to learn about E.P.I. you could read one of the authors' blogs. The definitive guide is Dr Conti's "Patterns First – How I Teach Lexicogrammar" which can be found on his blog (www.gianfrancoconti.com). There are also blogs on Dylan's wordpress site (mrvinalesmfl.wordpress.com) such as "Using sentence builders to reduce (everyone's) workload and create more fluent linguists" which can be read to get teaching ideas and to learn how to structure a course, through all the stages of E.P.I.

The book "Breaking the Sound Barrier: Teaching Learners how to Listen" by Gianfranco Conti and Steve Smith, provides a detailed description of the approach and of the listening and speaking activities you can use in synergy with the present book.

The basic structure of the book

The book contains 19 macro-units which concern themselves with a specific communicative function, such as 'Describing people's appearance and personality', 'Comparing and contrasting people', 'Saying what you like and dislike' or 'Saying what you and others do in your free time'. You can find a note of each communicative function in the Table of Contents. Each unit includes:

- a sentence builder modelling the target constructions;
- a set of vocabulary building activities which reinforce the material in the sentence builder;
- a set of narrow reading texts exploited through a range of tasks focusing on both the meaning and structural levels of the text;
- a set of translation tasks aimed at consolidation through retrieval practice;
- a set of writing tasks targeting essential writing micro-skills such as spelling, functional and positional processing, editing and communication of meaning.

Each sentence builder at the beginning of a unit contains one or more constuctions which have been selected with real-life communication in mind. Each unit is built around that construction <u>but not solely on it</u>. Based on the principle that each E.P.I instructional sequence must move from modelling to production in a seamless and organic way, each unit expands on the material in each sentence builder by embedding it in texts and graded tasks which contain both familiar and unfamiliar (but comprehensible and learnable) vocabulary and structures. Through lots of careful recycling and thorough and extensive processing of the input, by the end of each unit the student has many opportunities to encounter and process the new vocabulary and patterns with material from the previous units.

Alongside the macro-units you will find:

- grammar units: one or two pages of activities occurring at regular intervals. They explicitly focus on key grammar structures which enhance the generative power of the constructions in the sentence builders.
- question-skills units: one or two pages on understanding and creating questions. These micro-units too occur at regular intervals in the book, so as to recycle the same question patterns in different linguistic contexts;
- revision quickies: these are retrieval practice tasks aimed at keeping the previously learnt vocabulary alive. These too occur at regular intervals;
- self-tests: these occur at the end of the book. They are divided into two sections, one for less confident and one for more confident learners.

The point of all the above micro-units is to implement lots of systematic recycling and interleaving, two techniques that allow for stronger retention and transfer of learning.

Important *caveat*

1) This is a '**no frills**' book. This means that there are a limited number of illustrations (only on unit title pages). This is because we want every single little thing in this book to be useful. Consequently, we have packed a substantive amount of content at the detriment of its outlook. In particular, we have given serious thought to both **recycling** and **interleaving**, in order to allow for key constructions, words and grammar items to be revisited regularly so as to enhance exponentially their retention.

2) **Listening** as modelling is an essential part of E.P.I. There will be an accompanying listening booklet released shortly which will contain narrow listening exercises for all 19 units, following the same content as this book.

3) **All content** in this booklet matches the content on the **Language Gym** website. For best results, we recommend a mixture of communicative, retrieval practice games, combined with Language Gym games and workouts, and then this booklet as the follow-up, either in class or for homework.

4) An **answer booklet** is also available, for those that would like it. We have produced it separately to stop this booklet from being excessively long.

5) This booklet is suitable for **beginner** to **pre-intermediate** learners. This equates to a **CEFR A1-A2** level, or a beginner **Y6-Y8** class. You do not need to start at the beginning, although you may want to dip in to certain units for revision/recycling. You do not need to follow the booklet in order, although many of you will, and if you do, you will benefit from the specific recycling/interleaving strategies. Either way, all topics are repeated frequently throughout the book.

We do hope that you and your students will find this book useful and enjoyable.

Gianfranco, Dylan & Sharon

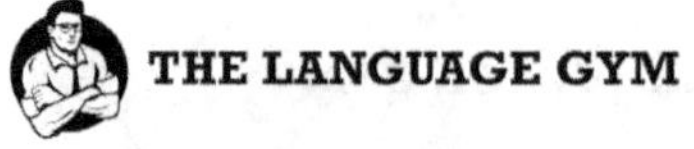

TABLE OF CONTENTS

UNIT 1
Talking about my age

> **In this unit you will learn:**
>
> - How to say your name and age
> - How to say someone else's name and age
> - How to count from 1 to 16
> - A range of common Indonesian names
> - The words for brother and sister

Umur saya satu tahun

Umur saya sepuluh tahun

Umur saya lima belas tahun

Umur saya enam tahun

THE LANGUAGE GYM

UNIT 1
Talking about my age

Siapa nama kamu* dan berapa umur kamu? *What is your name and how old are you?*
Siapa namamu dan berapa umurmu?

Siapa nama ……. kamu dan berapa umurnya? *What is your ….'s name and how old are they?*

Nama saya *My name is* **Saya bernama** *I am named*	**Anisa** **Bayu** **Dewi** **Gunadi** **Irfan**		**umur saya** *my age* **saya berumur** *I am aged* **saya berusia** *I am aged*	**satu** 1 **dua** 2 **tiga** 3 **empat** 4 **lima** 5 **enam** 6 **tujuh** 7	**tahun** *year/years old*
Nama adik saya **OR** **Adik saya bernama** *My younger sibling's name is* **Nama kakak saya** **OR** **Kakak saya bernama** *My older sibling's name is*	**Iva** **Kadek** **Kristiono** **Mahmud** **Melati** **Ratu** **Sari**	**dan** *and*	**umur dia** *his/her age* **umurnya** *his/her age* **dia berumur** *he/she is aged* **dia berusia** *he/she is aged*	**delapan** 8 **sembilan** 9 **sepuluh** 10 **sebelas** 11 **dua belas** 12 **tiga belas** 13 **empat belas** 14 **lima belas** 15 **enam belas** 16	
Saya punya *I have a*	****adik** *younger* ****kakak** *older* *****saudara** *sibling/s*			**laki-laki** *brother* **perempuan** *sister*	

Author's notes:

*****Anda** *or* **kamu***? In general, the exercises in this book are designed to prompt conversation between students, therefore* **kamu** *has been used. When a social connection is unknown, the formal word* **Anda** *must be used in interactions.* **Kamu** *can be shortened to* **mu** *and added to the end of a noun, e.g.* **namamu** *– your name*

***In Indonesian, siblings are primarily referred to as 'older' or 'younger' rather than as 'brothers' or 'sisters' as in English.* **Adik** *is a younger brother or sister while* **kakak** *is an older brother or sister. The terms* **laki-laki** *or* **perempuan** *can be added to* **adik** *or* **kakak** *to indicate if the sibling is a brother or sister, e.g.* **adik laki-laki** *'little brother' or* **kakak perempuan** *'older sister'.*

****The word* **saudara** *can be used to identify a relative and in this case a sibling. It is especially useful when it is not indicated whether the sibling is older or younger. (It can also be used as a formal word for 'you'.)*

Unit 1. Talking about my age: VOCABULARY BUILDING

1. Match up

satu tahun	seven years
dua tahun	four years
tiga tahun	five years
empat tahun	six years
lima tahun	eleven years
enam tahun	ten years
tujuh tahun	nine years
delapan tahun	two years
sembilan tahun	eight years
sepuluh tahun	one year
sebelas tahun	twelve years
dua belas tahun	three years

2. Complete with the missing word

a. Umur saya __________ tahun — *I am fourteen years old*

b. Nama adik __________ Irfan — *My brother is called Irfan*

c. __________ Melati — *My name is Melati*

d. Umur __________ dua tahun — *My little brother is two*

e. Umur __________ sebelas tahun — *My older sister is eleven*

f. __________ saya Dewi — *My older sister's name is Dewi*

Nama saya	saya	adik saya
kakak saya	Nama kakak	empat belas

3. Translate into English

a. Umur saya tiga tahun

b. Saya berumur lima tahun

c. Saya berusia sebelas tahun

d. Umurnya lima belas tahun

e. Dia berumur tiga belas tahun

f. Umur dia tujuh tahun

g. Adik saya

h. Kakak saya

i. Nama saya

4. Broken words

a. Dua be_____ *twelve*

b. Nama say____ *my name is*

c. Kak______ *my older sibling*

d. Lim_____ *fifteen*

e. Ena______ *sixteen*

f. Seb_____ *eleven*

g. Sem_____ *nine*

h. Emp______ *fourteen*

i. Du_____ *twelve*

5. Rank the people below from oldest to youngest as shown in the example

Umur Iva lima belas tahun	1
Bayu berumur tiga belas tahun	
Umur Kristiono dua tahun	
Umur Anisa empat tahun	
Sari berusia satu tahun	
Umur Gunadi lima tahun	
Umur Melati sembilan tahun	
Ratu berumur tiga tahun	

6. For each pair of people write who is the oldest, as shown in the example

A	B	OLDER
Umur saya sebelas tahun	Umur saya tiga belas tahun	B
Saya berumur tiga tahun	Saya berumur enam tahun	
Umur dia sebelas tahun	Umur dia dua belas tahun	
Umur saya lima belas tahun	Umur saya tiga belas tahun	
Umur saya empat belas tahun	Umur saya sebelas tahun	
Saya berusia delapan tahun	Saya berusia sembilan tahun	
Umurnya sebelas tahun	Umurnya tujuh tahun	

Unit 1. Talking about my age: READING

Nama saya Ali. Saya orang Indonesia. Saya berumur dua belas tahun dan saya tinggal di Jakarta, ibu kota negara Indonesia. Saya punya seorang kakak yang bernama Iriana. Iriana berumur empat belas tahun.

Nama saya Ruben. Saya orang Indonesia. Umur saya sepuluh tahun dan saya tinggal di Sentani, di provinsi Papua. Saya punya seorang adik bernama Markus dan seorang kakak bernama Ndeli. Umur Markus lima tahun dan umur Ndeli sembilan belas tahun.

Nama saya Kadek. Saya orang Bali. Saya berumur tiga belas tahun dan saya tinggal di Denpasar, ibu kota provinsi Bali. Saya punya kakak yang bernama Wayan. Wayan berumur lima belas tahun.

Nama saya Marina. Saya orang Malaysia. Saya berumur sepuluh tahun dan saya tinggal di Kuala Lumpur, ibu kota negara Malaysia. Saya punya seorang kakak bernama Izzati. Izzati berusia sebelas tahun. Saya juga punya seorang adik bernama Azfar. Azfar berusia delapan tahun.

Nama saya Ferlyn. Saya orang Singapura. Saya berumur tujuh tahun dan saya tinggal di pulau Sentosa. Saya punya seorang kakak perempuan yang bernama Huan. Huan berumur tiga belas tahun. Saya juga mempunyai seorang kakak laki-laki yang bernama Devan. Devan berumur sepuluh tahun.

Nama saya Jasmin. Saya berasal dari Brunei. Saya berumur empat belas tahun dan saya tinggal di Bandar Seri Begawan. Saya punya dua kakak. Nama kakak saya Nazif dan Zaini. Nazif berumur enam belas tahun dan umur Zaini lima belas tahun.

1. Find the Indonesian for the following items in Ali's text

a. I am Indonesian

b. I am called

c. the capital city

d. in Jakarta

e. who is called Iriana

f. I am twelve

g. is fourteen years old

2. Answer the following questions about Ruben

a. Where is Ruben from?

b. How old is he?

c. How many siblings does he have?

d. What are their names and ages?

3. Complete the table below

	Age	Nationality	How many siblings	Ages of siblings
Ali				
Ruben				
Marina				

4. Marina, Kadek, Ferlyn or Jasmin?

a. Who is from Brunei?

b. Who has an 13-year-old sister?

c. Who is 11?

d. Who has an older brother aged 16?

e. Who has a 15-year old brother?

Unit 1. Talking about my age: TRANSLATION

1. Faulty translation: spot and correct (in the English) any translation mistakes you find below

a. Nama kakak saya Anisa: *Her name is Anisa*

b. Saya punya dua kakak perempuan: *I have two brothers*

c. Kakak saya bernama Dian: *My mother is called Dian*

d. Umur adik laki-laki saya lima tahun: *My sister is 5 years old*

e. Umur saya lima belas tahun: *I am five years old*

f. Umur adik laki-laki saya delapan tahun:

My brother is seven years old

g. Saya punya seorang kakak: *I don't have a sister*

h. Saya berumur enam belas tahun: *I am 17*

i. Umur saya dua belas tahun: *I am 13*

j. Nama kakak saya Junaidi: *My name is Junaidi*

2. From Indonesian to English

a. Nama kakak laki-laki saya Mahmud.

b. Umur saya lima belas tahun.

c. Umur adik saya enam tahun.

d. Nama adik perempuan saya Maria.

e. Umur saya tujuh tahun.

f. Saya tinggal di kota Bandung.

g. Umur kakak saya empat belas tahun.

h. Saya punya dua adik dan satu kakak.

i. Ratu berumur dua belas tahun.

j. Iskandar berusia sembilan tahun.

3. English to Indonesian translation

a. My name is Gunadi. I am six.

b. My brother is fifteen years old.

c. I am twelve.

d. My sister is called Kartika.

e. I am fourteen.

f. I have a brother and a sister.

g. My name is Dewi and I am fourteen.

h. My name is Ahmad and I am eleven.

i. My name is Devan. I am ten. I have a brother and a sister.

j. My sister is called Balqis. She is twelve.

Unit 1. Talking about my age: WRITING

1. Complete the words

a. Na__________ sa__________ Anisa

b. Saya beru______ tiga be______ ta________

c. Umur adik saya li__________ ta____________

d. Na________ kakak saya Mahmud

e. Na________ saya Reza

f. Nama ad________ saya Irfan

g. U__________ saya tiga ta________

h. Na______ saya Sari

2. Write out the numbers in Indonesian

nine	s__________________
seven	t__________________
twelve	d__________________
five	l__________________
fourteen	e__________________
sixteen	e__________________
thirteen	t__________________
four	e__________________

3. Spot and correct the spelling mistakes

a. Nana saya Melati.

b. Umur kakak saya lila tahun.

c. Nama kadak saya Ali.

d. Namo adik saya Dewi.

e. Nama soya Muklis.

f. Umur kakak saya sapuluh tahun.

4. Complete with a suitable word

a. ______________ kakak saya Bayu.

b. Umur kakak saya lima belas __________.

c. ________ saya Rizal.

d. Nama adik __________ Yusuf.

e. ________ adik saya Susi.

f. __________ kakak saya empat belas tahun.

5. Guided writing – Write 4 short paragraphs describing these children and their siblings

	Age	Lives in	Nationality or Ethnicity	Brother's name and age	Sister's name and age
Novita	12	Jakarta	Indonesia	Agus 9	Fifi 8
Wayan	15	Lovina	Bali	Kadek 13	Nyoman 5
Martinus	11	Flores	Indonesia	Markus 7	Lidya 12
Benny	10	Surabaya	Tionghoa	Rizal 6	Siti 1

6. Describe this person in the third person:

Name: Susi

Age: 12

Lives in: Bandung

Brother: Irfan, 13 years old

Sister: Iva, 15 years old

UNIT 2
Saying when my birthday is

In this unit you will learn to say:

- Where you and another person (e.g. a friend) are from
- When your birthday is
- Numbers from 17 to 31
- Months
- I am / He is / She is
- Names of Indonesian speaking locations
- Where you live

THE LANGUAGE GYM

UNIT 2
Saying when my birthday is

Siapa nama kamu? *What is your name?*

Kamu berasal dari mana? *Where do you come from?*

Kapan hari ulang tahun kamu ? *When is your birthday?*

Kamu lahir pada bulan apa? *You were born in what month?*

Siapa nama temanmu? *What is your friend's name?*

Dia berasal dari mana? *Where does he/she come from?*

Hari ulang tahun temanmu pada tanggal berapa? *When is your friend's birthday ?*

Dia lahir pada bulan apa? *He/she was born in what month?*

Nama saya ... *My name is ...*	**Saya berasal dari ....** *I am from ...* **Umur saya ... tahun** *I am ... years old*	**dan hari ulang tahun saya pada tanggal** *and my birthday is on the* **dan saya lahir pada tanggal** *and I was born on the*	**1 - satu** **2- dua** **3 - tiga** **4 - empat** **5 - lima** **6 - enam** **7 - tujuh** **8 - delapan** **9 - sembilan** **10 - sepuluh** **11 - sebelas** **12 - dua belas** **13 - tiga belas** **14 - empat belas** **15 - lima belas** **16 - enam belas** **17 - tujuh belas** **18 - delapan belas** **19 - sembilan belas** **20 - dua puluh** **21 - dua puluh satu** **22 - dua puluh dua** **23 - dua puluh tiga** **24 - dua puluh empat** **25 - dua puluh lima** **26 - dua puluh enam** **27 - dua puluh tujuh** **28 - dua puluh delapan** **29 - dua puluh sembilan** **30 - tiga puluh** **31 - tiga puluh satu**	**Januari** **Februari** **Maret** **April** **Mei** **Juni** **Juli** **Agustus** **September** **Oktober** **November** **Desember**
Nama teman saya ..... *My friend's name is ....*	**Dia berasal dari ....** *he/she comes from .....* **Umur dia* ... tahun** *he/she is ... years old*	**dan hari ulang tahun dia pada tanggal** *and his/her birthday is on the* **dan dia lahir pada tanggal** *and he/she was born on the*		

dan *and*	**saya** *I was* **dia** *he/she was*	**lahir pada** *born in the*	**bulan** *month of*

Author's note:

Remember! The Indonesian language uses the word **dia to describe all genders. You will see it many times throughout this booklet!* ☺

Unit 2. Saying when my birthday is: VOCABULARY BUILDING

1. Complete with the missing word

a. Nama _______Gunadi   *My name is Gunadi*

b. _________ teman saya Siti   *My friend's name is Siti*

c. Nama _________ saya Ruben.   *My friend's name is Ruben*

d. Hari ulang tahun _____ pada …   *My birthday is on …*

e. pada tanggal lima _______   *on the fifth of May*

f. tanggal__________ November   *the 8th of November*

g. _________ empat belas Juli   *the 4th of July*

h. Hari ulang _______ dia pada…   *His/her birthday is on the…*

2. Match up

bulan	May
November	birthday
Desember	my friend
Mei	month
Januari	November
Februari	he/she is called
hari ulang tahun	December
teman saya	My name is
pada tanggal	February
nama saya	January
nama dia	on the date

3. Translate into English

a. empat belas Januari

b. dua puluh delapan Juli

c. tujuh Februari

d. dua puluh delapan Maret

e. hari ulang tahun saya

f. pada bulan Mei

g. dia lahir pada tanggal

h. pada tanggal tiga Juni

4. Add the missing letter

a. Januar_   c. M_ret   e. M_i   g. Jul_   i. Se_tember   k. No_ember

b. Februar_   d. Ap_il   f. Jun_   h. A_ustus   j. O_tober   l. De_ember

5. Broken words

a. t________ t__________ J____________   *3ʳᵈ January*

b. t________ l_________ J____________   *5ᵗʰ July*

c. t________ s__________ A____________   *9ᵗʰ August*

d t________ d____ b______ M__________   *12ᵗʰ March*

e. t________ e_____ b_____ A________   *16ᵗʰ April*

f. t_________ s______ b_____ D______   *19ᵗʰ December*

g. t________ d___ p______ O_________   *20ᵗʰ October*

h. t________ d___ p______ e_____ M___   *24ᵗʰ May*

i. T________ T_____p_____ S__________   *30ᵗʰ September*

6. Complete with a suitable word

a. Nama ____________ Anisa

b. Saya ______ pada tanggal 2 April

c. Nama teman _________ Bayu

d. Hari ulang _____ saya tanggal 13 Mei

e. _________ ulang tahun dia

f. _______dia dua belas tahun

g. Saya lahir _______ tiga belas Juni

h. Teman _____________ bernama

i. Dia lahir pada __________ Maret

j. Dia ____________ dari Jakarta

k. _____________ dia Wayan

Nama saya Susi. Saya berumur dua belas tahun dan saya tinggal di Bandung. Hari ulang tahun saya pada tanggal dua belas September. Nama teman saya Kristiyana dan dia berumur empat belas tahun. Hari ulang tahunnya pada tanggal dua puluh delapan Mei. Pada waktu luang saya selalu bermain gitar. Kristiyana juga! Teman saya bernama Cinta. Dia berumur tiga puluh lima tahun dan dia seorang guru. Dia lahir pada tanggal dua puluh satu Juni. Cinta punya seorang kakak laki-laki. Dia lahir pada tanggal delapan Januari.

Nama saya Niki. Saya berumur dua puluh dua tahun dan saya tinggal di Palembang, di Sumatra Selatan. Hari ulang tahun saya pada tanggal sepuluh September. Teman saya bernama Natasya dan dia berumur lima belas tahun. Hari ulang tahunnya pada tanggal dua puluh delapan Mei. Pada waktu luang saya selalu menonton televisi.

Nama saya Aminah. Saya berumur tujuh tahun dan saya tinggal di Kuala Lumpur, ibu kota Malaysia. Hari ulang tahun saya pada tanggal lima Desember. Saya punya dua orang kakak, Nahmad dan Rahmad. Nahmad berumur sebelas tahun dan dia sangat baik. Dia lahir pada tanggal tiga puluh September. Rahmad sangat nakal. Dia berumur tiga belas tahun dan hari ulang tahunnya pada tanggal lima Januari.

Nama saya Nara. Saya berusia delapan tahun dan saya tinggal di Balikpapan, di Kalimantan. Hari ulang tahun saya pada tanggal sembilan Agustus. Adik perempuan saya berusia empat tahun. Dia anak yang baik. Hari ulang tahunnya juga pada tanggal sembilan Agustus. Sama dengan saya! Nama teman saya Mamut dan dia berusia tujuh belas tahun. Dia lahir pada tanggal dua puluh lima Oktober.

1. Find the Indonesian for the following items in Susi's text

a. I am called:

b. I am 12 years old:

c. I live in Bandung:

d. My birthday is:

e. the twelfth of:

f. her birthday is on:

g. in my free time:

h. my friend:

i. is called:

j. she is 35:

k. the 21st of June:

l. has an older brother:

m. the eighth of January:

3. Answer these questions about Aminah

a. How old is she?

b. Where is Kuala Lumpur?

c. When is her birthday?

d. How many brothers does she have?

e. Which brother is good?

f. How old is Rahmad?

g. When is his birthday?

2. Complete with the missing words

Nama _____________ Nara.

_________ saya delapan

______ dan saya tinggal

_______ Balikpapan. ______

teman saya Mamut. Saya lahir

pada __________ Agustus.

4. Find Someone Who...

a. ...has a birthday in December

b. ...is 22 years old

c. ...shares a birthday with a sibling

d. ...likes to play the guitar with their friend

e. ...has a friend who is 35 years old

f. ...has a birthday in late September

g. ...has a little sister

h. ...has one good and one bad sibling

i. ...is from the South Sumatra

Unit 2. Saying when my birthday is: WRITING

1. Complete with the missing letters

a. Na_ _ saya Paulus

b. Say_ tinggal d_ Bandung

c. Saya lah_ _ pada tanggal li_ _ Jun_

d. Ha_ _ ula_ _ tah _ _ saya

e. Tem_ _ saya bern_ _ _ Cinta

f. Cinta tingg _ _ di Surabaya

g. T _ man saya tin _ _ al d_ Jayapura

h. Hari la_ _ r Mahmut semb_ _ an A_ _stus

2. Spot and correct the spelling mistakes

a. Saya lehir pada tanggal empat Januari

b. Namo saya Putu

c. Saya berasal di Jakarta

d. Taman saya bernama Cinta

e. Iva berumur sebelas tahan.

f. Umur saya emat belas tahun.

g. Hari ulang tahun saya satu Marat

h. Umur saya lima balas tahun

3. Answer the questions in Indonesian

Siapa nama kamu?

Berapa umurmu?

Hari ulang tahun kamu pada tanggal berapa?

Berapa umur adik atau kakakmu?

Adik atau kakakmu lahir pada bulan apa?

4. Write out the dates below in words as shown in the example

a. 15.05 *lima belas Mei*

b. 10.06

c. 20.03

d. 19.02

e. 25.12

f. 01.01

g. 22.11

h. 14.10

5. Guided writing – write 4 short paragraphs in the 1st person singular 'I' describing the people below

Name	Town/City	Age	Birthday	Name of brother	Brother's birthday
Rizal	Medan	11	25.12	Ismail	19.02
Sanja	Palu	14	21.07	Mahmud	21.04
Yohanes	Ambon	12	01.01	Markus	20.06
Ratu	Salatiga	16	02.11	Agus	12.10

6. Describe this person in the third person:

Name: Lestari

Age: 12

Lives in: Surabaya, East Java

Birthday: 21.06

Brother: Mahmud, 16 years old

Birthday: 01.12

Unit 2. Saying when my birthday is: TRANSLATION

1. Faulty translation: spot and correct (in the English) any translation mistakes you find

a. Hari ulang tahun saya pada dua puluh delapan April: *His birthday is on the 28th April*

b. Nama saya Robert dan saya berasal dari Kuala Lumpur: *Your name is Robert and you are from Kuala Lumpur*

c. Saya berumur dua puluh tiga tahun: *I am 22 years old*

d. Nama teman saya Jordi: *My friend I am called Jordi*

e. Dia berumur dua puluh enam tahun: *I have 26 years old*

f. Hari ulang tahunnya 4 April: *My birthday is the 14th April*

g. Saya tinggal di Merauke: *I come from Merauke*

2. Translate from Indonesian to English

a. tanggal delapan Oktober

b. Hari ulang tahun saya pada...

c. Nama teman saya ...

d. Hari ulang tahun dia pada...

e. sebelas Januari

f. empat belas Februari

g. dua puluh lima Desember

h. lahir pada bulan Juni

i. pada tanggal satu Juni

3. Phrase-level translation

a. My name is

b. I am ten years old

c. My birthday is the...

d. ...the seventh of May

e. My friend is called Balqis

f. She is twelve years old

g. Her birthday is the...

h. The 23rd of August

i. The 29th April

4. Sentence-level translation

a. My name is Kristiono. I am 30 years old. I live in Palembang. My birthday is on the 11th March.

b. My brother is called Mahmud. He is 14 years old. His birthday is on the 18th August.

c. My friend is called Agus. He is 22 years old and his birthday is on the 14th January.

d. My friend is called Nana. She is 18 years old and her birthday is on the 25th July.

e. My friend is called Gede. He is 20 years old. His birthday is on the 24th September.

UNIT 3
Describing hair and eyes

In this unit you will learn:

- To describe what a person's hair and eyes are like
- To describe details about their faces (e.g. beard and glasses)
- Colours
- I wear
- He/she wears

You will also revisit:
- Common Indonesian names
- Numbers from 1 to 16

UNIT 3
Describing hair and eyes

Siapa nama kamu? *What is your name?*		**Siapa namanya?** *What is his/her/their name?*	
Berapa umur kamu? *How old are you?*		**Berapa umurnya?** *How old is he/she (are they)?*	

Nama saya ... *My name is* **Nama dia** or **Namanya** *His/Her name is*	**Ahmad** **Cici** **Dilah** **Ismail** **Mariam** **Lestari** **Yusuf** **Yuliah**	**dan** *and*	**saya berumur** *my age is* **dia berumur** *he/she is aged*	**sepuluh tahun** *10 years* **sebelas tahun** *11 years* **dua belas tahun** *12 years* **tiga belas tahun** *13 years* **empat belas tahun** *14 years* **lima belas tahun** *15 years* **enam belas tahun** *16 years*

Bagaimana rambut kamu? *What is your hair like?* **Bagaimana rambutnya?** *What is his/her hair like?*

Saya berambut *I have hair (that is)* **Dia berambut** *He/She has hair that is*			**cokelat** *brown*	**dan** *and*	**berombak, ikal** *wavy* **keriting** *curly* **lurus** *straight* **panjang** *long* **pendek** *short* **sangat pendek** *very short / crew-cut* **setengah panjang** *medium length*
Rambut saya *My hair* **Rambut dia** or **Rambutnya** *His/Her/Their hair*	**berwarna** *is coloured*		**cokelat tua** *dark brown* **hitam** *black* **jingga** *red* **pirang** *blond*		

Dia botak. *He/She is bald.*

Apa warna mata kamu? *What colour are your eyes?* **Apa warna matanya?** *What colour are his/her eyes?*

Saya bermata *I have eyes that are* **Dia bermata** *He/She has eyes that are*			**abu-abu** *grey* **biru** *blue*	**dan** *and*	**saya** *I* **saya tidak** *I don't*	**berjenggot** *have/has a beard*
Mata saya *My eyes* **Mata dia** or **Matanya** *His / Her eyes*	**berwarna** *are coloured*		**cokelat** *brown* **cokelat muda** *light brown* **hijau** *green*		**dia** *he/she* **dia tidak** *he/she doesn't*	**berkacamata** *wear/s glasses* **berkumis** *have/has a moustache*

Unit 3. Describing hair and eyes: VOCABULARY BUILDING

1. Complete with the missing word/s

a. Rambut saya berwarna _________   *I have brown hair*

b. Saya berambut _______________   *I have blond hair*

c. Dia _______________________   *He has a beard*

d. Mata saya _______________ biru   *I have blue eyes*

e. Saya _____________ berkacamata   *I don't wear glasses*

f. Rambut saya _________ _________   *My hair is mid-length*

g. _______________ berwarna hijau   *Her eyes are green*

h. _________ _______________ merah   *She has red hair*

2. Match up

rambut pirang	brown hair
rambut hitam	black eyes
rambut cokelat	moustache
mata hitam	green eyes
kacamata	black hair
kumis	short hair
mata biru	long hair
mata hijau	red hair
rambut pendek	blond hair
rambut panjang	glasses
rambut merah	blue eyes

3. Translate into English

a. rambutnya

b. mata biru

c. berkumis

d. berwarna pirang

e. cokelat dan keriting

f. rambut sangat pendek

g. tidak berkacamata

h. mata berwarna cokelat gelap

4. Add the missing letter

a. ber_arna   c. _endek   e. lu_us   g. hit_m   i. panj_ng   k. _erah

b. ti_ak   d. ber_umis   f. cok_lat   h. ram _ ut   j. keri_ing   l. ma_a

5. Broken words

a. S______ b____________ k_________   *I have curly hair*

b. S______ b______________________   *I wear glasses*

c. R_________ s________ p________   *My hair is short*

d. S______ t______ b__________   *I don't have a moustache*

e. M_______ d____ b_________ c________   *His eyes are brown*

f. D_______ b__________________   *He has a beard*

g. S______ b_____ s______ t_______   *I am eleven years old*

h. N______ s______ Y__________   *My name is Yusuf*

i. S____ b______ s_______ t_______   *I am ten years old*

6. Complete with a suitable word

a. _______________ saya Mariam

b. _______________ berjenggot

c. Saya __________ berkacamata

d. _______________ saya keriting

e. Saya _______________ panjang

f. Rambutnya __________ hitam

g. Mata dia ___________cokelat

h. _______ saya berwarna pirang

i. __________ dia berwarna biru

j. Saya berambut hitam ___ pendek

k. _______________ Ahmad

l. Dia ___________ delapan tahun

Unit 3. Describing hair and eyes: READING

Nama saya Melati. Saya berumur dua belas tahun dan saya tinggal di Sentosa, di negara Singapura. Saya punya rambut hitam, lurus, pendek dan bermata cokelat. Saya berkacamata. Hari ulang tahun saya pada tanggal sepuluh September. Rambut kakak saya lurus. Dia berumur sepuluh tahun.

Nama saya Iva. Saya berumur lima belas tahun dan saya tinggal di Bandung, di provinsi Jawa Barat. Rambut saya merah, panjang, berombak dan mata saya berwarna cokelat. Saya tidak berkacamata. Saya lahir pada tanggal lima belas Desember.

Nama saya Joey. Saya berumur sembilan tahun dan saya tinggal di Adelaide, ibu kota negara bagian Australia Selatan. Rambut saya berwarna cokelat, sedang panjang, ikal dan mata saya berwarna cokelat. Saya tidak berkacamata. Saya lahir pada tanggal lima Desember. Nama kakak saya Travis. Dia berumur lima belas tahun. Rambutnya merah, lurus dan panjang dan dia bermata hijau. Dia berkacamata. Hari ulang tahunnya pada tanggal tiga belas November.

Nama saya Alina. Saya berumur delapan tahun dan saya tinggal di Ambon, di provinsi Maluku. Saya berambut pirang, kerinting, panjang dan mata saya berwarna hijau. Saya berkacamata. Saya lahir pada tanggal sembilan Mei. Di rumah saya, ada tiga hewan, seekor kuda, seekor anjing dan seekor kucing. Nama kakak saya Sazlan. Dia berumur empat belas tahun. Rambut dia berwarna pirang, panjang, lurus dan matanya berwarna hijau, sama seperti saya. Dia berkacamata, seperti bapak saya. Hari ulang tahunnya pada tanggal dua Juni.

Nama saya Pahmi. Saya berusia sepuluh tahun dan saya tinggal di Denpasar, ibu kota provinsi Bali. Rambut saya berwarna pirang, pendek, lurus dan mata saya berwarna hijau. Saya berkacamata. Hari ulang tahun saya pada tanggal delapan April.

1. Find the Indonesian for the following items in Melati's text

a. I am called:

b. In:

c. I wear glasses:

d. My birthday is:

e. The tenth of:

f. I have:

g. Straight:

h. Black:

i. Eyes:

2. Answer the following questions about Iva's text

a. How old is she?

b. Where is Bandung?

c. What colour is her hair?

d. Is her hair wavy, straight or curly?

e. What length is her hair?

f. What colour are her eyes?

g. When is her birthday?

3. Complete with the missing words

Nama saya Pahmi. Saya _______ sepuluh tahun dan saya tinggal di _________ ibu kota, ______ ______. Rambut saya _________ pirang, lurus, pendek dan __________ saya berwarna hijau. Saya ________________. ______ ______ ______ saya pada tanggal delapan April.

4. Answer the questions below about all five texts

a. Who has a brother called Sazlan?

b. Who is eight years old?

c. Who celebrates their birthday on 9 May?

d. How many people wear glasses?

e. Who has red hair and green-coloured eyes?

f. Who has a fifteen year old brother?

g. Whose birthday is in April?

h. Who has brown, wavy hair and brown eyes?

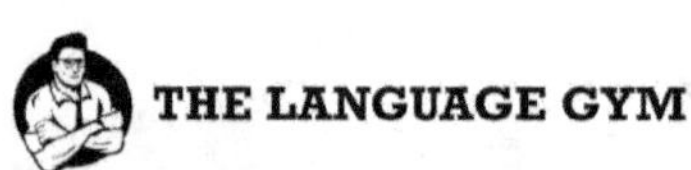

Unit 3. Describing hair and eyes: TRANSLATION

1. Faulty translation: spot and correct (in the English) any translation mistakes you find

a. Rambut saya pirang: *I have black hair*

b. Matanya berwarna biru: *He/she has brown eyes*

c. Saya berjenggot: *He has a beard*

d. Namanya Paulus: *I am called Paulus*

e. Dia botak: *He has long hair*

f. Matanya berwarna hijau: *I have green eyes*

g. Saya tinggal di Jakarta: *I am from Jakarta*

2. From Indonesian to English

a. Saya berambut pirang

b. Mata saya berwarna hitam

c. Rambut saya lurus

d. Saya berkacamata dan berjenggot.

e. Saya berkumis.

f. Saya berkacamata.

g. Saya tidak berjenggot.

h. Rambut saya keriting.

i. Saya berambut panjang.

3. Phrase-level translation

a. blond hair

b. my name is

c. my hair

d. blue eyes

e. straight hair

f. he/she has

g. ten years old

h. dark brown hair

i. wears glasses

j. brown eyes

k. black hair

4. Sentence-level translation

a. My name is Fahrul. I am ten years old. I have black and curly hair and blue eyes.

b. I am twelve years old. I have green eyes and blond, straight hair.

c. I am called Kemala. I live in Kendari. I have long blond hair. My eyes are brown.

d. My name is Sofi. I live in Lombok. I have black hair, very short and wavy.

e. I am fifteen years old. I have black, curly long hair and green eyes.

f. I am thirteen years old. I have red, straight long hair and brown eyes.

Unit 3. Describing hair and eyes: WRITING

1. Split sentences

a. Rambut saya	saya berwarna hijau
b. Saya	saya pirang
c. Rambut	berjenggot
d. Rambut saya	keriting
e. Saya berambut pirang dan mata	berwarna hitam
f. Nama saya	sepuluh tahun
g. Saya berumur	Lestari

2. Rewrite the sentences in the correct order

a. saya rambut keriting

b. tidak saya berjenggot

c. saya nama Dilah

d. berambut saya merah

e. dia nama Ismail

3. Spot and correct the grammar and spelling errors

a. Mata saya bewarna hitam

b. Adik saya nama Ahmad

c. Dia berrambut keriting

d. Dia nama Yuliah.

e. Saya beumur empat belas

f. Rambut lurus saya

g. Mata saya hijua

h. Saya berjengot

i. Saya bekacamata

j. Saya tidak berkummis

4. Anagrams

a. trambu

b. tengjog

c. tama

d. nutha

e. rubi

f. ripgan

g. thima

h. rinktige

5. Guided writing – write 3 short paragraphs in the first person singular 'I' describing the people below

Name	Age	Hair	Eyes	Glasses	Beard	Moustache
Ahmad	12	Brown Curly Long	Green	Wears	Does not have	Has
Fira	11	Blond Straight Short	Blue	Doesn't wear	Does not have	Does not have
Agus	10	Red Wavy Medium-length	Black	Wears	Does not have	Does not have

6. Describe this person in the third person:

Name: Yusuf

Age: 15

Hair: Black, curly, very short

Eyes: Brown

Glasses: No

Beard: Yes

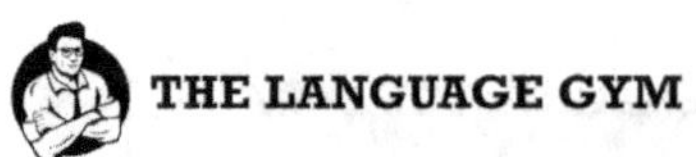

UNIT 4
Saying where I live and am from

In this unit you will learn to talk about:

- Where you live and are from
- If you live in an apartment or a house
- What your accommodation looks like
- Where it is located
- The names of cities and islands in Indonesia

You will also revisit:

- Introducing yourself
- Telling age and birthday

UNIT 4 Saying where I live and am from

Nama saya … dan *My name is … and*	**saya tinggal di** *I live in*	**rumah** *a house* **apartemen** *a flat* **gedung** *a building*	**baru** *new* **besar** *big* **indah** *beautiful* **kecil** *small* **mewah** *luxurious* **modern** *modern* **sederhana** *simple* **tua** *old*	**sekali** *very*	**di pedesaan** *in the countryside* **di pantai** *on the coast* **di pinggiran kota** *on the outskirts* **di pusat kota** *in the city centre*

saya berasal dari *I am from* **saya tinggal di** *I live in*	**kota*** *the city*	**Canberra** **Dili** **Jakarta **** **Kuala Lumpur** **Manila** **Singapura** *Singapore*	**ibu kota** *capital city of*	**negara** *the country*	**Australia** **Timor-Leste** **Indonesia** **Malaysia** **Filipina** *the Philippines* **Singapura** *Singapore*
		Denpasar **Ubud**			**Bali**
		Ende			**Flores**
		Bandung **Surabaya** **Yogyakarta**	**yang terletak di** *which is located on* **di** *on*	**pulau*** *the island*	**Jawa**
		Banjarmasin **Pontianak**			**Kalimantan**
		Ambon **Ternate**			**Maluku**
		Jayapura **Merauke**			**Papua**
		Kendari **Makassar** **Manado**			**Sulawesi**
		Banda Aceh **Medan** **Padang**			**Sumatra**

Author's note:
* **kota** and **pulau** *are optional, but give clarity to the sentence*
***In 2022 the Parliament of Indonesia passed a Bill to relocate the capital city of Indonesia. The new capital city, Nusantara, will be built on the east coast of Kalimantan.*

Unit 4. Saying where I live and am from: VOCABULARY BUILDING

1. Complete with the missing word

a. Saya tinggal _______ Surabaya   *I live in Surabaya*

b. Saya suka _______________ saya   *I like my flat*

c. Saya berasal dari _________ Bali   *I am from the island Bali*

d. Saya ________ di apartemen kecil   *I live in a small flat*

e. Apartemen saya di _________tua   *My flat is in an old building*

f. Saya_____________ dari ibu kota   *I come from the capital city*

g. Saya tinggal di rumah mewah _____   *I live in a very luxurious house*

h. Saya tinggal di ___________   *I live in the countryside*

2. Match up

berasal dari	very big
besar sekali	very small
sederhana	old
gedung	luxurious
mewah	city centre
kecil sekali	the coast
pantai	come from
pinggiran	the outskirts
pulau	live in
pusat kota	simple
tinggal di	building
tua	island

3. Translate into English

a. di gedung modern di pedesaan

b. di rumah besar sekali

c. Apartemen di gedung modern

d. Saya berasal dari negara Singapura

e. Saya tinggal di Jakarta, ibu kota negara Indonesia

f. Saya berasal dari Canberra, ibu kota negara Australia

g. Saya tinggal di apartemen di pantai

h. Saya berasal dari Medan di pulau Sumatra

4. Add the missing letters

a. J_ka_t_   c. d_s_   e. r_ m _ h   g. s_ k_ l _   i. p_ la _

b. i_u k_t_   d. p_s_t k_t_   f. p_nt_i   h. y_ ng   j. n_ g _ r_

5. Broken words

a. S____ t_______ d__ k _____M_____ d__S ________
I live in Medan in Sumatra

b. S______ t_________ d___ r_______ t_____ s ____
I live in a very old house

c. S___ b___ d____ A______, tetapi s_____ t______ d__
J_________   *I am from Ambon, but I live in Jakarta*

d. S__ t______ d__ a__________ d__ p_____ B______
I live in a flat on the island of Bali

e. N__ s__ D___ d__s_ t_____ d__ r____ k____
My name is Daud and I live in a small house

f. S___ b____ d____ K______ d__ s__ t_____ d__
g____ t____   *I'm from Kendari and I live in an old building*

g. S____ b___ d____ n________ S___________
I come from Singapore

6. Complete with a suitable word

a. Saya _________ dari Denpasar

b. Saya tinggal ____ Jakarta

c. Canberra, ibu ________ negara Australia

d Medan yang terletak di pulau _________

e. Makassar di ________ Sulawesi

f. _______ ______ , ibu kota negara Malaysia

g. Bandung terletak di pulau ___________

h. Saya _________ di apartemen kecil

i. ___________ ibu kota negara Indonesia

j. Saya tinggal di_________ mewah di pusat kota

Unit 4. Geography : Using your own knowledge (and a bit of help from the Internet or your teacher) match the numbers to the cities and countries

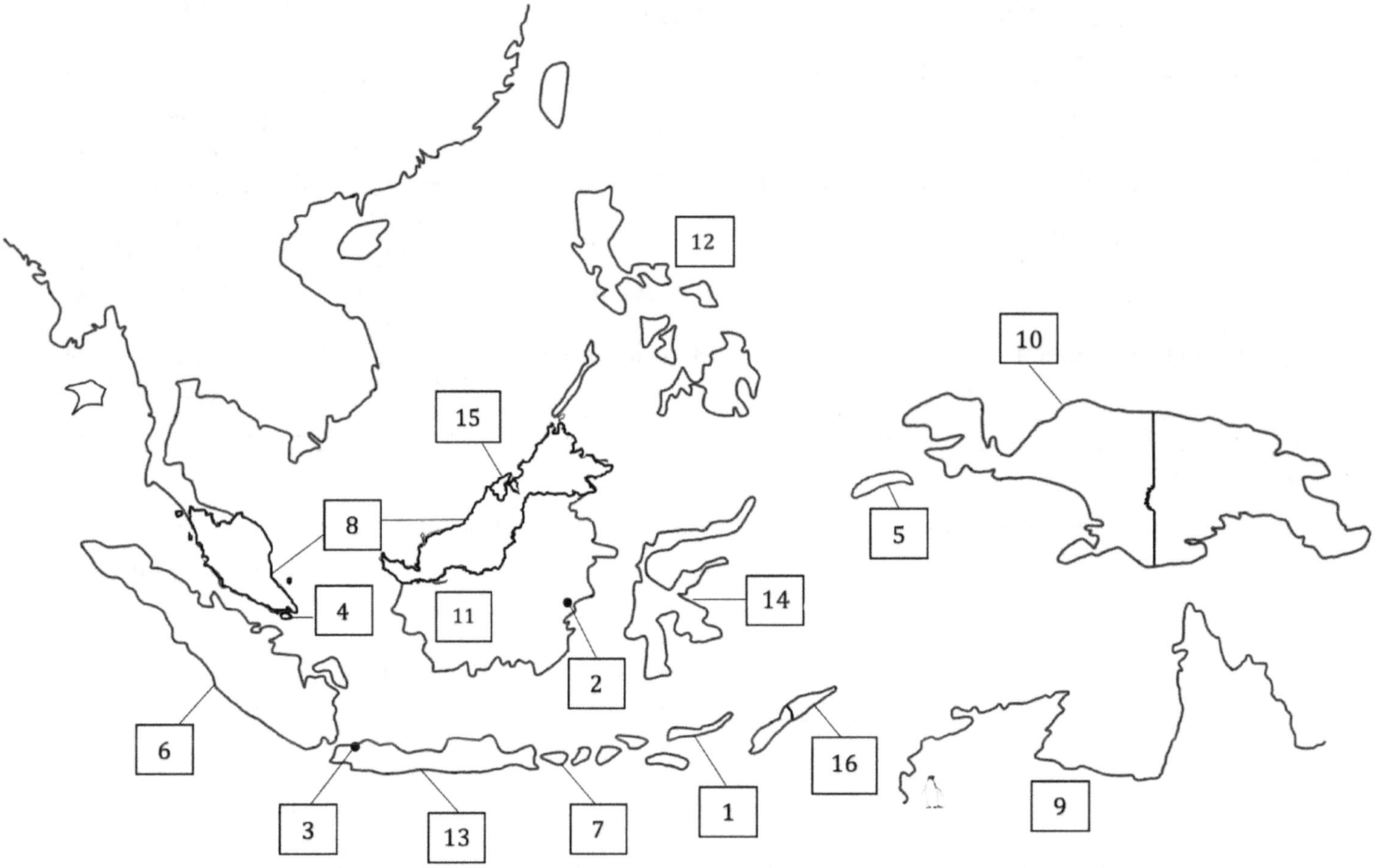

Indonesia		
No.	**IBU KOTA** *Capital Cities*	
	Jakarta	
	Nusantara	
No.	**PULAU** *Island*	**No.**	**PULAU** *Island*

No.	PULAU Island	No.	PULAU Island
	Bali		Maluku
	Flores		Papua
	Jawa		Sulawesi
	Kalimantan		Sumatra

Negara di Asia Tenggara	
Countries in South East Asia	
No.	**NEGARA** *Country*
X	Indonesia
	Australia
	Brunei
	Filipina
	Malaysia
	Singapura
	Timor Leste

Unit 4. Saying where I live and am from: READING

Nama saya Pramana. Saya berumur dua puluh dua tahun dan hari ulang tahun saya pada tanggal sembilan Agustus. Saya tinggal di kota Ende di Flores. Saya tinggal di rumah indah di pusat kota. Saya punya dua adik laki-laki, Ed dan Rob. Saya sangat suka Ed tetapi Rob sangat nakal. Teman saya Joni tinggal di kota Ambon, yang terletak di pulau Maluku. Dia tinggal di sebuah apartemen di gedung tua, di pusat kota.

Nama saya Iva. Saya berumur dua puluh satu tahun dan saya tinggal dengan teman baik saya, Dian di kota Bandung, di Jawa. Kami tinggal di apartemen besar dan modern di pinggiran kota. Hari ulang tahun saya pada tanggal dua Juni dan hari ulang tahun Dian pada tanggal dua belas Juli. Saya punya seekor kadal bernama Gnarls 'Barkley'. Dia sangat besar dan lucu. Ulang tahunnya pada tanggal satu April. Gnarls 'Barkley' berusia tiga tahun. Saya juga punya seekor laba-laba besar tetapi sangat jelek, namanya Lulu. Ulang tahun laba-laba saya juga pada tanggal satu April. Jadi saya mengadakan pesta untuk kedua hewan peliharaan saya secara bersamaan. Hal ini sangat praktis.

Nama saya Rangga. Saya berusia lima belas tahun. Saya orang Indonesia tetapi saya tinggal di Manila, ibu kota negara Filipina. Di keluarga saya, ada empat orang: orang tua saya, saudara laki-laki saya, Mahmud, dan saya. Hari ulang tahun Mahmud dan saya pada tanggal sebelas September. Kami saudara kembar!

Nama saya Aminah. Saya berusia sembilan tahun dan saya tinggal di Medan, di pulau Sumatra. Saya tinggal dengan keluarga saya: orang tua saya, kakak saya, Hayati, dan saya. Hari ulang tahun saya pada tanggal sembilan Mei dan hari ulang tahun Hayati pada tanggal tiga puluh Maret. Dia berusia sebelas tahun. Rumah saya besar dan mewah di pantai. Sangat menyenangkan!

1. Find the Indonesian for the following in Iva's text

a. My name is

b. I am 21 years old

c. We live in…

d. A big flat

e. On the outskirts

f. The 2nd of June

g. I have a lizard

h. He is very big

i. His birthday is on the 1st April

j. He is 3 years old

k. I also have a spider

2. Complete the statements below based on Pramana's text

a. I am _______ years old

b. My birthday is the ____of ____________

c. I live in a ________ house

d. My house is in the _________ of town

e. I like Ed but Rob is ____________

f. My friend Joni lives in ________ in Maluku

g. His flat is in an old ________

3. Answer the questions on the four texts above

a. How old is Rangga?

b. Why do Rangga and Mahmud have the same birthday? *(what do you think a 'saudara kembar' is?)*

c. Who only likes one of his siblings?

d. Who has two pets that share a birthday?

e. Why is it convenient that they share a birthday?

f. Who has a friend that lives in a different city?

g. Who lives with their really good friend?

h. Who does not live in Indonesia?

i. Whose birthday is on the twelfth of July?

4. Correct any incorrect statements about Aminah's text

a. Aminah tinggal di Medan di pusat Sumatra.

b. Di keluarga Aminah ada lima orang

c. Ulang tahunnya pada bulan Maret

d. Ulang tahun Hayati pada tanggal tiga Maret

e. Aminah tinggal di rumah besar tetapi sederhana di pantai

f. Dia tidak suka rumahnya

Unit 4. Saying where I live and am from: TRANSLATION/WRITING

1. Translate into English

a. saya tinggal di

b. rumah

c. pulau

d. indah

e. besar

f. di sebuah rumah

g. tua sekali

h. modern

i. di pusat kota

j. ibu kota

k. di pinggiran kota

l. saya berasal dari

m. di pulau Jawa

n. di negara Singapura

2. Gapped sentences

a. Saya tinggal di ______ sederhana   *I live in a simple house*

b. apartemen di _______ baru   *A flat in a new building*

c. Saya tinggal di _________ kecil   *I live in a small flat*

d. Rumah di ________ _____   *A house on the outskirts*

e. Saya ______ _____ Jakarta   *I come from Jakarta*

f. Ibu ___________ Indonesia   *The capital city of Indonesia*

3. Complete the sentences with a suitable word

a. Saya tinggal di _____________ , ibu kota Indonesia

b. Saya berasal dari __________Sydney, di Australia

c. Saya tinggal di apartemen besar ______

d. Saya tinggal _____ rumah sederhana sekali

e. Saya_______ di Canberra, ______ kota Australia

f. Saya tinggal di rumah modern ______ pedesaan

4. Phrase-level translation Eng to Ind

a. I live in…

b. I am from…

c. a house…

d. a flat…

e. luxurious…

f. very small …

g. in an old building…

h. in the city centre…

i. on the outskirts…

j. on the coast…

k. in the countryside…

5. Sentence-level translation Eng to Indonesian

a. I am from Jayapura, on the island of Papua in Indonesia. I live in a big and beautiful house on the coast.

b. I am from Kuala Lumpur, the capital of the country Malaysia. I live in a small flat in the city centre.

c. I am from the town of Makassar which is located on the island of Sulawesi. I live in a flat in a new building on the outskirts. My flat is big and modern.

d. I am from Manila the capital city of the Philippines. I live in a flat in an old building on the outskirts. I like my flat.

Unit 4. Saying where I live and am from: WRITING

1. Complete with the missing letters

a. N_m_ saya Iskandar

b. Sa_ _ tinggal di rum_ _ _ ind_h

c. Saya tin_ _al di ap_ _temen b_s_r dan t_a

d. S_y_ tinggal d_ pu_ _t k_t_

e. S_ _ _ t_ngg_l di Jakar_ _ di Indone_ _a

f. Sa _ a ber_s_l d_ri D_np_sar di Bal_

g. S_ _ _ b_ ras _l d_ _ i Fil_p_n_

h. _aya bera_a_ dar_ Me_ _n di Sum_ _ra

2. Spot and correct the spelling mistakes

a. Saya berasal diri Kendari, di Sulawesi

b. Saya tinggal di Jakata, iba kota Indonesia

c. Saya tinggal di sebuah rumuh tua

d. Saya tinggal di sebuah apartemen basar

e. Saya tinggal di gedang modern

f. Saya tinggal di pulua Jawa

g. Saya berasal dari Kula Lumpur di Malaysia

h. Saya berasal dari Denpeser di pulau Bali

3. Answer the questions in Indonesian

a. Siapa namamu?

b. Berapa umurmu?

c. Kapan kamu lahir?

d. Kamu berasal dari mana?

e. Di mana kamu tinggal?

f. Apakah kamu tinggal di rumah atau di apartemen?

4. Anagrams (islands of Indonesia and neighbouring countries)

a. waaJ   *Jawa*

b. mSuarat

c. mnKiaanalt

d. wauleSsi

e. laBi

f. aapPu

g. gniauSpra

h. ipFilian

i. kuMalu

j. yaliaasM

5. Guided writing – write 4 short paragraphs in the 1st person singular 'I' describing the people below

Name	Age	Birthday	City	Country or region
Sanja	12	20.06	Jakarta	Indonesia
Nur	14	14.10	Kuala Lumpur	Malaysia
Andrew	11	14.01	Sydney	Australia
Hendri	13	17.01	Medan	Sumatra
Made	15	19.10	Denpasar	Bali

6. Describe this person in the third person:

Name: Anisa

Age: 16

Birthday: 15 May

Place of origin: Java, Indonesia

Country of residence: Sydney, Australia

UNIT 5
Talking about my family members, saying their age and how well I get along with them. Counting to 100.

Revision Quickie: Numbers 1-100 / Dates / Birthdays

In this unit you will learn to talk about:
- How many people there are in your family and who they are
- If you get along with them
- Words for family members
- What their age is
- Numbers from 31 to 100

You will also revisit
- Numbers from 1 to 31
- Hair and eyes description

UNIT 5
Talking about my family members, saying their age and how well I get along with them. Counting to 100.
Unit 5. Talking about my family + Counting to 100: VOCAB BUILDING

Di keluarga kamu ada berapa orang? *In your family there are how many people?*
Ada siapa saja di keluargamu? *Who is in your family?*
Berapa umurnya? *How old is he/she? How old are they?*

| Di keluarga saya ada *In my family there are* | dua *2*   empat *4*   enam *6*
 tiga *3*   lima *5*   tujuh *7* | orang, *people,* | **bapak** *father*
 ibu *mother*
 adik *younger sibling*
 kakak *older sibling*
 kakek *grandfather*
 nenek *grandmother* | |
| **Ada** *There is / are* | | | | |

Saya dekat* dengan *I am close to* **Saya tidak dekat* dengan** *I am not close to*	**bapak saya.** *my father* **ibu saya.** *my mother* **kakek saya.** *my grandfather* **nenek saya.** *my grandmother* **paman saya.** *my uncle* **bibi saya.** *my aunt*	**Dia berumur** *He/She is aged* **Mereka berumur** *They are aged* **Umurnya** *He/She is aged* *They are aged*	satu 1 dua 2 tiga 3 empat 4 lima 5 enam 6 tujuh 7 delapan 8 sembilan 9 sepuluh 10 sebelas 11 dua belas 12 tiga belas 13 empat belas 14 lima belas 15 enam belas 16 tujuh belas 17 delapan belas 18 sembilan belas 19 dua puluh 20 dua puluh satu 21 dua puluh dua 22 tiga puluh 30 tiga puluh satu 31 empat puluh 40 lima puluh 50 enam puluh 60 tujuh puluh 70 delapan puluh 80 sembilan puluh 90 seratus 100	**tahun** *years old*
Saya akrab dengan…** *I get along well with…* **Saya tidak akrab dengan…** *I don't get along well with*	**adik saya** *my younger sibling* **adik laki-laki saya.** *my little brother* **adik perempuan saya.** *my little sister* **kakak saya.** *my older sibling* **kakak laki-laki saya.** *my older brother* **kakak perempuan saya.** *my older sister*			
Saya bertengkar dengan *I quarrel with* **Saya tidak bertengkar dengan** *I don't quarrel with*	**sepupu saya.** *my cousin* **sepupu laki-laki saya.** *my male cousin* **sepupu perempuan saya.** *my female cousin*			

Author's note: *Remember,* he or she *is replaced by* **dia,** *and* his/her *is* **-nya** *Watch out for it!*
The formal word for father is **bapak,** *but* **ayah** *is also used as a less formal word (more like* Dad*).* **Bapak** *and* **Ibu** *are also used politely to address adults as Mr and Mrs/Ms.*
***dekat** *is used when referring to someone older*   ****akrab** *is used when the relationship is very close and often within the same generational level*

 THE LANGUAGE GYM

1. Complete with the missing word

a. Di _________ saya ada   *In my family there are...*

b. Ada____________ orang   *There are five people*

c. _____________ saya, Abdul   *My grandfather, Abdul*

d. Kakek saya berumur _________ tahun   *My grandfather is 80*

e. __________ saya, Aminah   *My mother Aminah*

f. Dia _________ lima puluh tahun   *She is 50 years old*

g. Saya _______ dengan adik saya   *I get on well with my bro*

2. Match up

enam belas	12
dua belas	48
dua puluh satu	13
sepuluh	16
tiga puluh tiga	10
tiga belas	21
empat puluh delapan	15
lima puluh dua	5
lima	33
lima belas	52

3. Translate into English

a. Di keluarga saya ada

b. Ibu saya, Aminah

c. Dia berumur lima puluh tahun

d. Saya akrab dengan

e. Nenek saya, Fatimah

f. Dia berumur lima puluh tahun

g. Bapak saya

h. Kakek saya

4. Add the missing letter/s

a. ke_ _ _ _ ga   c. d_   e. ta_ _n   g. de_ _ _t   i. a_ _h   k. _ _a

b. i_ _u   d. u_ _ur   f. pu_ _h   h. n_ _ _ _k   j. d_a   l. a_ _k

5. Broken words

a. A_ _ e____ o_____ d_________k______s________
There are 6 people in my family

b. K_______ p_______ s______ b_______d_ b_____ t______
My sister is 12 years old

c. D_______ k________ s_______ a_______...
In my family I have...

d. S_______ l____-_____ s_____ b_________
My male cousin is called

e. B______ s_____ b________ l___ p______ l____ t______
My father is 55 years old

f. S _____ t_____ a_______ d______ k______ l____-_____ saya
I get on badly with my older brother...

g. S______ a _______ d________ ...
I get on well with my...

6. Complete with a suitable word

a. Di keluarga ____________

b. ___________ empat orang

c. ___________ kakek saya Abdul

d. Dia _______ 50 tahun

e. Saya akrab _________ adik saya

f. Saya _________ akrab dengan kakak

g. Kakak _______ berumur 10 tahun

h. Adik saya _____________ 12 tahun

i. Saya bertengkar _________adik saya

j. Sepupu laki-laki saya ______ 15 tahun

k. Kakek saya ___________ 70 tahun

Unit 5. Talking about my family + Counting to 100: VOCABULARY DRILLS

1. Match up

tiga puluh	there are
akrab dengan	my cousin
keluarga	with
sepupu saya	family
ada	get along well with
dengan	thirty

2. Complete with the missing word

a. ________ lima orang — *There are five people*

b. Bapak saya berumur enam ______ tahun — *My father is 60 years old*

c. Saya __________ dengan paman saya — *I get along with my uncle*

d. Saya ________ akrab dengan... — *I don't get along with ...*

e. Bibi saya ________ empat puluh tahun — *My aunt is 40 years old*

f. Dia berumur __________ belas tahun — *He is 18 years old*

g. Dia berumur dua _____ enam tahun — *She is 26 years old*

h. Umurnya ______ saya delapan puluh tahun — *My grandma is 80 years old*

3. Translate into English

a. Dia berumur sembilan tahun

b. Dia berumur empat puluh tahun

c. Umur bapak saya empat puluh empat tahun

d. Saya tidak dekat dengan kakek saya

e. Saya bertengkar dengan adik laki-laki saya

f. Adik perempuan saya berumur lima belas tahun

g. Saya dekat dengan nenek saya

h. Ada delapan orang di keluarga saya

4. Complete with the missing letters

a. Ka _ _ k laki-laki saya   *My older brother*

b. Di kel _ _ rga saya _ d_ tiga orang
In my family there are three people

c. Se _ _pu saya dela _ _ _ belas tahun
My cousin is eighteen years old

d. Saya ti _ _k akrab d _ _ gan kakak saya
I don't get along with my older brother

e. Pa_ _ n saya berumur empat puluh _a_un
My uncle is 40 years old

f. S _ _a a_ _ ab dengan sepupu saya
I get along with my cousin

g. _ _ _upu saya ber_ _ ur l_ _a belas tahun
My cousin is 15 years old

h. Saya akrab dengan _ _ _
I get along well with her

i. Saya d_ _ _ t dengan ...   *I am close to ...*

5. Translate into Indonesian

a. in my family

b. there are

c. my father

d. is 40 years old

e. I get along well...

f. close to

6. Spot and correct the errors

a. Di keluarga saya ini tiga orang

b. Nanak saya Anisa

c. Adik laki-laki saya berumur sembilan tahan

d. Saya akrab dengan saya sepupu

e. Umur sepupu saya delepan tahun

f. Kekek laki-laki saya, Bakti

Unit 5. Talking about my family + Counting to 100: TRANSLATION

1. Match up

dua puluh	30
tiga puluh	70
empat puluh	100
lima puluh	50
enam puluh	20
delapan puluh	80
sembilan puluh	40
seratus	60
tujuh puluh	90

2. Write in the missing number in words

a. Saya berumur _____________________ tahun   *I am 31 yrs old*

b. Umur bapak saya _______________ tahun   *My dad is 57 yrs old*

c. Ibu saya berumur _______________ tahun   *My mum is 48 yrs old*

d. Kakek saya berumur_______________ tahun   *My grandad is 100 old*

e. Umur paman saya_______________ tahun   *My uncle is 62 yrs old*

f. Mereka berumur _______________ tahun   *They are 90 yrs old*

g. Sepupu-sepupu saya berumur_______tahun   *My cousins are 44*

h. Berapa umurnya, _______________ tahun?   *How old is she, 70?*

3. Write out in Indonesian

a. 35 tiga puluh lima

b. 63 e_____________________

c. 89 d_____________________

d. 74 t_____________________

e. 98 s_____________________

f. 100 s_____________________

g. 82 d_____________________

h. 24 d_____________________

i. 17 t_____________________

4. Correct the translation errors

a. *My father is forty*   Bapak saya berumur tiga puluh tahun

b. *My mother is fifty-two* Ibu saya berumur lima belas dua tahun

c. *We are forty-two*   Kami berumur dua puluh tahun

d. *I am forty-one*   Umur saya empat puluh tahun

e. *They are thirty-four*   Umur mereka tiga puluh tiga tahun

5. Translate into Indonesian (please write out the numbers in words)

a. In my family there are six people:

b. My mother's name is Sari and she is 43 years old:

c. My father is called Hartono and he is 48 years old:

d. My older sister is called Yohana and she is 31 years old:

e. My younger brother's name is Ali and he is 18 years old:

f. My name is Mahmud and I am 27 years old:

g. My grandfather is called Yusuf and he is 87 years old:

Unit 5. Talking about my family + Counting to 100: WRITING

1. Spot and correct the spelling mistakes

a. empat pulah   *empat puluh*

b. tiga puluh sata

c. dalapan puluh dua

d. due puluh satu

e. semblan puluh

f. emam

g. tujoh puluh

h. enam puloh

3. Rearrange the sentences below in the correct word order

a. ada orang keluarga Di saya empat
In my family there are four people

b. laki-laki Saya tidak saya dengan akrab kakak
I don't get along with my brother

c. umurnya Bapak saya Markus bernama dan puluh lima dua
My father is called Markus and is 52 years old

d. ibu saya Di tiga saya ada bapak keluarga orang: dan
In my family there are three people: my mother, my father and I

e. puluh Nama saya Paulus sepupu umurnya dan tujuh tiga
My cousin is called Paulus and is 37 years old

f. delapan bernama saya dan Fernando umurnya Kakek puluh tujuh
My grandfather is called Fernando and is 87 years old

2. Complete with the missing letters

a. I__u sa_a b_rum_r em_at p__ _uh t_h_n

b. Um_r ba__k s_y_ li_a p_luh s_tu __hun

c. K_ _ _k _ _ ya beru_ur del__an p__uh tah_ _

d. U__ _r ad_k _ _ya seb_ _as ta_ _n

e. Ne_ _k saya be_ _mur se_ _ilan pul_ _ ta_un

f. Um_ _ ka_ak s_ _a d_a p_ _ _uh ti_a _a_un

4. Complete

a. In my family: D__ k____________ s _______

b. There are: A______

c. Is called: B____________

d. My mother: I___ s____________

e. My father: B____________ s____________

f. He is fifty: D___ b_______ l______ p________

g. I am sixty: U_______ s_______ e______ p _______

h. He is forty: D___ b_______ e______ p _______

5. Write a relationship sentence for each person as shown in the example

e.g. Teman baik saya yang bernama Bayu, berumur lima belas. Saya sangat dekat dengan dia.

Name	Relationship to me	Age	How I get along with them
e.g. Bayu	*Best friend*	*15*	*Very well*
Steve (Smith)	Father	57	Close to
Ana	Mother	45	Not close to
Dewi	Aunt	60	Quarrel
Irfan	Cousin	15	Well
Iskandar	Older brother	20	Not well

Revision Quickie 1:
Numbers 1-100, dates and birthdays, hair and eyes, family

1. Match up

11	lima belas
12	dua belas
13	enam belas
14	delapan belas
15	sebelas
16	sembilan belas
17	empat belas
18	dua puluh
19	tujuh belas
20	tiga belas

2. Translate the dates into English

a. tanggal tiga puluh Juni

b. tanggal satu Juli

c. tanggal lima belas Mei

d. tanggal dua puluh dua Maret

e. tanggal tiga puluh satu Desember

f. tanggal lima Januari

g. tanggal enam belas Oktober

h. tanggal dua puluh sembilan Februari

3. Complete with the missing words

a. Hari ulang tahun saya pada ______ lima belas April

b. Umur saya empat belas _________

c. Rambut adik saya __________ ___________

d. Kamu berasal dari ___________ ?

e. Di keluarga saya _________ empat orang

f. Ibu_______ _______ cokelat

g. Saya berasal ___________ Jakarta

h. Kakak saya __________ Ratna

mana	tanggal	dari	saya	bernama
pirang	bermata	tahun	ada	berwarna

4. Write out the solution in words as shown in the example

a. empat puluh – tiga puluh =

b. tiga puluh – sepuluh =

c. empat puluh + tiga puluh =

d. dua puluh x dua =

e. delapan puluh – dua puluh =

f. sembilan puluh – lima puluh =

g. tiga puluh x tiga =

h. dua puluh + lima puluh =

i. dua puluh + tiga puluh =

5. Complete the words

a. k _ _ _ _ s _ _ _ _   *my grandfather*

b. se _ _ _ _ _ s_ _ _   *my cousin*

c. ma _ _   *eyes*

d. hi _ _ _ _   *green*

e. jen _ _ _ _ _   *beard*

f. kac _ _ _ _ _ _   *glasses*

g. adik per_ _ _ _ _ _ _   *sister*

h. kel_ _ _ _ _ _ s_ _ _ _   *my family*

6. Translate into English

a. Ibu saya berambut cokelat

b. Mata saya berwarna biru

c. Saya berumur empat puluh tahun

d. Kakek saya berumur sembilan puluh tahun

e. Bapak saya berkacamata

f. Kakak saya berkumis

g. Kakak saya berambut hitam

h. Mata kakak saya berwarna abu-abu

UNIT 6: Describing myself and another family member (physical and personality)

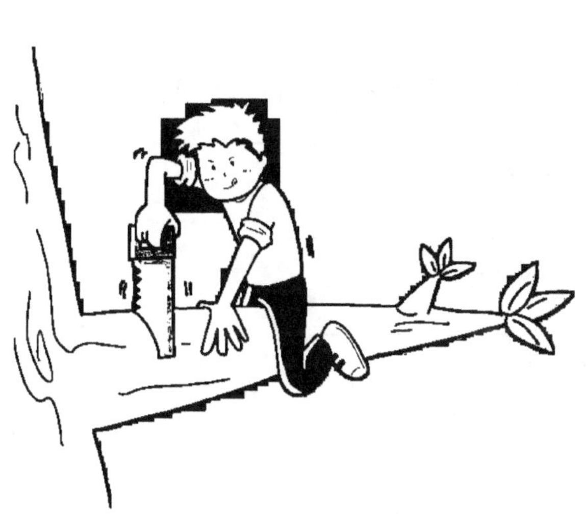

UNIT 6 (Part 1/2)
Introduction to describing myself and another family member

Bagaimana sifat kamu? *What are you like?*			
Bagaimana sifatnya? *What are his/her characteristics?*			

Saya *I (am)*	**cantik** *beautiful*	**dan** *and*	**aktif** *active*
	ganteng *handsome*		**artistik** *artistic*
Bapak saya *My father is*	**gemuk** *fat*	**dan juga** *and also*	**bijaksana** *wise*
	jelek *ugly*		**cengeng** *crybaby*
Ibu saya *My mother is*	**kuat** *strong*		**cerewet** *nagging, talkative*
	kurus *slim*	**dan selalu** *and always*	
Adik perempuan saya *My younger sister is*	**pendek** *short*		**kreatif** *creative*
	tinggi *tall*		**malas** *lazy*
		tetapi *but*	**pemalu** *shy*
Adik laki-laki saya *My younger brother is*			**nakal** *naughty*
	baik hati *kind*	**tetapi tidak** *but not*	**pandai** *clever*
	baik *nice*		
Kakak laki-laki saya *My older brother is*	**jahat** *bad, mean*		**rajin** *diligent*
	keras kepala *stubborn*		**ramah** *friendly*
	lucu *funny, cute*		**sabar** *patient*
Kakak laki-laki saya *My older brother is*	**membosankan** *boring*		**sombong** *arrogant*
	pemurah *generous*		

Unit 6. Describing Myself and Family: VOCABULARY BUILDING

1. Match up	
Saya baik	I am funny
Saya jahat	I am slim
Saya keras kepala	I am kind
Saya ganteng	I am mean
Saya lucu	I am nice
Saya baik hati	I am short
Saya kuat	I am strong
Saya jahat	I am handsome
Saya pendek	I am bad
Saya tinggi	I am tall
Saya kurus	I am stubborn

2. Complete the sentences

a. Adik laki-laki saya k_________________
My younger brother is slim

b. Bapak saya tidak r_______________
My father is unfriendly

c. Kakak perempuan saya k_________ k___________
My older sister is stubborn

d. Bapak saya b_____________ *My father is wise*

e. Kakak laki-laki saya l______ tetapi tidak s_________
My older brother is funny but not arrogant

f. Paman saya Harto k__________ *My Uncle Harto is strong*

3. Categories – sort the adjectives below in the categories provided

a. kuat; b. bijaksana; c. baik; d. keras kepala; e. ganteng;
f. pandai; g. cantik; h. jahat; i. pemurah; j. membosankan;
k. gemuk; l. jelek; m. lucu

Fisik *physical characteristics*	Kepribadian *personality*

4. Complete the words

a. Saya membos__ __ __ __ __

b. Dia tidak j__ __ __ __

c. Saya pem__ __ __

d. Ibu saya keras k __ __ __ __ __ __

e. Saya jah__ __

f. Mereka can__ __ __

g. Teman saya b__ __ __

h. Kakak dia ge__ __ __

5. Translate into English

a. Kakak perempuan saya pemurah

b. Adik perempuan saya tidak gemuk

c. Kakak perempuan saya ramah

d. Ibu saya lucu

e. Saya tidak jelek

f. Saya selalu keras kepala

g. Saya ganteng dan juga pandai

h. Teman saya Gunadi kuat sekali

6. Spot and correct the translation mistakes

a. Saya kuat: *He is strong*

b. Dia gemuk: *He is slim*

c. Saya sangat cantik: *I am very ugly*

d. Ibu saya tinggi: *My mother is short*

e. Nenek saya baik hati: *My grandma is funny*

f. Adik saya pemalu: *My sister is three*

g. Bapak saya kuat: *My father is mean*

7. Complete with an adjective

a. Saya pem__ __ __

b. Dia k__ __ __ __

c. Ibu saya b__ __ __   h__ __ __

d. Ibu Susi c__ __ __ __ __

e. Dia k__ __ __ __ __ k __ __ __ __ __

f. Saya r__ __ __ __

8. English to Indonesian translation

a. I am strong and funny

b. My mother is very stubborn

c. My older sister is short and slim

d. My younger brother is clever

e. I am kind and fun

f. My father is tall and not fat

g. Gargamel is ugly and always mean

h. I am tall and strong

Grammar Time 1: Pronouns

PERSONAL PRONOUNS		
Saya *I (formal) am* **Aku** *I (inf., conversational) am*		
Anda *You (formal) are* **Kamu** *You (informal) are*		**artistik** *artistic*
Dia *He, She is*		**baik hati** *kind*
		bijaksana *wise*
Kami *We (excluding listener) are* **Kita** *We (including listener) are*	**agak** *rather*	**cerdas** *intelligent*
		cerewet *talkative*
Semua *You all are* **Anda semua** *All of you (formal) are*	**cukup** *quite*	**keras kepala** *stubborn*
	sangat *very*	**kreatif** *creative*
Mereka *They are*		**lucu** *funny*
POSSESSIVE PRONOUNS	**sedikit** a *little*	**malas** *lazy*
	sungguh *really*	**nakal** *naughty*
Orang tua <u>saya</u> *My (formal) parents are* **Ibu<u>ku</u>** *My (inf., conversational) mother is* **Saudara <u>saya</u>** *My relatives are / My sibling is*	**tidak** *not*	**pemalu** *shy*
		pemurah *generous*
Pekerjaan <u>Anda</u> *Your (formal) job is* **Bapak <u>kamu</u>** *Your (inf.) father is* **Teman<u>mu</u>** *Your (inf.) friend is*		**rajin** *diligent*
		ramah *friendly*
Adik<u>nya</u> *His/her younger sibling is* **Kakak<u>nya</u>** *His/her older sibling is*		**sabar** *patient*
		streng *strict*
Kakek-nenek <u>kami</u> *Our (excl.) grandparents are* **Keluarga <u>kita</u>** *Our (incl.) family is*		
Bibi <u>mereka</u> *Their aunt is* **Paman<u>nya</u>** *Their uncle is*		

Author's note:
Due to cultural complexity, the use of pronouns in Indonesian is very different to English. The use of pronouns depends on the social context of the interaction as well as the age, relationship and social position of the person addressed.

*Whether to use **Anda** or **kamu** is subject to understanding the connection between the speakers. **Anda** can accommodate all kinds of people but **kamu** can only be used once a level of intimacy has been reached. Generally, children and young people of the same age and social standing will use **kamu**, however, if addressing a friend's older sibling it may not be appropriate to use **kamu** unless you know them very well.*

*In communicative exchanges between people of various social roles, instead of a pronoun, a personal name can be used, or kinship terms such as **Ibu** and **Bapak**, or **Kakek** and **Nenek**. In addition, rank or position names can be used, e.g. **Dokter** (doctor), **Profesor** (professor).*

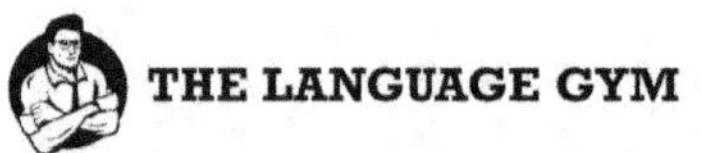

Grammar Time 1. Personal Pronouns: DRILLS

1. Match up

Dia	I (am)
Kami	You (are)
Kita	He/She (is)
Kamu	They (are)
Mereka	We [exc.] (are)
Saya	We [inc.] (are)

2. Complete with the missing pronoun

a. ________________ sangat cerewet   *I am very talkative*

b. ________________ sungguh lucu   *You (inf.)are really funny*

c. ________________ sangat cerdas   *They are very intelligent*

d. ________________ berasal dari Bali   *We (exc)come from Bali*

e. ________ berumur tiga belas tahun   *He is 13 years old*

f. ________________ tinggal di mana?   *Where do they live?*

g. Bagaimana________________?   *What is she like?*

h. ________________ sangat ramah!   *You all are very friendly!*

3. Translate into English

a. Dia baik hati

b. Saya sedikit cerewet

c. Mereka cukup malas

d. Dia tidak streng

e. Anda sangat pemalu

f. Kamu agak nakal

g. Aku tidak keras kepala!

h. Anda semua sangat kuat!

4. Complete with the missing letters

a. K_ _ i sangat ramah   *We are very friendly*

b. D _ _ cukup keras kepala *She is quite stubborn*

c. M _ _ _ _ _ tidak sabar *They are not patient*

d. D _ _ tidak ramah *He is not friendly*

e. K _ _ _ _   cukup artistik *You are quite artistic*

f. A _ _ _ _ s _ _ _ _ _ sangat cerewet
You all are very talkative

g. S _ _ _ sedikit malas *I am a bit lazy*

h. M _ _ _ _ _ _ sangat baik hati dan pemurah
They are very kind and generous

i. Apakah k _ _ _ _ dekat dengan bapak _ _ _? *Are you close to your father?*

5. Translate into Indonesian

a. You (inf.) are funny.

b. He is intelligent

c. You all are really creative

d. They are quite friendly

e. We are not talkative

f. She is very shy

6. Spot and correct the errors

a. Dia streng sangat

b. Kamu dan sabar kreatif

c. Meraka sedikit pemalu

d. Agak saya cerewet

e. Apakah sungguh dia rajin?

Grammar Time 1. Possessive Pronoun Drills

1. Complete with the missing pronouns

a. Orang tua____ ramah *Her parents are friendly*

b. Bapak__ agak tinggi *His father is rather tall*

c. Anjing__ gemuk *Her dog is fat*

d. Guru-guru___ sangat baik
My teachers are very good

e. Kakak perempuan___ cantik *Your sister is pretty*

f. Teman ____tidak pemalu *Their friends are not shy*

g. Adik _______ dan_______ sangat rajin
My brother and I are very hard-working

2. Complete with the missing pronouns

a. Ibu ______   *My mother (formal)*

b. Orang tua _____   *My (inf) parents*

c. Teman _____   *Your (inf. abbr.) friend*

d. Sepupu ______   *Her cousins*

e. Nenek _______   *Our (incl.) grandma*

f. Keluarga ______   *His family*

g. Kakek-nenek _____   *Our (exc) grandparents*

h. Bibi_______   *Their aunt*

i. Saudara _______   *Your (formal) relatives*

3. Complete with the missing pronouns

a. Apakah teman__ *(your abbr.)* tinggal di Indonesia?

b. Ibu _____________ *(my)* sedikit keras kepala

c. Bapak _________________ *(his)* sangat streng

d. Kakak ___________ *(your abbr.)* sungguh lucu

e. Rumah _________________ *(my)*sedikit kecil

f. Orang tua_________________ *(their)* pendek

g. Kakak _________ *(my)* dan __________ *(I)* kuat

h. Sepupu ___________ *(his)* berasal dari Jakarta

4. Translate into Indonesian.

a. My mother is tall

b. Your (inf.) father is short

c. Her brother is not funny

d. My sister is nice

e. Their grandfather is very strict

f. Your (form.) grandmother is quite patient

g. My mother is intelligent

5. English to Indonesian translation. The pronouns are underlined and they are a mix of personal and possessive pronouns, so be careful!

a. *My mother and her sister are very tall:*

b. *She is kind and generous:*

c. *Her parents come from the Philippines:*

d. *My friend is talkative but I am shy:*

e. *Your (form.) father is very tall:*

f. *She lives in Singapore and her parents live in Indonesia:*

g. *They live in a large house but my house is small:*

Grammar Time 2: Noun Phrases

Bagaimana rambut dan matanya? *Describe his/her/their hair and eyes.*

Saya *I*	**punya** *has / have*	**rambut** *hair*	**cokelat** *brown* **hitam** *black* **merah** *red* **pirang** *blond* **putih** *white* **berombak** *wavy* **keriting** *curly* **lurus** *straight* **tebal** thick **tipis** thin **pendek** *short* **panjang** *long* **pendek** *short*
Kamu *You (informal)* **Anda** *You (formal)*			
Dia *He / She*			
Adik saya *My younger siblilng*			
Kakak saya *My older sibling*			
Saudara saya *My sibling*			
Ibu saya *My mother*			
Bapak saya *My father*			
Ayah saya *My father (informal)*			
Kami *We (excl.. listener)* **Kita** *We (incl. listener)* **Bapak saya dan saya** *My father and I* **Ibu saya dan saya** *My mother and I*	**tidak punya** *does not have*	**mata** *eyes*	**biru** *blue* **cokelat** *brown* **hitam** *black* **hijau** *green* **besar** *big* **kecil** *small*
Anda semua *You all*			
Mereka *They* **Orang tua saya** *My parents* **Saudara-saudara saya** *My relatives*			

Grammar Time 2. Noun phrases : DRILLS 1

1. Translate into English	**2. Spot and correct the mistakes (note: not all sentences are wrong)**
a. Kami punya rambut hitam	a. Ibu saya tidak punya putih rambut
b. Dia punya rambut pirang	b. Saudara-saudara saya punya pirang rambut
c. Mereka punya rambut sangat panjang	c. Saya punya panjang rambut
d. Kamu punya rambut yang sangat pendek	d. Dia punya hitam rambut
e. Mereka tidak punya mata hijau	e. Kami punya tidak rambut pendek
f. Dia punya rambut merah	f. Saya orang tua punya rambut keriting
g. Kita tidak punya rambut keriting	

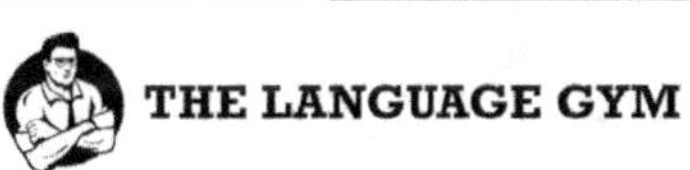

Grammar Time 2. Noun phrases : DRILLS 2

3. Complete with the missing pronoun or noun phrase according to the word in the bracket

a. ___________ *(I)* punya rambut pirang dan tebal

b. ______________ *(She)* tidak punya mata biru

c. _______________ *(They)* punya rambut merah

d. ___________ *(My father)* punya rambut pirang

e. ______________ *(They)* punya rambut hitam

f. ___________ *(My grandma)* punya rambut putih

g. _________ *(We excl)* tidak punya rambut hitam

h. ___________ punya rambut cokelat *(My cousin)*

i. Apakah___ ___ punya rambut panjang? *(You all)*

j. _________ *(My older sis)* punya rambut keriting

k. ___________ *(My friend Agus)* punya mata hijau

l. ___________ *(My parents)* punya rambut pendek

m. _______________ *(I)* tidak punya rambut lurus

n. Apakah_______ *(you inf)* punya mata biru yang sama dengan_______________ *(your inf. mother)?*

4. Translate into English

a. Ibu saya punya rambut merah

b. Orang tua saya punya mata cokelat

c. Kakak dan saya punya rambut hitam

d. Kakek-nenek saya punya rambut putih

e. Orang tua saya tidak punya rambut merah

f. Saudara-saudara saya punya rambut keriting

g. Adik saya dan saya punya rambut berombak

h. Sepupu saya tidak punya mata cokelat

i. Kedua adik saya punya rambut lurus

j. Teman saya dan saya punya mata biru

5. Translate into Indonesian

a. We have black hair

b. You (form.) have long hair

c. You all have blue eyes

d. She does not have green eyes

e. My father has curly hair

f. My sister has straight hair

g. My uncle has white hair

h. My grandfather has no hair

i. My father and I have blond hair

j. My Uncle Bakti has green eyes

6. Guided writing: write a text in the first person singular (I) including the details below:

- Say you are 13 years old
- Say you have a brother and a sister
- Say your older brother is 15
- Say he has brown, straight, short hair and green eyes
- Say he is tall and handsome
- Say your younger sister is 12
- Say she has black, curly, long hair and brown eyes
- Say your parents are short, have dark brown hair and brown eyes

7. Write an 80 to 100 words text in which you describe four relatives, or friends. You must include their:

a. Name
b. Age
c. Hair (colour, length and type)
d. Eye colour
e. If they wear glasses or not
f. Their physical description
g. Their personality description

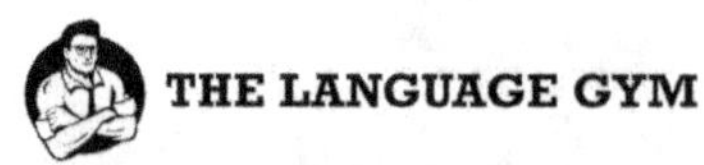

Ada berapa orang di keluargamu? *There are how many people in your family?*		
Ada *There are*	**tiga** *three* **lima** *five* **empat** *four* **enam** *six*	**orang di keluarga saya** *people in my family*

Bagaimana saudaramu. *Describe your relatives.* **Apakah kamu dekat dengan…** *Are you close to …?* **Apakah kamu akrab dengan…** *Do you get along with …?* **Mengapa kamu suka …** **?** *Why do you like … ?*			
Saya dekat* dengan *I am close to* **Saya tidak dekat dengan** *I am not close to*	**bapak saya, Yohanes.** *my father, Yohanes.* **ibu saya, Lia.** *my mother, Lia.* **nenek saya, Mila.** *my grandmother, Mila.* **kakek saya, Ari.** *my grandfather Ari* **paman saya, Irfan.** *my uncle, Irfan.* **bibi saya, Dinda.** *my aunt, Dinda.*	**Saya suka ____ saya karena dia** *I like my ____ because he/she is* **Saya tidak suka ____ saya karena dia** *I do not like my ____ because he/she is* **________ saya agak** *My ______ is quite* **________ saya sangat** *My ______ is very* **________ saya juga sedikit** *My ______ is also a little*	**baik hati** *kind* **bijaksana** *wise* **cerdas** *intelligent* **jahat** *bad, mean* **keras kepala** *stubborn* **kreatif** *creative* **lucu** *funny, cute* **menjengkelkan** *annoying* **pandai** *clever* **pemalas** *lazy* **pemurah** *generous* **ramah** *friendly* **sabar** *patient* **streng** *strict*
Saya akrab dengan** *I get along with* **Saya tidak akrab dengan** *I don't get along with*	**adik laki-laki, Yudi** *my younger brother Yudi.* **adik perempuan, Siti.** *my younger sister, Siti.* **kakak laki-laki saya, Eko.** *my older brother, Eko.* **kakak perempuan saya, Maya.** *my older sister, Maya.* **sepupu saya, Idris.** *my cousin, Idris.*		

Author's Note:
***dekat** *is used when referring to someone older*
****akrab** *is used when referring to someone on the same generational level*

Unit 6. Part 2 Describing my family: VOCABULARY BUILDING

1. Complete with the missing word

a. Di keluarga saya_______   *In my family there are...*

b. Ada___________ orang   *There are four people...*

c. _________ saya, Lia   *My mother, Lia*

d. Saya _________ dengan   *I get along well with*

e. Saya tidak _______ dengan   *I don't get along with*

f. Paman saya ____ tinggi   *My uncle is very tall*

g. _______ saya baik hati sekali *My aunt is very kind*

h. Sepupu saya Clara_________   *My cousin Clara is funny*

2. Match up

Bibi saya	My cousin
Kakek saya	My mum
Ibu saya	My aunt
Bapak saya	My little bro
Kakak laki-laki saya	My big sis
Sepupu saya	My granddad
Kakak perempuan saya	My dad
Paman saya	My big bro
Adik perempuan saya	My uncle
Adik laki-laki saya	My little sis

3. Translate into English

a. Saya suka paman saya

b. Sepupu saya pemurah

c. Dia keras kepala

d. Saya akrab dengan...

e. Saya tidak suka...

f. Saya tidak akrab dengan...

g. Ibu saya sedikit menjengkelkan

h. Dia agak cerewet

4. Add the missing letter

a. keras __epala   c. baik __ati   e. __epupu   g. ka__ak   i. jug__   k. pa__a__

b. __kra__   d. __akek   f. __dik   h. i__u   j. __aya   l. kar__na

5. Broken words

a. A______ e_________ o_________ ...

There are four people ...

b. d_________ k_____________ s __________

in my family

c. I___ s_________ s_________ b _____ h_________

My mother is very kind

d. S______ a________ d______ ...

I get on well with...

e. P_________ s_________ s________ p__________

My uncle is very generous

f. S______ t_________ a_________ d_______...

I don't get along with...

g. A____ p_________ s_____ b________ p_________

My younger sister has long hair

h. B_______ s________ j______ a_________ s _______

My father is also quite strict

6. Complete with a suitable word

a. Ada empat _____________

b. Dia _________ hati

c. Saya _________ baik

d. Sangat _____________

e. Saya tidak _________ dengan paman

f. Ibu _________sedikit streng

g. Saya dekat ________ bibi

h. Rambut saya ________ hitam dan tebal

i. Mata saya __________ biru

j. Sepupu __________ agak lucu

k. Kakak ________ sangat pandai

l. Nenek berumur delapan puluh ______

Unit 6. Part 2 Describing my family: READING

Saya Amir. Saya berumur sepuluh tahun dan saya tinggal di Kuala Lumpur, ibu kota Malaysia. Di keluarga saya, ada lima orang, bapak saya Jon, ibu saya Alya dan dua saudara saya, Ashraf dan Haziq. Saya akrab dengan Ashraf karena dia baik hati dan pemurah. Tetapi, saya tidak akrab dengan Haziq karena dia sangat menjengkelkan.

Nama saya Edith. Saya berusia empat belas tahun dan saya tinggal di kota Manila, di Filipina. Saya sangat suka kakek saya karena dia sangat lucu. Dia cerdas tetapi sangat pemalu. Bapak saya, dia sangat gemuk dan sangat keras kepala. Dia punya mata cokelat dan rambut yang pendek sekali.

Nama saya Matt. Saya berumur lima belas tahun dan saya tinggal di kota Perth, di Australia. Saya punya rambut pirang dan sangat pendek. Di keluarga saya ada enam orang. Saya tidak akrab dengan adik saya karena dia menjengkelkan dan keras kepala. Saya akrab dengan sepupu saya karena mereka sangat baik. Sepupu favorit saya bernama Ian dan dia tinggi, besar dan kuat. Dia sangat lucu dan baik. Dia punya rambut hitam pendek dan berkacamata.

Saya Iskandar. Saya berumur sepuluh tahun dan saya tinggal di Jakarta, ibu kota Indonesia. Saya sangat ganteng. Di keluarga saya, saya ada delapan orang. Saya suka paman saya tetapi saya tidak suka bibi saya. Saya dekat dengan paman saya Yusuf karena dia lucu dan ramah. Tetapi, bibi saya tidak ramah dan menjengkelkan. Bibi saya Maya punya rambut hitam, panjang dan keriting. Matanya hijau seperti saya. Hari ulang tahunnya pada tanggal lima Mei.

Nama saya Zay. Saya berusia sembilan tahun dan saya tinggal di kota Makassar, di Sulawesi. Di keluarga saya, ada empat orang. Saya punya satu kakak laki-laki. Saya tidak dekat dengan bapak saya karena dia sangat keras kepala dan tidak ramah. Saya sangat suka nenek saya karena dia sangat baik.

1. Find the Indonesian for the following items in Edith's text

a. I am called:

b. live in:

c. my grandfather:

d. but:

e. very:

f. my father:

g. brown eyes:

h. very short hair:

2. Answer the following questions about Iskandar

a. How old is he?

b. Where is he from?

c. How many people are there in his family?

d. Who does he get along well with?

e. Why does he like Yusuf?

f. Who does he not like?

g. When is her birthday?

3. Complete with the missing words

Nama saya Agung.

__________ saya sepuluh

tahun dan saya tinggal ___

Denpasar. Di keluarga

saya ada empat _______.

Saya ________ dengan

kakek saya karena ___

sangat baik hati dan lucu.

Bapak saya punya

__________ pendek dan

matanya _______ cokelat.

4. Find Someone Who...

a. ...has a grandma who is very good

b. ...is fifteen years old

c. ...celebrates their birthday on 5th May

d. ...has a favourite cousin

e. ...is from the Philippines

f. ...only gets along well with one of his brothers

g. ...is very handsome

h. ...is tall, big and strong

i. ...has green eyes

Unit 6. Part 2 Describing my family: TRANSLATION

1. Faulty translation: spot and correct any translation mistakes (in the English)

a. Di keluarga saya ada empat orang: *In my family there are fourteen people*

b. Ibu saya Iva dan adik saya Dian: *My mother Iva and my cousin Dian*

c. Saya tidak akrab dengan bapak saya: *I get along well with my father*

d. Paman saya bernama Agus: *My father is called Agus*

e. Irfan sangat baik dan lucu: *Irfan is very mean but fun*

f. Ahmad punya rambut yang tebal: *Ahmad has long hair*

2. From Indonesian to English

a. Saya suka kakek saya

b. Nenek saya sangat baik

c. Sepupu saya bertengkar dengan ibunya

d. Saya akrab dengan kakak laki-laki saya

e. Saya tidak akrab dengan sepupu saya

f. Saya suka kakek saya karena dia pemurah

g. Bapak saya baik hati dan lucu

h. Saya tidak suka adik laki-laki saya

i. Saya bertengkar dengan sepupu saya karena dia menjengkelkan

3. Phrase-level translation

a. He is nice

b. She is generous

c. I get along well with…

d. I do not get along with…

e. My uncle is funny

f. My little brother

g. I like my cousin Maya

h. She has short and black hair

i. He has blue eyes

j. I don't like my granddad

k. He is very stubborn

4. Sentence-level translation

a. My name is Iskandar. I am nine years old. In my family there are four people.

b. My name is Iva. I have blue eyes. I get along well with my brother.

c. I do not get along with my brother because he is stubborn.

d. My name is Firda. I live in Singapore. I do not like my uncle Gunadi because he is mean.

e. I like my cousin a lot because she is very good.

f. In my family there are five people. I like my father but I do not like my mother.

Unit 6. Part 2 Describing my family: WRITING

1. Split sentences

Bapak saya	hitam
Ibu	dengan adik
Saya berambut	karena dia streng
Saya	saya baik hati
Saya tidak suka paman saya	bermata hijau
Saya sangat suka	pemurah
Saya akrab	bibi saya

2. Rewrite the sentences in the correct order

a. orang keluarga di ada saya enam

b. saya kakak dengan saya akrab

c. suka tidak saya saya paman

d. biru saya punya ibu mata

e. baik hati saya pemurah bibi dan

f. hitam dia mata punya

3. Spot and correct the grammar and spelling errors

a. Di saya keluarga punya…

b. Saya akrab dangan…

c. Saya tidak suka saya bibi…

d. Adik laka-laka saya lucu

e. Saya tidak akab dengan…

f. Bapak saya baik hata

g. Dia punya biru mata

h. Kakak saya tinggi and lucu

i. Rambut ibu panjang dan luras

j. Saya suka sangat kakek saya

4. Anagrams

a. laakerug

b. rkusu

c. kraab

d. nangteg

e. rdceas

f. kbai hait

g. rskea ekalpa

h. cluu

5. Guided writing – write 3 short paragraphs describing the people below in the first person:

Name	Age	Family	Likes	Likes	Dislikes
Idris	12	4 people	Mother because very nice. Has long blond hair.	Older brother because fun and very good.	Cousin Cinta because very mean.
Ratna	11	5 people	Father because very fun. Has short black hair.	Grandmother because very nice and generous.	Uncle Eko because stubborn and ugly.
Harto	10	3 people	Grandfather because very funny. Has very short hair.	Younger sister because very good and relaxed.	Aunt Dewi because very strong but stubborn.

6. Describe this person in the third person:

Name: Uncle Agus
Hair: Blond, short hair
Eyes: Blue
Opinion: Like a lot
Physical: Tall and strong
Personality: Nice, fun, generous.

UNIT 7
Talking about pets

Grammar Time 3: To Have – Ada, Punya (Mempunyai) & Memiliki

Pets and descriptions

Question Skills: Age / Descriptions / Pets

In this unit will learn how to say in Indonesian

- What pets you have at home
- What pet you would like to have
- What its name is
- More adjectives to describe appearance and personality
- Key question words

You will also learn how to ask questions about
- Name / age / appearance / quantity

You will revisit the following
- Introducing oneself
- Family members
- Describing people
- The verbs 'Ada', 'Punya (Mempunyai)' and 'Memiliki' (to have)

UNIT 7
Talking about pets

Apakah kamu <u>punya/mempunyai</u> binatang peliharaan? *Do you <u>have</u> pets?*
Apakah kamu <u>memiliki</u> seekor anjing? *Do you <u>own</u> a dog?*
Apakah kamu <u>ada</u> kucing di rumah? *Do you <u>have</u> a cat at home?*
Apakah <u>ada</u> tiga ayam putih di rumahmu? *<u>Are there</u> three white chickens in your house?*

Di rumah saya ada *In my house there is/are*	**binatang peliharaan** *pet*	**yang bernama Tabby** *that is called Tabby*
	seekor anjing *a dog*	
Saya memelihara *I look after*	**seekor ayam** *a chicken*	**kecil** *small*
	seekor bebek *a duck*	**besar** *big*
Saya punya/mempunyai *I have*	**seekor burung** *a bird*	**biru** *blue*
	seekor burung kakaktua *a cockatoo*	**cokelat** *brown*
Saya tidak punya/mempunyai *I don't have*	**seekor burung nuri** *a parrot*	**hijau** *green*
	seekor hamster *a hamster*	**hitam** *black*
	seekor ikan *a fish*	**jingga** *orange*
Teman saya Paulus punya *My friend Paulus has*	**seekor ikan emas** *a goldfish*	**kuning** *yellow*
	seekor kadal *a lizard*	**merah** *red*
Saya memiliki *I have (own)*	**seekor kelinci** *a rabbit*	**putih** *white*
	seekor kucing *a cat*	
Saya tidak memiliki *I don't have (own)*	**seekor kuda** *a horse*	**cantik** *pretty*
	seekor kura-kura *a turtle*	**jelek** *ugly*
Teman saya Paulus memiliki *My friend Paulus has*	**seekor laba-laba** *a spider*	**jinak** *tame*
	seekor marmut *a guinea pig*	**liar** *wild*
	seekor penguin *a penguin*	**lincah** *lively*
Saya ada *I have*	**seekor tikus** *a mouse*	**lucu** *funny, cute*
	seekor tikus besar *a rat*	**malas** *lazy*
Saya tidak ada *I do not have*	**seekor ular** *a snake*	**manja** *affectionate*
		membosankan *boring*
Saya ingin punya *I want to have*		**menjengkelkan** *annoying*
		nakal *naughty*
Saya tidak ingin punya *I wouldn't want to have*		

Unit 7. Talking about pets: VOCABULARY BUILDING

1. Complete with the missing word

a. Di rumah saya ada seekor b_____   *At home I have a bird*

b. Saya tidak ada k__________   *I don't have a rabbit*

c. Saya ingin punya seekor a________   *I'd like to have a dog*

d. Saya ingin memiliki seekor k_____   *I would like to have a turtle*

e. Di r_____ saya ada seekor k______   *At home I have a cat*

f. Saya tidak punya s________ ular   *I don't have a snake*

g. Saya ada l______- l_______ di rumah   *I have a spider at home*

h. Saya i___ punya seekor marmut   *I'd like to have a guinea-pig*

2. Match up

seekor kucing	a rat
dua ekor anjing	a lizard
seekor kuda	two fish
seekor burung	a cat
seekor ikan	a turtle
seekor kura-kura	a fish
seekor kadal	a guinea pig
seekor kakaktua	two dogs
dua ekor ikan	a cockatoo
seekor tikus besar	a bird
seekor marmut	a horse

3. Translate into English

a. Saya memiliki seekor anjing

b. Teman saya Lia ada seekor kucing

c. Saya punya dua ekor ikan emas

d. Saya tidak ada binatang peliharaan di rumah

e. Saya ada tiga ekor anjing

f. Saya ingin memiliki seekor marmut

g. Adik saya punya seekor kura-kura

h. Kucing saya berumur lima tahun

4. Add the missing letter

a. Te__an saya

b. Ku__a-ku__a

c. Bu__ung nuri

d. I__an

e. An__ing

f. Ku__ing

g. Mar__ut

h. Se__kor

5. Anagrams

a. amay

b. stiuk

c. dkua

d. dkala

e. arul

f. urubng

g. onymet

h. bebke

6. Broken words

a. D_ r_____ s_____ a_____ s_____ a_______

At home I have a dog

b. T_____ s_____ F_____ p___ s___ b___ n___

My friend Firda has a parrot

c. A____ l____-l___ s____ m______ s____ k___-k____

My younger brother has a turtle

d. S____ t____ p_____ s____ k______   *I don't have a rabbit*

e. S____ a____ s_____ u____   *I have a snake*

f. Ahmad p____ s____ k____   *Ahmad has a cat*

g. S____ m_______ s_____ i_____ e_____   *I have a goldfish*

h. S____ p____ d____ e____ b_______   *I have two animals*

7. Complete with a suitable word

a. Saya _________ seekor kucing

b. Ikan emas ______ sangat lucu

c. Teman saya ______ seekor burung

d. Adik saya punya________ kucing

e. Di ________ ada dua ekor bebek

f. ___rumah ada dua binatang peliharaan, seekor anjing _____ seekor kucing

g. Di rumah saya ada_____ marmut

h. Di rumah ada dua_____ burung

i. Kakak saya ________ seekor kuda

j. Anjing saya ________ putih dan cokelat

Unit 7. Talking about pets: READING

Nama saya Alina. Saya berumur delapan tahun dan saya tinggal di kota Madrid. Ada empat orang di keluarga saya: orang tua saya dan adik laki-laki saya, yang bernama Hendri. Hendri tidak ramah dan kurus. Kami mempunyai dua binatang peliharaan: seekor anjing bernama Bueno dan seekor kucing bernama Malo. Bueno, dia sangat manja. Malo menjengkelkan, seperti saudara saya!

Nama saya Rahmad. Saya berumur sembilan tahun dan saya tinggal di Kuala Lumpur. Ada empat orang di keluarga saya: ibu, bapak dan adik saya, namanya Fredy. Dia berumur dua belas tahun. Kami punya dua binatang peliharaan: seekor burung kakaktua lucu bernama Rico dan seekor kucing bernama Si Putih yang nakal.

Nama saya Jalil. Saya berumur sembilan tahun dan saya tinggal di Bandung. Ada lima orang di keluarga saya: ibu, bapak dan dua kakak laki-laki yang bernama Harto dan Mahmud. Harto cerewet dan lucu. Mahmud sangat serius dan rajin. Kami ada dua binatang peliharaan: seekor marmut bernama Sam dan seekor kura-kura bernama Dexter. Marmut sangat lucu dan lincah. Dexter sangat serius, seperti kakak saya Mahmud.

Nama saya Selene. Umur saya sepuluh tahun. Ada empat orang di keluarga saya: ibu, bapak dan dua adik perempuan saya, namanya Sari dan Lian. Sari sangat pemurah dan suka membantu. Lian sangat keras kepala dan membosankan. Kami memiliki dua binatang peliharaan: seekor kelinci bernama Busy dan seekor bebek bernama Loco. Busy sangat jinak dan ramah. Loco sangat liar dan malas. Seperti adik saya!

1. Find the Indonesian in Alina's text

a. two pets

b. which is called

c. a cat

d. a dog

e. very affectionate

f. like my sibling

g. my parents

h. my name is

i. not friendly

j. four people

2. Find Someone Who...

a. ...has a cat

b. ...has a cockatoo

c. ...has a duck

d. ...has a guinea pig

e. ...has a rabbit

f. ...has a dog

3. Answer the following questions about Jalil's text

a. Where does Jalil live?

b. What is his brother Mahmud like?

c. Who is cute and lively?

d. Who is like Mahmud?

e. Who is Harto?

f. Who is Dexter?

g. Who is Sam?

5. Fill in the blanks

Saya ____________ Wayan. Saya berumur sebelas t________ dan t_________ di Bali. Di k_________ saya ada lima orang: ibu, bapak dan dua adik perempuan s____, n__________ Putu dan Made. Putu cerewet dan ramah. Made malas d___ tidak menyenangkan. Kami p__________ dua binatang peliharaan di rumah: seekor tikus yang bernama Maya dan seekor kucing bernama Swift. Swift lucu d____ lincah. Maya s_____ baik, sama seperti a________ saya Made.

4. Fill in the table below

Name	Alina	Rahmad
Age		
City		
Pets		
Description of pets		

Unit 7. Talking about pets: TRANSLATION

1. Faulty translation: spot and correct any translation mistakes you find below

a. Di keluarga saya ada empat orang dan dua binatang peliharaan *In my family there are four people and three pets.*

b. Di rumah kami punya dua binatang peliharaan: seekor anjing dan seekor tikus *At home we have two pets: a dog and a rabbit*

c. Teman saya Putu mempunyai seekor kura-kura bernama Speedy. Speedy sangat lucu. *My friend Putu has a duck called Speedy. Speedy is very boring.*

d. Kakak perempuan saya ada seekor kuda yang bernama Dylan *My sister has a parrot called Dylan*

e. Ibu saya memiliki seekor marmut yang bernama Nicole *My father has a frog called Nicole*

f. Saya punya seekor kucing yang bernama Sleepy. Sleepy sangat lincah *I have a dog called Sleepy. Sleepy is very beautiful*

2. Translate into English

a. seekor kucing lucu

b. seekor anjing manja

c. dua ekor bebek putih

d. seekor kura-kura malas

e. seekor kuda cantik

f. dua ekor tikus lincah

g. tiga ekor marmut hitam dan cokelat

h. Saya punya dua binatang peliharaan

i. Saya tidak ada bintang peliharaan di rumah

j. Saya tidak ingin punya seekor anjing

k. Saya ingin punya banyak ikan

l. Saya punya dua ekor marmut tetapi saya ingin punya seekor ular

3. Phrase-level translation En to Indonesian

a. A cute dog

b. A lively duck

c. At home

d. We *(ex. listener)* have

e. A pretty horse

f. A lazy cat

g. I have

h. I don't have

i. I want to have

4. Sentence-level translation En to Indonesian

a. My brother has a horse called Coco.

b. My sister has an ugly turtle called Miko.

c. I have a fat guinea pig called Felix

d. At home we have three pets: a duck, a rabbit and a parrot.

e. I have a rat called Roxy

f. At home we have three pets: a cat, a dog and a guinea pig

g. I have two fish called Nemo and Dory

Unit 7. Talking about pets: WRITING

1. Split sentences

Saya punya anjing yang	emas
Di rumah kami	peliharaan
Saya punya seekor ikan	bernama Speedy
Saya punya seekor kucing	marmut
Saya suka binatang	ada laba-laba
Adik saya punya seekor	rumah kami
Kami tidak punya binatang peliharaan di	hitam

2. Rewrite the sentences in the correct order

a. punya binatang tiga peliharaan Kami di rumah

b. seekor ingin Saya tikus punya

c. kucing mempunyai Saya seekor anjing dan seekor

d. hitam Teman marmut saya Putu seekor punya

e. Fran hijau yang Kami ada burung seekor bernama

f. dua Kami punya ikan emas ekor

g. saya yang Kakak bernama memiliki seekor Nicole burung nuri

3. Spot and correct the grammar and spelling note: in several cases a word is missing

a. Di rumah ada seekor anjing seekor kucing

b. Saya punya seekor hitam marmut

c. Saya ingin mempunyai ular seekor

d. Saya adik memiliki kucing putih

e. Teman Agus saya punya dua ekor ikan emas

f. Kuda saya nama Graham

g. Saya ada hitam kuda

h. Di rumah kami punya peliharaan bintang

4. Anagrams

a. ucinkg

b. likenic

c. itusk

d. liharaanpe

e. laru

f. kani

g. atbingan

6. Describe this person in the third person:

Name: Juliani

Hair: Blond, short

Eyes: Green

Personality: Very nice

Physical: Short, fat

Pets: A dog, a cat and two fish and would like to have a spider

5. Guided writing – write 3 short paragraphs (in 1st person) describing the pets below

Name	Animal	Age	Colour	Character or appearance
Reza	Dog	4	White	Affectionate
Sanja	Duck	6	Blue	Cute
Niki	Horse	1	Brown	Beautiful

Grammar Time 3:
To Have - ADA, PUNYA (MEMPUNYAI), MEMILIKI
Pets and Descriptions

1. Translate

a. I have: s_ _ _ punya

b. You have: k _ _ _ p_ _ _ _ _

c. She has: d _ _ m_ _ _ _ _ _ _ _

d. We (inc.) have: k _ _ _ a _ _

e. We (exc.) have: k _ _ _ p _ _ _ _

f. They have: m _ _ _ _ _ _ p_ _ _ _

2. Translate into English

a. Saya punya seekor kuda yang sangat cantik. Namanya Jai.

b. Adik saya memiliki seekor kucing yang sangat lucu.

c. Ibu saya punya seekor kelinci berwarna putih.

d. Sepupu saya ada seekor kuda yang sangat gemuk.

e. Di rumah kami mempunyai dua ekor ayam yang jinak.

f. Teman saya Ali punya seekor kura-kura yang sangat besar.

3. Complete the translation

a. *I have a cat*   Saya p____________ seekor kucing.

b. *It is two years old*   D______ berumur dua tahun.

c. *We (exc.) have a turtle. It is 4 years old* K_____ ada kura-kura. U____________ empat tahun.

d. *My older sister has a dog*   Kakak perempuan saya m____________ seekor anjing.

e. *My uncle has two cats*   Paman saya m____________ dua ekor kucing.

f. *They are three years old*   M____________ berumur tiga tahun.

g. *My brother and I have a snake*   Saya dan adik saya p____________ seekor ular.

h. *Do you guys have pets?*   Apakah A______ s____________ punya binatang peliharaan?

i. *What animals do you have?*   Kamu p____________ binatang apa?

4. Translate into Indonesian

a. I have a guinea pig. It is three years old.

b. We don't have pets at home.

c. My dog is three years old. It is very big.

d. I have three brothers. They are very mean.

e. My cousins have a duck and a guinea pig.

f. My auntie has blond, curly and long hair. She is very pretty.

g. My brother and I have black hair and green eyes.

Question Skills 1: Age / Descriptions / Pets

1. Match question and answer

a. Berapa umurmu?	Mereka berumur delapan puluh tahun
b. Mengapa kamu tidak dekat dengan ibumu?	Baik-baik saja, terima kasih
c. Apa warna rambut dia?	Umur saya lima belas tahun
d. Berapa umur kakek-nenekmu?	Mata saya biru
e. Apa warna matamu?	Karena dia sangat keras kepala
f. Apa warna favoritmu?	Anjing
g. Apa kabar?	Tidak, saya tidak punya binatang peliharaan
h. Apakah kamu punya binatang peliharaan?	Dia berambut merah
i. Yang mana binatang favoritmu, kucing atau anjing ?	Tanggal dua puluh Juni
j. Kamu punya berapa binatang peliharaan?	Tidak, karena dia sangat serius dan malas
k. Bagaimana sifatmu?	Biru
l. Bagaimana ciri-cirimu?	Saya punya dua, seekor kucing dan burung nuri
m. Apakah kamu dekat dengan bapakmu?	Saya ramah dan cerewet
n. Kapan ulang tahunmu?	Saya pendek dan sedikit gemuk

2. Complete with the missing words

a. Kamu berasal dari ____________?
Where are you from?

b. ______________ sifatmu?
What are you like in terms of character?

c. Berapa____________ bapakmu?
How old is your father?

d. _______kamu dekat dengan ibumu?
Do you get along with your mum?

e. ____________ ulang tahunmu?
When is your birthday?

f. ___________ anjingmu?
What is your dog like?

g. Kamu punya _________ binatang peliharaan? *How many pets do you have?*

3. Translate the following question words into English

a. Yang mana?

b. Kapan?

c. Di mana?

d. Bagaimana?

e. Dari mana?

f. Apakah?

g. Berapa?

h. Apa ?

i. Mengapa?

5. Translate into Indonesian

a. What is your name?

b. How old are you?

c. What is your hair like?

d. What is your favourite animal?

e. Do you get along with your father?

f. Why don't you get along with your mother?

g. How many pets do you have?

h. Where are you from?

4. Complete the questions

a. B____________ u__________mu?

b. A________ k______________ ?

c. A______ w________ r____________mu?

d. B________________ s________mu?

e. A_________ w_____________ favoritmu?

f. K________ u________ t________ mu ?

g. A______ w__________ m______ mu ?

UNIT 8
Saying what jobs people do, why they like/dislike them and where they work

Grammar Time 4: Question Words & BER- verbs
Grammar Time 5: Auxiliary Verbs

In this unit will learn how to say:

- What jobs people do
- Why they like/dislike those jobs
- Where they work
- Adjectives to describe jobs
- Words for useful jobs
- Words for types of buildings
- The verb "Bekerja" (to work)
- Other BER- verbs
- Auxiliary Verbs
- Words to indicate past, present and future

You will revisit the following:
- Family members
- Description of people and pets

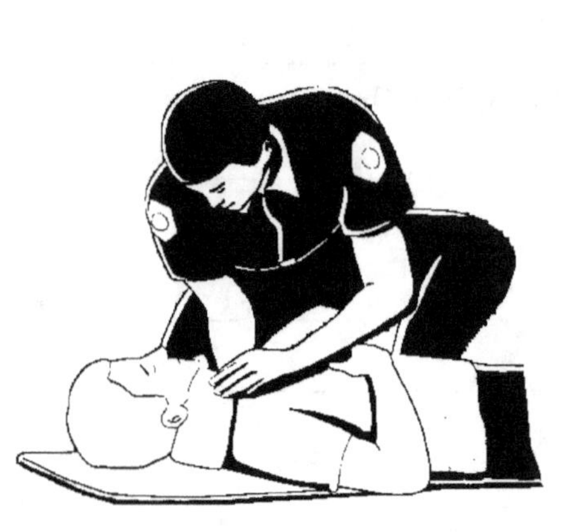

UNIT 8
Saying what jobs people do, why they like/dislike them and where they work

Dia bekerja sebagai apa? *He/She works as what?* **Dia bekerja di mana?** *Where does he/she/they work?*					**Dia bekerja di** He/*she works in/at*
Bapak saya *My father*		**aktor** *actor*	**dan dia suka pekerjaannya karena** *he/she likes the job because it is*	**aktif** *active*	**bengkel** *garage*
		akuntan *accountant*			
Ibu saya *My mother*		**dokter** *doctor*		**berulang-ulang** *repetitive*	**pedesaan** *countryside*
		dokter gigi *dentist*			
Adik laki-laki saya *My younger brother*		**guru** *teacher*		**membosankan** *boring*	**hotel** *hotel*
		ibu/bapak rumah tangga *housewife/husband*	**dan dia tidak suka pekerjaannya karena** *he/she doesn't like the job because it is*		**kantor** *office*
Adik perempuan saya *My younger sister*		**insinyur** *engineer*		**memuaskan** *rewarding*	**kebun** *garden*
		karyawan *office worker*		**menghilangkan stres** *stress relieving*	**kota** *city*
	bekerja sebagai seorang *works as a*	**montir** *mechanic*		**menyenangkan** *fun*	**lapangan terbang** *airport*
Kakak laki-laki saya *My older brother*		**pemadam kebakaran** *firefighter*	**dan dia sangat suka pekerjaannya karena** *he/she loves the job because it is*	**mudah** *easy*	**perusahaan** *company*
		pemasak *chef*		**menarik** *interesting*	**restoran** *restaurant*
Kakak perempuan saya *My older sister*	**adalah seorang** *is a*	**penata rambut** *hairdresser*			
		pengacara *lawyer*	**dan dia benci pekerjaannya karena** *he/she hates the job because it is*	**suasananya nyaman** *pleasant environment*	**ruang kerja** *workshop*
		pengusaha *businessperson*			**rumah** *at home*
Paman saya *My uncle*		**perawat** *nurse*		**ada banyak stres** *stressful*	**rumah makan** *restaurant*
		petani *farmer*			
Bibi saya *My aunt*		**pilot** *pilot*		**susah/sulit** *difficult*	**rumah sehat** *hospital*
		pramugari *flight attendant*			
		tukang cukur *barber*			**sekolah** *a school*
					teater *theatre*

Unit 8. Saying what jobs people do: VOCABULARY BUILDING

1. Complete with the missing word

a. Bapak saya seorang _____________ *My father is a lawyer*

b. Bibi saya seorang _______________ *My aunt is a hairdresser*

c. Adik saya bekerja sebagai ______________
My younger brother works as a mechanic

d. Ibu saya seorang _____________ *My mother is a doctor*

e. Kakak _________ saya bekerja sebagai _______________
My older sister works as an engineer

f. Bibi saya seorang ______________*My aunt is an accountant*

g. _________ saya seorang _____________ *My uncle is a farmer*

2. Match up

membosankan	stressful
aktif	difficult
sulit	fun
menyenangkan	active
nyaman	rewarding
ada banyak stres	boring
mudah	interesting
memuaskan	easy
menarik	pleasant

3. Translate into English

a. Ibu saya seorang montir

b. Paman saya seorang petani

c. Dia bekerja di garasi

d. Kakak saya seorang akuntan

e. Dia tidak suka pekerjaannya

f. Sepupu saya seorang tukang cukur

g. Dia sangat suka perkerjaannya

h. karena menarik

4. Add the missing letter

a. N_aman

b. Men_ rik

c. In_inyur

d. _okter

e. st_es

f. Pe_erjaan

g. Pe_awat

h. Akti_

5. Anagrams

a. kDtoer ggii

b. otirMn

c. ngacPeara

d. rotkA

e. taniPe

f. aunAktn

g. urGu

h. asPemak

6. Broken words

a. D_____ b_______ r_______ t______ *He is a house husband*

b. D__ s__________ p________nya *He likes his job*

c. K_____ l___ - l_____ s______ p___ *My brother is a farmer*

d. D_____ b_________ *He/she works*

e. D__ p____________ *In the countryside*

f. D_______ b_____ p_______nya *He hates his job*

g. K_______ s_________ n_______ *Because it is a pleasant environment*

h. S_______ m______________ *It is very rewarding*

7. Complete with a suitable word

a. Ibu saya seorang _____________

b. Saya_________ pekerjaan saya

c. Dia suka pekerjaannya _____ menarik

d. Bekerja di _______________

e. _____ saya seorang penata rambut

f. Saya tidak_____ pekerjaan ini

g. Karena sangat _____________

h. Bibi _____ seorang dokter

i. Dia suka bekerja ______ petani

j. Paman saya seorang montir, dia bekerja di _______________

Unit 8. Saying what jobs people do: READING

Nama saya Arif. Saya berumur dua puluh tahun dan saya tinggal di Yogyakarta, di pulau Jawa. Di keluarga saya ada empat orang. Saya punya anjing yang sangat lucu, Davi. Bapak saya bekerja sebagai dokter di kota. Dia suka pekerjaannya karena memuaskan dan menyenangkan. Paman saya seorang petani dan dia suka juga pekerjaannya. Kadang-kadang pekerjaannya susah, tetapi dia suka bekerja dengan binatang.

Nama saya Sofi. Ada empat orang di keluarga saya. Nama bapak saya Mateo dan dia seorang pengacara. Dia suka pekerjaannya karena menarik, walaupun pekerjaanya membuat dia banyak stres. Ibu saya seorang ibu rumah tangga dan dia sangat suka pekerjaannya karena menjadi ibu rumah tangga membuat hati ibu saya senang. Saya punya seekor anjing bernama Dani. Dia sangat besar dan lucu! Saya tidak suka kucing.

Nama saya Samuel. Saya berasal dari Ambon. Orang favorit di keluarga saya adalah ibu saya. Dia pemalu tetapi sangat baik. Ibu saya seorang insinyur tetapi sekarang dia tidak bekerja. Saya benci paman saya, dia cerdas tetapi sangat menjengkelkan. Paman saya seorang guru tetapi dia benci pekerjaannya karena sulit dan membosankan. Dia bekerja di sebuah sekolah di Ambon, tetapi dia tidak suka anak-anak. Di rumah saya punya seekor kura-kura bernama Speedy. Dia lambat tetapi sangat lucu, seperti kakak saya Casandra.

Nama saya Camila. Ada empat orang di keluarga saya. Nama ibu saya Valeri dan dia seorang penata rambut. Dia suka pekerjaannya karena menarik dan aktif. Bapak saya seorang bapak rumah tangga tetapi dia tidak begitu suka pekerjaannya karena sangat sukar dan agak membosankan. Di rumah saya tidak ada binatang tetapi saya ingin punya seekor kuda. Sepupu saya punya seekor kuda bernama Kristian dan dia besar dan kuat. Sungguh keren!

1. Find the Indonesian in Arif's text

a. I am 20

b. I have a dog

c. my dad works as...

d. a doctor

e. in the city

f. he likes his work

g. it is rewarding

h. sometimes

i. with animals

2. Answer the questions on ALL texts

a. Who is Kristian?

b. Whose mum is a housewife?

c. Who has an uncle that is in the wrong job?

d. Whose father is a doctor?

e. Who has a turtle?

f. Who has a dog?

3. Answer the following questions about Samuel

a. Where does Samuel live?

b. Who is his favourite person?

c. What does his mum do? - 2 details

d. Why does he hate his uncle?

e. Why is his uncle a bad teacher?

f. Who is Speedy?

g. What is Casandra like?

4. Fill in the blanks

N______ saya Mila. Umur saya tiga belas t_____ dan saya t______ di Medan. Di k______ saya ada lima orang. Sepupu saya Karman sangat cere___ dan baik h___, umurnya tiga p____ tahun. Dia bekerja sebagai s______ dokter. Dia tinggal di London di Inggris. Dia suka p_______nya karena menar___ dan memuas___. Bapak saya tidak b______ sekarang. Di r____ kami p_____ bintang yang bernama Damian, seekor laba-l___: seekor tarantula!

5. Fill in the table below using information in Ex.4

Name	Mila	Karman
Age		
City		
Pets/Job		
Opinion of job	- - -	

Unit 8. Saying what jobs people do: TRANSLATION

1. Faulty translation: spot and correct IN THE ENGLISH any translation mistakes you find below

a. Bapak saya bekerja sebagai aktor dan dia sangat suka pekerjaannya karena itu memuaskan. Dia bekerja di teater. *My father works as a cook and he really likes his job because it is interesting. He works in a school.*

b. Bibi saya bekerja sebagai seorang pengusaha di sebuah kantor. Dia suka pekerjaannya tetapi itu sulit. *My aunt works as a business woman in a hair salon. She hates her job but it's hard.*

c. Teman saya Fran bekerja sebagai perawat. Dia bekerja di rumah sehat dan dia suka pekerjaannya. *My enemy Fran works as a nurse. She lives in a hospital and likes his work.*

d. Paman saya Gianfranco adalah seorang pemasak di sebuah restoran Italia dan dia suka pekerjaannya. *My uncle Gianfranco is a lawyer in an Italian restroom and he likes it.*

e. Ibu saya Angela adalah seorang akuntan dan bekerja di sebuah kantor. Dia membenci pekerjaannya karena membosankan dan berulang-ulang. *My mother Angela is an actress and works in an office. She loves her work because it is boring and repetitive.*

3. Phrase-level translation English to Indonesian

a. my big brother

b. works as

c. a farmer

d. he likes

e. his job

f. because it's active

g. and fun

h. but it's tough

2. Translate into English

a. Paman saya bekerja

b. Bapak saya bekerja sebagai

c. Ibu rumah tangga

d. Perawat

e. Tukang cukur

f. Montir

g. Dia suka pekerjaannya

h. Bekerja di bengkel

i. Bekerja di teater

j. Bekerja di ladang

k. Memuaskan

l. Susah tetapi menyenangkan

4. Sentence-level translation En to Ind

a. My brother is a mechanic

b. My father is a business man

c. My uncle is a farmer and hates his job

d. My brother Darren works in a restaurant

e. At home I have a snake called Sally

f. At home I have a fun dog and a mean cat

g. My aunt is a nurse. She likes her job…

h. …because it is rewarding

i. My aunt works in a hospital

Unit 8. Saying what jobs people do: WRITING

1. Split sentences/phrases

a. Kakak saya punya	memuaskan
b. Bibi saya adalah	sebagai seorang pengacara
c. Sepupu saya berkerja	seorang guru
d. Dia suka	restoran
e. karena	di kantor
f. bekerja di	pekerjaanya
g. bekerja	bebek hitam

2. Rewrite the sentences in the correct order

a. Dia sangat pekerjaannya suka

b. Dia bekerja seorang sebagai akuntan

c. menjadi Dia rumah ibu tangga

d. saya sebagai bekerja Paman petani

e. Kakak bekerja di teater saya

f. saya Kakek suka pekerjaannya tidak

g. saya Teman bekerja rumah sehat di sebagai dokter seorang

3. Spot and correct the grammar and spelling note: in several cases a word is missing

a. Ibu saya seorang rumah

b. Pekerjaan itu membosankan susah

c. Kakak saya bekerja sebagai rambut

d. Dia tidak sukah pekerjaannya karena sesah dan berulang-ulang.

e. Dia bekerja rumah sehat di kota

f. Dia suka sangat pekerjanya karena mudah

g. Saya teman benci pekerjaannya

h. Saya suka pekerjaannya karena memuaskan

4. Anagrams

a. ruGu

b. ulBerang-ungla

c. torDek

d. tnorKa

e. kelBeng

f. steorRan

g. maRuh hseta

6. Describe this person in Indonesian in the 3rd person:

Name: Maya

Hair: Blond + green eyes

Physique: Tall and slim

Personality: Hard-working

Job: Nurse

Opinion: Likes her job a lot

Reason: Hard but rewarding

5. Guided writing – write 3 short paragraphs describing the people below using the details in the box in 1st person

Person	Relation	Job	Like/Dislike	Reason
Yohanes	My dad	Mechanic	Loves	Active and interesting
Lukas	My brother	Lawyer	Hates	Boring and repetitive
Maya	My aunt	Farmer	Likes	Tough but fun

Grammar Time 4: Question Words & BER- Verbs

Siapa	namamu *your name*		?
What is (Who)	nama temanmu *your friend's name*		
	nama bapak kamu *your dad's name*		
Siapa *Who*	**bekerja** **sebagai** *works as*	seorang guru *a teacher*	?
		seorang pengacara *a lawyer*	
		seorang montir *a mechanic*	
	memiliki *has/owns*	binatang peliharaan *pets*	
		seekor anjing *a dog*	
	mempunyai has **punya** *has* **ada** *has*	rambut hitam *black hair* rambut keriting *curly hair* mata cokelat *brown eyes* mata biru *blue eyes*	
Berapa *How many is*	umurmu *your age* umur temanmu *your friend's age* orang di keluarga kamu *people in your family*		?
Bagaimana *Describe*	binatang peliharaan kamu *your pets* keluargamu *your family*		

Di mana *Where do/ were*	kamu *you*	lahir *born* tinggal *live* bekerja *work*	?	
	temanmu *your friend*	memiliki *own/have* punya *have* ada *have*	binatang peliharaan *pets* seekor anjing *a dog* seekor kucing *a cat*	
Apakah *Do/Does*	Iva *Iva*	punya *have* ada *have*	rambut hitam *black hair* mata hijau *green eyes*	?
	ibu kamu / ibumu *your mum*	suka *like* tidak suka *not like*	pekerjaannya *that job* binatang peliharaan *pets*	
Mengapa *Why do/does*	dia *he/she*			

Grammar Time 4. Question Words: DRILLS

1. Match up

Siapa ...?	Describe ...?
Di mana ...?	Where ...?
Berapa ...?	Does ...?
Mengapa ...?	How many ...?
Apakah ...?	Who ...?
Bagaimana ...?	Why ...?

2. Translate into English

a. Kapan kamu lahir?

b. Siapa punya mata biru?

c. Apakah ibu kamu bekerja di toko?

d. Mengapa dia tidak pernah bekerja?

e. Apakah kamu bekerja sebagai seorang polisi?

f. Apakah kamu bekerja di kota?

3. Complete with the correct option

a. ___________ nama teman kamu?

b. ___________ umur bapakmu?

c. ___________ kamu lahir?

d. ___________ orang di keluargamu?

e. ___________ kamu memelihara seekor anjing?

f. ___________ punya mata cokelat?

g. ___________ dia tidak bekerja hari ini?

h. ___________ dia bekerja di toko setiap hari?

Siapa	Mengapa	Apakah	Berapa
Apakah	Berapa	Siapa	Di mana

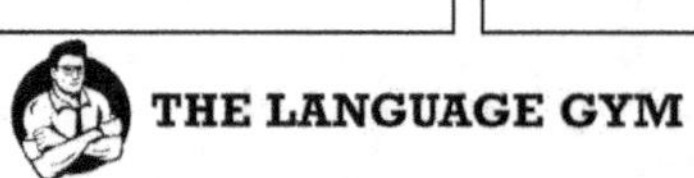

Grammar Time 4. Question Words: DRILLS

4. Match up these question phrases/sentences

a. Siapa namamu?	Describe his characteristics?
b. Siapa bekerja sebagai ...?	Does your friend ...?
c. Siapa mempunyai...?	When were you ...?
d. Siapa ada ...?	Where were you ...?
e. Berapa umur ...?	What is your name?
f. Di mana kamu ...?	How old ...?
g. Kapan kamu ...?	Who has ...?
h. Mengapa dia ...?	How many dogs ...?
i. Apakah temanmu ...?	Who works as ...?
j. Berapa ekor anjing ...?	Who owns ...?
k. Bagaimana ciri-cirinya?	Why is she ...?

5. Translate into Indonesian

a. What is your name?

b. Who works as a lawyer?

c. Who has two cats?

d. Who has brown hair?

e. How old is your friend?

f. Where do you live?

g. When were you born?

h. Does your friend have a rabbit?

i. What is your friend's name?

6. Spot and correct the errors in the English translation

a. Di mana ibumu lahir?   *Where was your father born?*

b. Bagaimana binatang peliharaanmu?   *Describe your family.*

c. Apakah teman kamu punya seekor kucing?   *Does your friend have a dog?*

d. Apakah kamu punya banyak binatang peliharaan?   *Why do you have many pets?*

e. Di mana orang tuamu bekerja?   *Where do your grandparents work?*

f. Siapa nama gurumu?   *What is the name of your friend?*

g. Siapa memiliki dua ekor kucing dan seekor kadal?   *Who has cats and lizards?*

h. Siapa punya rambut keriting dan mata hijau?   *Who has straight hair and brown eyes?*

i. Di mana kamu tinggal?   *Where do you work?*

Other Ber- Verbs

Belajar: to study

Berbahasa: to use the language

Berbelanja: to go shopping

Berenang: to swim

Beristirahat: to have a rest

Berjalan kaki: to walk

Berlatih: to practise

Berlibur: to go on holiday

Bermain: to play

1. Complete the sentences using one of the verbs in the grey box on the left

a. Saya ___________ di mal.   *I go shopping at the mall.*

b. Saya ________ Bahasa Inggris   *I study English*

c. Saya______ ke kantor   *I walk to the office.*

d. Apakah kamu____Indonesia?   *Do you speak Indonesian?*

e. Apakah dia ____setiap hari?   *Does she swim every day?*

f. Apakah Anda semua______ gitar?   *Do you all play the guitar?*

g. Dia ______pada sore hari   *He has a rest in the afternoon*

h. Saya _____ dengan keluarga saya   *I go on holiday with my family*

Grammar Time 5: Auxiliary Verbs & Using BER- Verbs (Part 2)

Subject	Auxiliary verb	Ber- Verb	
Saya *I* **Aku** *I (informal)* **Anda** *You (formal)* **Kamu** *You (informal)* **Dia** *She, He* **Bapak saya** *My father* **Kakak saya** My older sibling **Adik saya** *My younger sibling* **Ibu saya** *My mother* **Kami** *We (excl)* **Kita** *We (incl)* **Anda semua** *You all* **Mereka** *They*	**akan** *will, is going* **belum** *not yet* **sedang** *is (in the process of)* **sudah** *already* **barangkali** *probably, possibly* **bisa** *can, is able* **boleh** *may, is allowed* **dapat** *can, is able* **harus** *must* **ingin** *wishes* **mau** *want* **mungkin** *probably, possibly* **tidak bisa** *can not* **tidak boleh** *may not*	**bekerja** *works* **berbelanja** *to go shopping* **beristirahat** *to have a rest* **berjalan kaki** *walk* **berlibur** *have a holiday*	**bersama teman saya** *with my friend* **bersama sahabat saya** *with my close friend* **bersama keluarga saya** *with my family* **di mal** *in the mall* **di kantor** *in the office* **di pusat kota** *in the city centre* **di Bali** *in Bali* **pada akhir minggu** *on the weekend* **setiap hari** *every day*
		belajar *to study*	**Bahasa Jerman** *German* **Geografi** *Geography* **Ilmu Alam** *Science* **Matematika** *Mathematics* **Musik** *Music* **Sejarah** *History* **Seni** *Art*
	belum bisa *can't yet* **sudah bisa** *can already*	**berbahasa** *speak the language* **berbicara bahasa** *speak the language*	**Belanda** *Dutch* **Indonesia** *Indonesian* **Inggris** *English* **Jepang** *Japanese* **Melayu** *Malaysian* **Prancis** *French*

Grammar Time 5. Auxiliary Verbs & Using BER- Verbs (Part 2): TRANSLATION

1. Match up

belum	will
sedang	wish
sudah	want
akan	not yet
ingin	in the process of
mau	already

3. Translate into English

a. sedang belajar

b. akan berlibur

c. belum bekerja

d. ingin belajar

e. bisa berbahasa Jepang

f. akan beristirahat

g. mau berjalan kaki

h. mungkin berbelanja

i. boleh berbelanja

j. sedang beristirahat

k. harus bekerja

2. Complete with the missing auxiliary verb according to the word in the bracket

a. Ibu saya __________ (*is in the process of*) bekerja di bank

b. Saudara saya __________ (*wants*) berbelanja di mal

c. Kakak saya __________ (*wishes*) bekerja sebagai polisi

d. Saya __________ (*have already*) berlibur di pulau Bali

e. Apakah kamu __________ (*will*) belajar Musik tahun depan?

f. Adik saya _______ (*is able to*) berjalan kaki

g. Mereka tidak __________ (*allowed*) beristirahat

h. Apakah dia __________ (*not yet*) bisa berbahasa Indonesia?

i. Saya __________ (*possibly*) berbelanja hari ini

j. Saya __________ (*can*) bekerja setiap hari

4. Translate into Indonesian (easier)

a. My father wants to have a holiday

b. My parents are already having a rest

c. I will go shopping with my friend

d. My uncle must walk every day

e. My cousins are able to speak Dutch

f. My aunt is (in the process of) studying German

g. My friend Valentino is allowed to go shopping

5. Translate into Indonesian (harder)

a. My brother is tall and handsome. He is studying Music.

b. My older sister is very intelligent and hard-working. She wishes to work as a doctor.

c. My younger brother is very active. He is allowed to walk to the mall with his friends.

d. My mother is very hard-working. She can speak Japanese.

e. My father is very patient and diligent. He is working in the office as an accountant.

UNIT 9
Comparing Appearance and Personality

Revision Quickie 2: Family / Pets / Jobs

In this unit will learn how to say in Indonesian:
- More/less … than
- As … as
- New adjectives to describe people

You will revisit the following:
- Family members
- Pets
- Describing the appearance and character of animals

UNIT 9
Comparing Appearance & Personality

Subject	Comparative	Adjective	Connector	Object
Saya *I* **Anda** *You* **Kamu** *You (inf.)* **Dia** *He / She* **Mereka** *They*		**atletik** *athletic* **baik hati** *kind* **baik** *nice* **berisik** *noisy*		**saya** *me* **Anda** *you* **kamu** *you (inf.)* **dia** *him / her* **mereka** *them*
Adik saya *My younger sibling* **Anak laki-laki saya** *My son* **Anak perempuan saya** *My daughter* **Bapak saya** *My father* **Bibi saya** *My aunt* **Ibu saya** *My mother* **Kakak saya** *My older sibling* **Kakek saya** *My grandpa* **Kakek-nekek** *My grandparents* **Nenek saya** *My grandma* **Orang tua saya** *My parents* **Pacar saya** *My boy/girlfriend* **Paman saya** *My uncle* **Sepupu saya** *My cousin* **Teman saya** *My friend* **Teman-teman saya** *My friends*	**lebih** *more* **kurang** *less*	**cantik** *beautiful* **cerdas** *intelligent* **cerewet** *talkative* **ganteng** *handsome* **gemuk** *fat* **jelek** *ugly* **keras kepala** *stubborn* **kuat** *strong* **kurus** *slim* **lemah** *weak* **malas** *lazy* **membosankan** *boring* **menyenangkan** *fun* **muda** *young* **pendek** *short* **pintar** *smart* **manja** *affectionate* **rajin** *hard-working*	**daripada** *than*	**adik saya** *my younger sibling* **anak saya** *my child* **anak laki-laki saya** *my son* **anak perempuan saya** *my daughter* **bapak saya** *my father* **bibi saya** *my aunt* **ibu saya** *my mother* **kakak saya** *my older sibling* **kakek saya** *my grandpa* **kakek-nekek** *my grandparents* **nenek saya** *my grandma* **orang tua saya** *my parents* **pacar saya** *my boy/girlfriend* **paman saya** *my uncle* **sepupu saya** *my cousin* **teman saya** *my friend* **teman-teman saya** *my friends*
Anjing saya *My dog* **Bebek saya** *My duck* **Kucing saya** *My cat* **Kura-kura saya** *My turtle*	***sama** *the same* ****se-as…as**	**santai** *relaxed* **serius** *serious* **sportif** *sporty* **tinggi** *tall* **tua** *old*	**-nya dengan** *as*	**anjing saya** *my dog* **bebek saya** *my duck* **kucing saya** *my cat* **kura-kura saya** *my turtle*

*__Author's note:__ *sama __tingginya__ dengan the same __height__ as The addition of the suffix __-nya__ changes the adjective to a noun*
***se- is added to the adjective, e.g. __setinggi__ as tall as and __dengan__ is not required*

Unit 9. Comparisons : VOCABULARY BUILDING

1. Complete with the missing word

a. Bapak saya lebih tinggi _______ kakak laki-laki saya — *My father is taller than my older brother*

b. Ibu saya sama cerewetnya __________ bibi saya — *My mother as talkative as my aunt*

c. Kakek saya lebih pendek ______ bapak saya — *My grandfather is shorter than my dad*

d. Sepupu saya lebih malas _______ kami — *My cousins are lazier than us*

e. Anjing saya lebih _______ daripada _______ saya — *My dog is more noisy than my cat*

f. Bibi saya ________ cantik daripada ibu ______ — *My aunt is less pretty than my mother*

g. __________ saya lebih _________daripada saya — *My brother is more hard-working than me*

h. Orang tua saya lebih ____ ______ daripada paman saya — *My parents are more kind than my uncles*

i. Adik laki-laki saya _________ saya — *My younger brother is as tall as me*

2. Translate into English

a. sepupu saya

b. lebih

c. paman saya

d. kakek-nenek saya

e. kakak perempuan

f. teman baik saya

g. karyawan

h. kurang

i. tinggi

j. tua

k. keras kepala

l. malas

3. Match up

rajin	strong
cantik	lazy
baik hati	sporty
kuat	beautiful
sportif	old
tua	hard-working
malas	kind

4. Spot and correct any English translation mistakes

a. Dia lebih tinggi daripada saya — *He is taller than you*

b. Dia secantik saya — *He is as funny as me*

c. Dia lebih muda daripada saya — *She is stronger than me*

d. Saya segemuk dia — *I am fatter than him*

e. Mereka lebih pendek daripada kita — *They are as short as us*

f. Saya sama tuanya dengan dia — *She is as old as him*

g. Dia lebih atletik daripada saya — *You are more athletic than me*

5. Complete with a suitable word

a. Ibu saya ______ tinggi ______ saya

b. Bapak____ lebih muda daripada bibi saya

c. Orang tua saya ______ lucunya ______ kakek-nenek saya

d. Kakek_____ lebih sportif _______ sepupu saya

e. Bebek saya kurang ramah __________ kucing saya

f. Kakek-nenek saya _____ baik hati _______ orang tua saya

g. Pacar saya _______ cantik ______ adik saya

h. Bibi saya tidak __kuat ________

6. Match the opposites

ganteng	pendek
rajin	membosankan
muda	jelek
tinggi	gemuk
lucu	kurang
lemah	malas
lebih	tua
kurus	kuat

Unit 9. Comparisons : READING

Nama saya Gunadi. Saya berumur dua puluh tahun dan saya tinggal di Baubau. Di keluarga saya, kami ada lima orang: orang tua saya dan dua saudara laki-laki saya, Bakti dan Ali. Bakti lebih tinggi, ganteng, dan lebih kuat daripada Ali, tetapi Ali lebih baik hati, lebih pintar, dan lebih rajin daripada Bakti. Nama orang tua saya Agus dan Fifi. Keduanya sangat baik hati, tetapi bapak saya lebih keras kepala daripada ibu saya. Juga, ibu saya lebih sabar dan tidak sekeras kepala bapak saya. Saya sama keras kepalanya dengan bapak saya! Di rumah kami ada dua binatang peliharaan: kura-kura dan bebek. Keduanya sangat baik, tetapi bebek saya lebih berisik. Sama berisiknya dengan saya...

Nama saya Johanes. Saya berumur lima belas tahun dan saya tinggal di kota Kendari. Di keluarga saya ada lima orang: orang tua dan dua kakak laki-laki, Ruben, Ben dan saya. Ruben lebih kurus dan sportif daripada Ben, tetapi Ben lebih tinggi dan lebih kuat. Nama orang tua saya Iva dan Amir. Saya lebih suka bapak karena dia kurang serius daripada ibu. Juga, ibu lebih keras kepala daripada bapak. Saya sama keras kepalanya dengan dia! Di rumah kami punya dua binatang peliharaan: seekor burung nuri dan seekor marmut. Keduanya sangat baik, tetapi burung nuri saya jauh lebih cerewet. Sama dengan saya yang banyak berbicara...

Nama saya Dinda. Umur saya dua puluh tahun dan saya tinggal di Medan bersama dengan orang tua dan dua adik perempuan saya, Rina dan Sari. Rina lebih cantik dari Sari, tetapi Sari lebih ramah. Orang tua saya sangat pemurah dan baik hati, tetapi bapak saya lebih menyenangkan daripada ibu saya. Juga, bapak lebih lucu daripada ibu. Saya selucu bapak saya! Di rumah kami punya dua binatang peliharaan: seekor anjing dan seekor kelinci. Keduanya sangat gemuk, tetapi anjing saya lebih malas. Sama malasnya dengan saya...

1. Find the Indonesian for the following in Gunadi's text

a. I live in:

b. My parents:

c. Good-looking:

d. Hard-working:

e. More stubborn:

f. More patient:

g. But:

h. My duck:

i. Two pets:

j. Very kind:

k. As stubborn as:

2. Complete the statements below based on Dinda's text

a. I am _______ years old

b. Rina is more ________ than Sari

c. Sari is more _______

d. My parents are very __________ and ________

e. I am as _____________ as my father

f. We have _______ pets: a ______ and a ___________

4. Answer the questions on the three texts above

a. Where does Johanes live?

b. Who is stricter, his mother or his father?

c. Who is as talkative as their parrot?

d. Who is as noisy as their duck?

e. Who has a stubborn father?

f. Who has a rabbit?

g. Who has a guinea pig?

h. Which one of Johanes' brothers is sportier?

i. What are the differences between Gunadi's brothers?

3. Correct any of the statements below (about Johanes' text) which are incorrect

a. Johanes punya tiga binatang...

b. Ruben kurang gemuk daripada Ben

c. Ruben lebih malas daripada Ben

d. Johanes cerewet seperti marmutnya

e. Johanes lebih suka ibunya

f. Johanes lebih keras kepala daripada ibunya

Unit 9. Comparisons: TRANSLATION/WRITING

1. Translate into English

a. tinggi

b. kurus

c. pendek

d. gemuk

e. cerdas

f. keras kepala

g. pintar

h. cantik

i. jelek

j. lebih…daripada

k. kurang…daripada

l. kuat

m. sama kuatnya dengan

n. semalas

2. Gapped sentences

a. _________saya _______ tinggi ______ bibi saya

My mother is taller than my aunt

b. Bapak_____ lebih ___________ daripada kakak saya

My father is stronger than my older brother

c. ____________ saya kurang ____________ daripada kami

My cousins are less sporty than us

d. Adik _______ ________ pintar daripada _________

My brother is smarter than me

e. Ibu saya ________ baik hatinya _________ bapak saya

My mother is as kind as my father

f. _____________ saya ________ rajin daripada_____________

My sister is more hard-working than us

g. ___________ saya kurang _________ __________ saya

My girlfriend is less serious than me

h. ___________ saya _______ keras kepala _________ nenek saya

My grandfather is more stubborn than my grandmother

3. Phrase-level translation En to Indonesian

a. My mother is

b. Taller than

c. As slim as

d. Less stubborn than

e. I am shorter than

f. My parents are

g. My cousins are

h. As fat as

i. They are as strong as

j. My grandparents are

k. I am as lazy as

4. Sentence-level translation En to Indonesian

a. My older sister is taller than my younger sister.

b. My father is as stubborn as my mother.

c. My girlfriend is more hard-working than me.

d. I am less intelligent than my brother.

e. My best friend is stronger and sportier than me.

f. My friend is better-looking than me.

g. My cousins are smarter than us.

h. My duck is noisier than my dog.

i. My cat is more fun than my turtle.

j. My rabbit is not as fat as my guinea pig.

Revision Quickie 2 : Family, Pets and Jobs

1. Match up

Pekerja	Doctor
Pengacara	Waiter
Perawat	Journalist
Pelayan	Nurse
Wartawan	IT worker
Dokter	Worker
Pramugari	Flight Attd
Aktor	Lawyer
Pekerja IT	Actor

2. Sort the words listed below in the categories in the table

a. pekerja; b. tinggi; c. perawat; d. lucu; e. pendek; f. sepupu;
g. guru; h. merah; i. bibi; j. bapak ; k. biru; l. gemuk; m. anjing;
n. tukang pipa; o. ibu; p.kakek; q. kelinci; r. cokelat; s. bebek; t. kucing

Kata Sifat	Binatang	Pekerjaan	Keluarga

3. Complete with the missing adjectives

a. Bapak saya _______________ *fat*

b. Ibu saya _________________ *tall*

c. Kakak saya _________ *short*

d. Pacar saya _______________ *pretty*

e. Sepupu saya ______________ *annoying*

f. Guru Seni saya_____________ *boring*

4. Complete with the missing nouns

a. Bapak saya bekerja sebagai ________ *lawyer*

b. Ibu saya seorang _________________ *nurse*

c. Teman baik saya __________________ *journalist*

d. Kakak saya bekerja sebagai________*flight attendant*

e. Sepupu saya seorang _____________ *student*

f. Saya bekerja sebagai _____________ *doctor*

g. Marta _________________________ *chef*

h. Nenek saya seorang _____________ *singer*

5. Match the opposites

Tinggi	Rajin
Ganteng	Tua
Gemuk	Pendek
Malas	Pendiam
Muda	Jelek
Berisik	Tidak sabar
Sakit	Kurus
Sabar	Sehat

7. Complete with the correct verb

a. Ibu ________ tinggi   *My mother is tall*

b. Saya__________ rambut hitam *I have black hair*

c. Saya________sebagai tukang pipa *I work as a plumber*

d. Bapak saya ________ 40 tahun *My father is 40*

e. Berapa _______ ada di keluargamu?
How many people are there in your family?

f. Kakak ______ tinggi *My brothers are tall*

g. Kakak saya _______ bekerja *My brother doesn't work*

h. Pacar saya ________ Gabi *My girlfriend is called Gabi*

6. Complete the numbers below

a.E_ _ _ _ belas   14

b. E_ _ _ _ puluh   40

c. E_ _ _ puluh   60

d. L_ _ _ puluh   50

e. T_ _ _ _ puluh   70

f. S_ _ _ _ _ _ _ puluh   90

"

UNIT 10
Saying what's in my school bag / classroom/ describing colour

Grammar Time 6: Using Classifiers Ekor, Buah, Orang
Grammar Time 7: Classroom Expressions

In this unit will learn how to say:

- What objects you have is in your schoolbag/pencil case/classroom
- Words for classroom equipment
- What you have and don't have
- Grouping with classifiers

You will revisit the following:
- Colours
- How adjectives follow the noun they are describing
- Introducing yourself (e.g. name, age, town, country)

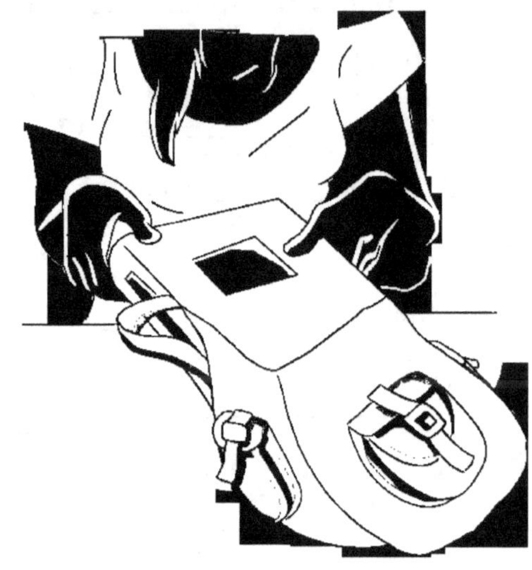

UNIT 10.
Saying what's in my school bag/ classroom/describing colour

Apa saja di dalam tas sekolahmu? *What is in your schoolbag?*
Apa saja di dalam kotak pensilmu? *What things are in your pencil case?*
Apa saja di ruang kelasmu? *What is in your classroom?*

Di dalam tas sekolah saya... *In my schoolbag*
Di kotak pensil saya... *In my pencil case*
Di ruang kelas saya... *In my classroom*

---

ada *there is / are*	**banyak pensil warna** *many coloured pencils* **beberapa pena** *some / several pens* **dua buah penghapus** *two erasers*	
tidak ada *there isn't a / aren't any*	**sebuah buku** *a book*	**abu-abu** *grey*
	sebuah buku latihan *an exercise book*	**biru** *blue*
	sebuah gunting *scissors*	**biru muda** *light blue*
Teman saya Ahmad ada *My friend Ahmad has*	**sebuah kertas** *a piece of paper*	**biru tua** *dark blue*
	sebuah kotak pensil *a pencil case*	**cokelat** *brown*
Teman saya Ahmad tidak ada *My friend Ahmad does not have*	**sebuah lem** *a gluestick*	**hijau** *green*
	sebuah pena *a pen*	**hitam** *black*
	sebuah penggaris *a ruler*	**jingga** *orange*
	sebuah penghapus *a rubber*	**kuning** *yellow*
Saya punya *I have*	**sebuah pensil** *a pencil*	**merah** *red*
	sebuah rautan pensil *a pencil sharpener*	**merah muda** *pink*
Saya tidak punya *I do not have*	**sebuah spidol** *a felt tip pen*	**putih** *white*
Saya perlu pinjam *I need to borrow*	**sebuah buku harian** *a diary* **sebuah kalkulator** *a calculator* **sebuah kamus** *a dictionary*	**berwarna-warni** *various colours*
Saya tidak perlu pinjam *I don't need to borrow*	**sebuah komputer** *a computer* **sebuah kursi** *a chair*	**warna** *coloured*
	sebuah meja *a table* **sebuah papan tulis** *a whiteboard*	**warna-warni** *colourful*

Author's note: *The use of* **sebuah / buah** *is optional in conversational Indonesian.*

Unit 10. Saying what's in my school bag: VOCABULARY BUILDING

1. Complete with the missing word

a. Saya ada sebuah______ _______   *I have an exercise book*

b. Saya perlu sebuah_________   *I need an eraser*

c. Saya tidak ___ sebuah pena   *I don't have a pen*

d. Saya ______ sebuah kertas   *I have a piece of paper*

e. Saya ____ sebuah kalkulator   *I have a calculator*

f. Saya perlu sebuah _________   *I need a chair*

g. Saya tidak ada sebuah _________   *I don't have a ruler*

h. Teman saya ada __________   *My friend has scissors*

2. Match up

penghapus	pencil
pensil	diary
buku harian	I have
kursi	sharpener
saya ada	pen
saya perlu	I don't have
saya tidak ada	chair
rautan pensil	eraser
pena	I need

3. Translate into English

a. Saya ada lem

b. Teman saya ada buku harian

c. Saya tidak ada buku latihan

d. Saya ada pensil

e. Saya tidak ada sebuah rautan pensil

f. Saya perlu pinjam spidol

g. Ada sebuah komputer

h. Saya tidak ada spidol

4. Add the missing letter

a. Gun__ing

b. L__m

c. Saya p__rlu

d. Tidak a__a

e. Buku h__rian

f. Te__an saya

g. Kamu __da

h. Pa__an tulis

5. Anagrams

a. aTs kSheola

b. taKok Psilen

c. gJigan

d. tuihP

e. erKtsa

f. mputKoer

g. naPerggis

h. iuHja

6. Broken words

a. D__ d______ t_____ s________ s____ a___ k_______ p______

In my bag I have a pencil case

b. D__ d______ k_______ p_______ a____ b______ p______

In my pencil case I have some pencils

c. S__ t_______ a____ s_____ p________   *I don't have an eraser*

d. S_____ p_______ s__________ p________   *I need a ruler*

e. A____ s_____ p______ t_______   *There is a whiteboard*

f. S_____ a____ b______ p____ b_______   *I have some blue pens*

g. S_____ p______ s_______ s__________   *I need a felt tip pen*

7. Complete with a suitable word

a. Saya ada ___________

b. Saya perlu________ pensil

c. Saya ada pena ______hitam

d. Saya ______ komputer

e. Sebuah ___________pensil

f. __________pena merah

g. Saya_____ sebuah kotak pensil

h. Dia_____ sebuah penggaris

i. Teman saya tidak ______ lem

j. Beberapa _________ warna

k. Tidak_______ papan tulis

Unit 10. Saying what's in my school bag: READING

Nama saya Renata. Saya berumur dua belas tahun dan saya tinggal di kota Roma, di Italia. Ada empat orang di keluarga saya. Saya punya kucing putih. Dia binatang favorit saya. Di tas sekolah saya, ada banyak buku. Saya ada sebuah pensil merah, sebuah pena kuning, sebuah penggaris merah, dan sebuah penghapus putih. Teman saya Zak hanya ada satu pena di kotak pensilnya. Di rumahnya dia punya seekor kuda abu-abu!

Nama saya Ndeli. Saya berusia sebelas tahun dan saya tinggal di kota Jayapura, ibu kota provinsi Papua. Kami berempat di keluarga saya. Saya mencintai ibu saya tetapi saya tidak menyukai bapak saya. Dia selalu streng. Dia seorang pengacara. Di kelas saya tidak ada banyak barang. Tidak ada papan tulis atau komputer. Ada dua puluh delapan meja, tetapi hanya ada dua puluh tujuh kursi. Ini masalah! Saya ada dua pensil berwarna-warni, dan buku latihan tetapi tidak ada kalkulator.

Nama saya Andrea. Saya berumur lima belas tahun dan saya tinggal di kota Paris di Prancis. Di keluarga saya ada tiga orang. Saya punya kelinci yang sangat lucu. Di ruang kelas saya ada papan tulis, komputer, dan tiga puluh meja. Ruang kelas saya sangat besar. Saya ada pensil biru, spidol kuning, penggaris baru, dan penghapus. Teman saya Martin ada banyak pensil warna.

Nama saya Lukas. Saya berusia delapan belas tahun dan tinggal di kota Cádiz, di Spanyol. Di keluarga saya ada lima orang. Di kelas saya ada sebuah papan tulis, dan dua puluh meja. Ada juga dua puluh kursi, yaitu satu untuk setiap siswa. Kelas saya baik dan guru saya sangat lucu. Saya tidak ada pensil, pena, penggaris, atau penghapus. Saya perlu semuanya. Di rumah saya punya seekor tikus putih yang sangat lucu, namanya Andi.

1. Find the Indonesian in Renata's text

a. I am 12

b. I live in Rome

c. There are 4 people

d. A white cat

e. A red pencil

f. A yellow pen

g. My favourite animal

h. Only has one pen

i. In his house

2. Find Someone Who…

a. …has a blue pencil

b. …has most tables in their class

c. …has a class with one less chair

d. …has no school equipment

e. …has a big pet

f. …doesn't like their dad

3. Answer these questions about Lukas' text

a. Where does Lukas live?

b. Who is Andi?

c. How many tables and chairs are there in his class?

d. How does he describe his class?

e. What school equipment does he have?

f. What pet does he have?

g. How does he describe his pet?

5. Fill in the blanks about Ketut

N_____ saya Ketut. Umur saya tiga belas t_______ dan saya tinggal d_ Denpasar Bali. Di keluarga saya a____ empat orang. Di ruang kelas saya a____ banyak benda. Ada s_____ komputer dan papan t_______. Di dalam t____ sekolah saya ada dua buah b_____ dan k_____ pensil saya. Teman saya a___ banyak pensil tetapi t_____ ada lem. Saya suka sekali guru s_____ karena dia l___ dan b____ h_____. Di rumah saya p______ seekor ular hijau.

4. Fill in the table below

Name	Renata	Andrea
Age		
City		
Items in pencil case		

Unit 10. Saying what's in my school bag: TRANSLATION

1. Faulty translation: spot and correct *in the English* any translation mistakes you find below

a. Di ruang kelas saya ada dua buah papan tulis dan sebuah komputer. Saya tidak suka guru saya. *In my class there is a whiteboard and a computer. I like my teacher.*

b. Saya tidak ada banyak pena di dalam kotak pensil saya. Saya ada sebuah pensil merah muda tetapi saya tidak punya sebuah penggaris. *I have many pens in my pencil case. I have a red pencil but I don't have an eraser.*

c. Teman saya Emir punya empat orang di keluarganya. Dia perlu sebuah spidol hitam dan buku harian. *My friend Emir has five people in his family. He needs a black pen and a diary.*

d. Saya perlu sebuah rautan pensil dan sebuah lem. Saya tidak ada sebuah penggaris atau sebuah pena. Saya sangat suka guru saya. *I need paper and an eraser. I don't have a ruler or a pencil. I don't like my teacher!*

e. Di ruang kelas saya ada tiga puluh meja dan tiga puluh kursi. Saya perlu buku harian tetapi saya ada kamus. *In my class there are thirty cats and thirty chairs. I need a calculator but I have a dictionary.*

2. Translate into English

a. Saya perlu sebuah

b. Saya ada pensil hitam

c. Saya ada pena biru

d. Penggaris hijau

e. Saya punya anjing di rumah

f. Teman saya ada buku

g. Bapak saya bekerja sebagai

h. Saya suka guru saya

i. Beberapa pensil merah

j. Sebuah papan tulis besar

k. Saya punya banyak spidol

l. Saya tidak ada gunting

m. Saya perlu sebuah kamus

3. Phrase-level translation En to Indonesian

a. A red book

b. A black calculator

c. I don't have

d. I need a…

e. I like

f. There are…

g. I have

h. My friend has…

4. Sentence-level translation En to Ind

a. There are 20 tables

b. There is a whiteboard

c. My teacher is nice

d. I have some blue pens

e. I have some orange pencils

f. I need an eraser and a sharpener

g. I need a chair and a book

h. My class is very big and pleasant

i. My father is a teacher

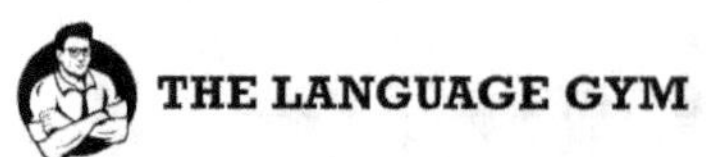

THE LANGUAGE GYM

Unit 10. Saying what's in my school bag: WRITING

1. Split sentences

Saya ada sebuah	pensil besar
Saya ada pensil	siswa di kelas saya
Di ruang kelas saya	sekolah besar
Ada tiga puluh	biru
Saya ada sebuah tas	ada papan tulis
Saya tidak ada pena	buku latihan
Saya ada sebuah kotak	berwarna-warni

2. Rewrite the sentences in the correct order

a. Saya perlu kalkulator sebuah

b. Saya punya penggaris sebuah dan hitam pensil

c. Saya ruang kelas sangat besar

d. Teman saya ada pena biru dua buah

e. Saya ada tidak sebuah buku harian biru

f. Di kura-kura hijau saya ada rumah

g. Bapak dokter saya dan dia bekerja di besar rumah sehat

3. Spot and correct the grammar and spelling note: in several cases a word is missing

a. Di kelas saya dua puluh meja ada.

b. Saya ada hitam kalkulator.

c. Pensil kotak saya ada banyak barang.

d. Teman saya perlu tidak kotak pensil.

e. Saya perlu pensil pengapus.

f. Teman saya banyak ada pensil berwarna-warni.

g. Ibu saya seorang montir dan dia bekerja garasi.

h. Saya tinggi dan kuat. Saya punya pirang rambut dan biru mata.

4. Anagrams

a. akkot enplsi

b. ppana tiuls

c. epna

d. maej

e. siopld

f. ntgguin

g. ekasrt

5. Guided writing – write 4 short paragraphs describing the people below using the details in the box

Person	Lives	Has	Hasn't	Needs
Heri	Jakarta	Exercise book	Pen	Diary
Ika	Medan	Ruler	Pencil	Paper
Julia	Makassar	Felt tip pen	Sharpener	A gluestick

6. Describe this person in Indonesian:

Name: Markus

Pet: A black horse

Hair: brown + blue eyes

School equipment: has pen, pencil, ruler, eraser

Does not have: sharpener, paper, chair

Favourite colour: blue

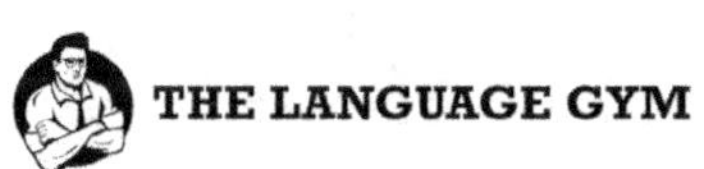

Grammar Time 6: Using Classifiers Ekor, Buah, Orang

Ada berapa ekor ayam? *There are how many chickens? / How many chickens are there?*			
Ada berapa buah pena biru? *There are how many blue pens? / How many blue pens are there?*			
Apa pekerjaannya? *What is his / her / their job?*			

Saya *I (formal)*			**anjing** *dog*
Aku *I (informal)*			**ayam** *chicken*
Anda *You (form)*			**bebek** *duck*
Kamu *You (inf)*	**seekor** *a, one*	**burung** *bird*
Dia *S/He*		**dua ekor** *two*	**ikan** *fish*
Kita *We (inc. listener)*	**ada** *have/has*	**tiga ekor** *three*	**kucing** *cat*
Kami *We (ex. listener)*	**mempunyai** *own/have*		**kuda** *horse*
Anda semua *You all*	**memiliki** *own/have*		**kura-kura** *turtle* **penguin** *penguin*
Mereka *They*	**tidak ada** *don't have*	**buku** *book*
Temanmu *Your friend*			**kalkulator** *calculator*
Bapakmu *Your dad*			**kamus** *dictionary*
Kakak saya *My older sibling*			**komputer** *computer*
		sebuah *a, one*	**kotak pensil** *pencil case*
Kakek saya *My grandpa*		**dua buah** *two*	**kursi** *chair*
		tiga buah *three*	**meja** *table*
Sepupu saya *My cousin*			**papan tulis** *whiteboard* **penghapus** *eraser*
			rautan pensil *pencil sharpener*
Teman saya <u>Alia</u> *My friend* <u>Alia</u>			**aktor** *actor*
			dokter *doctor*
			dokter gigi *dentist*
			guru *teacher*
Teman saya *My friend*	**bekerja sebagai** *work as …*		**ibu/bapak rumah tangga** *housewife/husband*
		seorang *a*	**insinyur** *engineer*
Teman-teman saya *My friends*	**mau menjadi** *wants to become*		**montir** *mechanic*
			pemasak *chef*
			pengacara *lawyer*
			penyanyi *singer*
			perawat *nurse*

Grammar Time 6. Using Classifiers: DRILLS

1. Match up

ada	a (things)
seorang	a (animals)
memiliki	don't have
tidak ada	own/have
seekor	has/have
sebuah	a (people)

2. Complete with the missing classifier

a. Kakak saya ada se _____ kuda — *My grandfather has a horse*

b. Saya memiliki se _____ kotak pensil — *I have a pencil case*

c. Kakak saya ada empat_____ kucing — *My sister has four cats*

d. Paman saya se _____ dokter — *My uncle is a doctor*

e. Saya mempunyai se_____ buku teks — *I have a textbook*

f. Ibu saya ada dua_____ ayam — *My mother has two chickens*

g. Ruang kelas ada se____ papan tulis — *The classroom has a blackboard*

h. Teman saya punya se_____ sapi — *My friend has a cow*

3. Translate into Indonesian

a. __________ __________: a doctor

b. __________ __________: a teacher

c. __________ __________: a book

d. __________ __________: a table

e. __________ __________: a horse

f. __________ __________: a rabbit

4. Spot and correct the errors

a. Kakak saya ada empat orang kucing

b. Kakek saya ada sebuah sapi

c. Saya mempunyai seekor buku teks

d. Saya memiliki seorang kotak pensil

e. Ibu saya seekor perawat

f. Saya punya dua ekor kalkulator

g. Apakah bapakmu sebuah dokter?

5. Complete with the missing letters

a. Bapak saya a_a se_kor anjing
My father has a dog

b. Ibu saya a_a dua b_ _h me_a.
My mother has two tables

c. Adik saya me_iliki dua _ua_ komputer
My brother has 2 computers

d. Adik perempuan saya s_o_a_g insi_ _ur
My younger sister is an engineer

e. _ _ _an baik saya ada s_ek_r _enguin
My good friend has a penguin

f. Kakek saya _emil_k_ se_ _ _ r ku_a-ku_a
My grandfather had a tortoise

g. Kakak saya m_ _ punyai _ _ _kor ku_a
My sister has a horse

6. Translate into English

a. Bapak saya ada seekor kelinci

b. Ibu saya punya dua buah komputer

c. Teman saya memiliki dua buah kamus

d. Adik perempuan saya ada seekor kucing

e. Kakak teman saya ada seekor kuda

f. Kakek saya memiliki seekor sapi

g. Kakak saya seorang perawat

h. Anda semua ada sebuah kotak pensil

i. Apakah bapakmu seorang pengacara?

j. Siapa punya dua ekor anjing?

Unit 10: Revision Drills

1. Translate the pronoun <u>and</u> verb into Indonesian

a. I like:

b. You look after:

c. She doesn't like:

d. He owns:

e. We (incl) work:

f. We (excl) have:

g. You all have the age:

h. They have the name:

2. Translate into Indonesian. Topic: Pets and colours

a. We have a blue parrot

b. I have two green turtles

c. My brother has a white guinea pig

d. My uncle has a black horse

e. My sister has a red and black spider

f. We don't have pets at home

g. Do you have pets at home?

3. Translate into Indonesian. Topic: family members

a. I don't have brothers

b. We have two grandparents

c. My mother has no sisters

d. Do you have any brothers or sisters?

e. Do you all have cousins?

f. I don't have any brothers

4. Translate into Indonesian. Topic: Age

a. They are fifteen years old

b. We are fourteen years old

c. I am sixteen years old

d. You guys are twelve years old

e. How old are you?

f. My mother is forty

5. Translate into Indonesian. Topic: Hair and eyes

a. I have black hair

b. We have blue eyes

c. She has curly hair

d. My mother has blond hair

e. Do you have grey eyes ?

f. They have green eyes

g. My brother has brown eyes

h. We have no hair

i. You all have beautiful eyes

j. My parents have red hair

k. You have no hair

l. My sister has very long hair

Grammar Time 7: Classroom Expressions, Being Polite and Apologizing in Indonesian

Teacher expressions				
Silakan *Please*	**masuk.** *come in* **duduk.** *sit down* **tunggu sebentar.** *wait a moment*	**Tolong** *Please*	**buka** *open* **tutup** *close*	**buku latihan** *exercise book* **buku teks** *text book* **kamus** *dictionary* **komputer** *computer* **pintu** *door* **jendela** *window*
			ambil *take*	**kertas dari meja** *paper from the table*
			nyalakan *turn on* **matikan** *turn off*	**lampu** *light*
			ulangi *repeat*	
			lihat *look at*	**papan tulis** *the board*
Ada *Are there*	**pertanyaan?** *questions*	**Coba** *Please (try)*	**jelaskan** *explain it* **baca** *read it* **ulangi** *repeat it*	**dulu** *first* **sekarang** *now*
Sudah *Already*	**selesai?** *finished* **siap?** *ready*		**lagi** *again*	

Student Expressions						Teacher response
Ma'af *I'm sorry* **Permisi** *Excuse me*	**Pak Guru** *(male teacher)* **Ibu Guru** *(female teacher)*	**Bolehkah** *May*	**saya** *I*	**ke** *go to*	**kantor?** *office* **kantor IT?** *IT office* **perpustakaan?** *library* **kamar kecil?** *toilet*	**Boleh** *You may* **Tidak boleh** *You may not*
				pinjam *borrow*	**buku?** *book* **pena?** *pen* **pensil?** *pencil* **penggaris?** *ruler* **penghapus?** *eraser*	
		Bisakah *Can*	**ulangi lagi** *repeat again*	**Pak?** *Sir* **Ibu?** *Ms*		**Bisa** *I can*
Terima kasih *Thank you*		**Kembali** **Sama-sama**	*You're welcome*			

Grammar Time 7: Classroom Expressions: TRANSLATION

1. Complete the table

English	Indonesian
repeat	
	silakan
	terima kasih
teacher	
	tolong
turn on	
questions	
	bolehkah saya
ready	
	matikan

2. Translate into English

a. Pinjam pena:

b. Tolong buka:

c. Silakan masuk:

d. Bolehkah saya…?:

e. Coba lagi:

f. Ulangi lagi:

g. Permisi Pak guru:

h. Lihat papan tulis:

i. Coba jelaskan:

j. Sudah selesai?:

3. Match the phrases

Indonesian	English
permisi Pak guru	please look at
tolong tutup	may I
ulangi dulu	take a paper
tolong lihat	excuse me Sir
bolehkah saya	repeat it first
ma'af	please close
ambil kertas	I'm sorry

4. Complete with the missing imperative/interrogative

a. ____________ masuk   *Please come in*

b. _________ nyalakan lampu   *Please turn on the light*

c. ____________ulangi   *Please repeat*

d. _________saya pinjam penghapus? *May I borrow an eraser?*

e. ______ Pak ulangi lagi?   *Can you please repeat it again Sir?*

f. ______ jelaskan dulu   *Please explain it first*

g. __________tunggu sebentar   *Please wait a moment*

h. _________ matikan komputer   *Please turn off your laptop*

5. Translate into Indonesian

a. borrow a blue pen

b. to the library

c. please explain it

d. please close

e. IT office

f. open the textbook

g. borrow a ruler

6. Translate into Indonesian

a. Please sit down

b. Are there any questions?

c. Please look at the board

d. Please repeat first

e. May I go to the office? You may

f. May I borrow a ruler?

g. Have you finished? Please read now

THE LANGUAGE GYM

UNIT 11
Talking about food (Part 1):
Likes / Dislikes / Reasons

Grammar Time 8: Adverbs of Frequency (Part 1)

In this unit will learn how to say:

- What food you like/dislike and to what extent
- Why you like/dislike it (old and new expressions)
- New adjectives
- How often you eat certain foods

You will revisit the following
- Time markers
- Providing a justification

UNIT 11: Talking about food - Part 1
Likes/ Dislikes / Reasons

Kamu lebih suka makanan apa, dan mengapa? *What food do you prefer and why?*				
Saya cukup suka *I quite like* **Saya kurang suka** *I don't really like* **Saya lebih suka** *I prefer* **Saya sangat suka** *I like a lot* **Saya sedikit suka** *I like a bit* **Saya suka** *I like* **Saya suka sekali** *I really like* **Saya tidak suka** *I don't like*	**air** *water* **apel** *apples* **ayam** *chicken* **bakso** *meatball soup* ***buah-buahan** *fruit* **daging** *meat* **gado-gado** *salad with peanut sauce* **permen** *lollies* **ikan** *fish* **jus buah** *fruit juice* **keju** *cheese* **kopi** *coffee* **kue** *cake* **madu** *honey* **makanan laut** *seafood* **nanas** *pineapple* **nasi** *rice* **nasi goreng** *fried rice* **rendang** *spicy beef curry* **pisang** *bananas* **roti** *bread* **sate ayam** *chicken satay* ****sayur-sayuran** *vegetables* **susu** *milk* **telur** *eggs* **tomat** *tomatoes* **udang** *prawns*	**karena rasanya** *because it's taste is*	**asam** *sour* **asin** *salty* **enak** *tasty* **gurih** *crispy, savoury* **lezat** *delicious* **manis** *sweet* **pahit** *bitter* **pedas** *spicy*	**sekali** *very*
			busuk *rotten* **menjijikkan** *disgusting* **tidak enak** *not tasty*	
		karena *because it is*	**bergizi** *nutritious* **kaya akan vitamin dan protein** *rich in vitamins and protein* **segar** *refreshing, fresh* **sehat** *healthy* **tidak sehat** *unhealthy* **berprotein tinggi** *high in protein*	

Author's note:

***Buah-buahan** is all kinds of fruit.

****Sayur-sayuran** is all kinds of vegetables and **sayuran** can be several different vegetables.

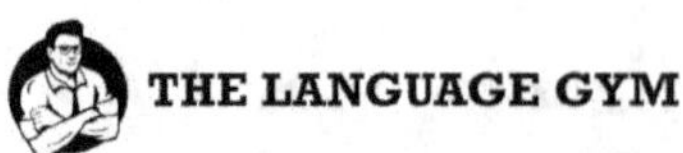

Unit 11. Talking about food (Part 1): VOCABULARY BUILDING (Part 1)

1. Match up

pisang	eggs
nasi	apple
daging	fish
sate ayam	milk
air	fruit
susu	water
telur	pineapple
ikan	chicken satay
nanas	meat
buah-buahan	bananas
apel	rice

2. Complete

a. Saya sangat suka ___________   *I like chicken a lot*

b. Saya suka _________________   *I like prawns*

c. Saya suka _________________   *I like vegetables*

d. Saya lebih suka ___________   *I prefer milk*

e. Saya suka _________________   *I like bananas*

f. Saya suka _________ mineral   *I like mineral water*

g. Saya tidak suka ___________   *I don't like tomatoes*

h. Saya sangat suka___________   *I really like chicken*

i. Saya suka _________________   *I like fruit*

j. Saya tidak suka ___________   *I don't like eggs*

3. Translate into English

a. Saya suka buah-buahan

b. Saya kurang suka telur

c. Saya suka sate ayam

d. Saya suka nasi

e. Saya tidak suka daging

f. Saya lebih suka nanas

g. Saya tidak suka tomat

h. Saya suka sekali susu

4. Complete the words

a. tel_________________

b. pis_________________

c. buah-b____________

d. sayur-s___________

e. nas_______________

f. ik_________________

g. ren_________

h. ba_________________

5. Fill the gaps with either 'saya suka' or 'saya tidak suka' as per your own preference

a. ___________________________telur

b. ___________________________air

c. ___________________________ayam

d. ___________________________kue

e. ___________________________sayur-sayuran

f. ___________________________daging

g. ___________________________buah-buahan

h. ___________________________ikan

i. ___________________________nasi

6. Translate into Indonesian

a. I like eggs

b. I quite like pineapple

c. I prefer tomatoes

d. I don't like seafood

e. I really like fruit

f. I don't like vegetables

g. I like milk a bit

Unit 11. Talking about food (Part 1): VOCABULARY BUILDING (Part 2)

1. Complete with the missing words. The initial letter of each word is given

a. Pisang ini rasanya m______________________________

These bananas are disgusting

b. Apel ini rasanya a______________________________

These apples are sour

c. Ayam ini rasanya sangat p______________________

This chicken is very spicy

d. Saya tidak suka d______________________________

I don't like meat

e. Kopi ini rasanya sangat m______________________

This coffee is very sweet

f. Kue tidak s______________________________

Cake is unhealthy

g. Sayur-sayuran s______________ s ________________

Vegetables are very healthy

h. Saya sangat suka s______________   *I really like milk*

2. Complete the table

Indonesian	English
susu	
	chicken satay
ikan	
telur	
	water
	bread
nasi goreng	
kue	
	vegetables

3. Complete with 'saya suka' or 'saya tidak suka' according to the icon

a. ______________________ apel ☺

b. ______________________susu ☹

c. ______________________roti ☹

d. ______________________nasi goreng ☺

e. ______________________________sayur-sayuran ☹

f. ______________________________ikan ☹

g. ______________________________nasi ☺

h. ______________________________kopi ☺

4. Broken words

a. S__________ t__________ s__________ t__________   *I don't like eggs*

b. S__________ s__________ a__________   *I like apples*

c. S__________ c______ s__________ u__________   *I quite like prawns*

d. S______ s__________ s________ k______   *I like cake a lot*

e. R__________ l__________ s________   *It's taste is very delicious*

f. I______ini r________ a________   *The taste of this fish is salty*

g. Rendang r__________ p________ s ________   *The taste of rendang is very spicy*

5. Complete each sentence in a way which is logical

a. Kue ____________ sehat

b. Pisang ini manis ____________

c. Saya kurang ____________ susu

d. Saya suka sekali sate ________

e. ______________ ikan karena sehat

f. ______________ daging merah karena tidak sehat

g. ______________ sayur-sayuran karena sehat dan rasanya lezat

Unit 11. Talking about food (Part 1): READING

Halo! Nama saya Ratna. Saya lebih suka makan apa? Saya suka makanan laut, jadi saya sangat suka udang dan cumi karena lezat. Saya juga sangat suka ikan karena rasanya enak dan bergizi. Saya lebih suka udang. Saya cukup suka sate ayam dan juga buah-buahan, terutama pisang dan nanas. Saya kurang suka sayur-sayuran karena rasanya tidak enak.

Halo! Nama saya Agung. Saya lebih suka makan apa? Saya suka sayur-sayuran. Saya makan sayur-sayuran setiap hari. Sayuran favorit saya adalah bayam, wortel dan tomat karena kaya akan vitamin dan mineral. Saya juga suka buah-buahan karena sehat dan rasanya enak. Saya tidak suka daging dan ikan. Daging dan ikan berprotein tinggi tetapi rasanya tidak enak.

Halo! Nama saya Lestari. Saya lebih suka makan apa? Saya suka daging, terutama daging domba karena rasanya sangat enak. Saya sangat suka ayam pedas karena enak dan berprotein tinggi. Saya cukup suka telur. Telur sehat dan kaya akan vitamin dan protein. Saya cukup suka buah-buahan, terutama pisang. Saya kurang suka apel. Saya lebih suka pisang karena rasanya pisang sangat enak dan kaya akan vitamin.

Halo! Nama saya Yusuf. Saya lebih suka makan apa? Saya lebih suka daging karena enak. Saya sangat suka sate ayam karena enak. Juga, saya sangat suka buah-buahan karena rasanya manis. Saya tidak suka sayur-sayuran. Saya kurang suka tomat dan wortel. Saya tidak suka telur. Telur kaya akan protein dan vitamin, tetapi rasanya menjijikkan. Saya tidak suka roti karena tidak sehat.

Halo! Nama saya Iva. Saya lebih suka makan apa? Saya suka daging merah karena sangat enak dan berprotein tinggi. Saya tidak makan banyak ikan karena saya tidak suka ikan. Saya cukup suka keju, tetapi makanan ini kurang sehat. Saya sangat suka buah-buahan, terutama pisang, karena enak, kaya akan vitamin dan tidak mahal. Saya tidak suka apel dan saya kurang suka nanas. Saya tidak makan sayuran.

1. Find the Indonesian in Ratna's text

a. I like seafood

b. I like prawns a lot

c. Are delicious

d. I like fish a lot

e. prawns

f. I quite like

g. Also

h. Especially

i. They are not tasty

2. Iva or Lestari? Write their name next to each statement below

a. I like spicy chicken a lot - *Lestari*

b. I don't really like pineapples

c. I like fruit a lot

d. I don't eat vegetables

e. I quite like eggs

f. I quite like cheese

g. I prefer bananas

h. I don't eat much fish

i. I like red meat

3. Complete the following sentences based on Agung's text

a. Agung likes ___________________

b. He eats them _______________________

c. His favourite vegetables are ___________________ ___________________and ___________________

d. He also likes ___________________because it is ___________________and ___________________

e. He doesn't like ___________and ___________________

4. Fill in the table below (in English) about Yusuf

Prefer	Likes a lot	Doesn't really like	Doesn't like

Unit 11. Talking about food (Part 1): TRANSLATION

1. Faulty translation: spot and correct IN THE ENGLISH any translation mistakes you find below

a. Saya sangat suka udang: *I don't like prawns*

b. Saya suka ayam : *I like meat*

c. Saya suka bakso: *I don't like meatball soup*

d. Saya suka nanas: *I like apples*

e. Telur menjijikkan: *eggs are tasty*

f. Pisang bergizi: *bananas are high in protein*

g. Ikan sangat sehat: *fish is unhealthy*

h. Saya lebih suka jus: *I prefer water*

i. Saya tidak suka sayur-sayuran: *I like vegetables*

j. Saya suka nasi: *I like fried rice*

k. Saya kurang suka buah-buahan: *I quite like fruit*

l. Nasi goreng rasanya sedikit pedas: *fried rice is a little salty*

2. Translate into English

a. Udang enak:

b. Ikan goreng:

c. Ayam kaya akan protein:

d. Saya suka nasi:

e. Daging merah tidak sehat:

f. Ikan goreng gurih:

g. Telur menjijikkan:

h. Saya lebih suka air:

i. Saya sedikit suka udang:

j. Saya tidak suka sayur-sayuran:

k. Saya suka tomat:

l. Rasanya kopi ini manis sekali:

m. Nanas ini busuk:

n. Apel ini asam:

3. Phrase-level translation Eng to Ind

a. Spicy chicken:

b. This coffee:

c. I quite like:

d. Very sweet:

e. Delicious seafood:

f. Rotten bananas:

g. I don't like:

h. I really like:

i. Tasty fish:

j. Fruit juice:

k. Sweet coffee:

4. Sentence-level translation Eng to Indonesian

a. I like meat curry a lot

b. I like pineapples because they are healthy

c. Meat is tasty but unhealthy

d. This cake is very sweet

e. Meatball soup is disgusting

f. I like bananas because they are tasty and nutritious

g. I really like fish. Fish is tasty and high in protein

h. These vegetables are rotten

i. I prefer bananas

j. This fruit juice is very sweet

Unit 11. Talking about food (Part 1): WRITING

1. Split sentences

Saya suka sate	buah-buahan
Saya tidak suka sayur-sayuran karena	ayam
Saya lebih suka	manis
Kopi ini	menjijikkan
Saya cukup suka	enak tetapi tidak sehat
Ayam goreng	pisang
Saya suka	daging

2. Rewrite the sentences in the correct order

a. (Example) ayam Saya sate suka

Saya suka sate ayam

b. sayur-sayuran suka Saya

c. ini manis Kopi

d. sehat Permen tidak

e. suka Saya air

f. menjijikkan Sayur-sayuran

g. lezat buah-buahan Saya karena suka rasanya

3. Spot and correct the grammar and spelling

a. Saya suka nenes

b. Saya tidak suku sayur-sayuran

c. Menjijikkan telur

d. Suka saya kopi

e. Saya suka lebih gado-gado

f. Saya suka tidak daging

4. Anagrams

a. iPgasn

b. ggniDa

c. naasRya

d. zigiBre

e. saePd

f. hiurG

g. nKeraa

5. Guided writing – write 3 short paragraphs describing the people below using the details in the box using the first person

Person	Likes	Quite likes	Doesn't really like	Doesn't like
Kartika	Rendang because spicy	Milk because healthy	Chicken	Eggs because disgusting
Subagio	Chicken because healthy	Pineapple because sweet	Fish	Meat because unhealthy
Dian	Honey because sweet	Fish because nutritious	Fruit	Vegetables because not tasty

6. Write a paragraph on Harto in Indonesian using the third person singular

Name: Harto
Age: 18
Description: Tall, good-looking, sporty, nice
Occupation: Student
Food he really likes: Chicken
Food he likes: Vegetables
Food he doesn't really like: Red meat
Food he dislikes: Fish

Grammar Time 8: Adverbs Of Frequency
Talking about food (Part 1)

Berapa kali seminggu kamu makan/minum …? *How many times a week do you eat/drink…?*
Berapa sering kamu makan/minum…? *How often do you eat/drink…?*
Apakah kamu sering makan/minum …? *Do you often eat/drink…?*

Saya *I* **Aku** *I (informal)* **Anda** *you (formal)* **Kamu** *you (inf.)* **Dia** *He/She* ****Kami** *We* *****Kita** *We* **Mereka** *They*	***selalu** *always* ***sering** *often* ***kadang-kadang** *sometimes* ***sekali-sekali** *from time to time* **belum pernah** *never* **jarang** *rarely* ***setiap hari** *every day*	**minum** *drink*	**air** *water* **es kelapa muda** *iced coconut drink* **es teler** *fruit cocktail* **jamu** *herbal drink* **jus jeruk** *orange juice* **kopi** *coffee* **susu** *milk* **teh** *tea*
		makan *eat*	**apel** *apples* **bakso** *meatball soup* **buah-buahan** *fruit* **daging** *meat* **gado-gado** *salad with peanut sauce* **permen** *lollies* **ikan** *fish* **nanas** *pineapple* **nasi goreng** *fried rice* **nasi** *rice* **pisang** *bananas* **roti** *bread* **sate ayam** *chicken satay* **sayur-sayuran** *vegetables* **telur** *eggs* **tomat** *tomatoes*

Author's note:
* These adverbs of frequency can also be positioned at the end of the sentence.
** **Kami** means *'we'* excluding the listener/reader
*****Kita** means *'we'* including the listener/reader

Grammar Time 8. Adverbs Of Frequency Food (Part 1): TRANSLATION

1. Match up

Saya makan	They eat
Kamu makan	He/she eats
Mereka makan	We eat
Aku makan	You eat
Dia makan	I (inf.) eat
Kita makan	I eat

2. Translate into English

a. Saya makan nasi

b. Dia minum jus

c. Saya jarang makan daging

d. Kamu minum apa?

e. Mereka selalu minum air

f. Mereka jarang makan ayam

g. Saya sering makan bakso

h. Apakah kamu makan ayam?

i. Apakah kamu sering makan ikan?

j. Saya kadang-kadang makan roti

3. Spot and correct the mistakes

a. Ibu saya makan nasa.

b. Adik saya kadang-kadung makan kue

c. Teman saya sarong makan sate ayam

d. Keluarga saya sering makan teh

e. Dia suka makan kopi manis

f. Maraka selalu minum jamu

g. Kamu suka makan berapa untuk sarapan?

h. Kamu minum siapa?

4. Complete

a. Bapak saya ___________ banyak buah-buahan

b. Saya kadang-kadang ___________ jus nanas

c. Kamu sekali-sekali ___________ ayam?

d. Ibu saya selalu ___________ banyak nasi

e. Orang tua saya selalu ___________ bakso

f. Kakak saya sering ___________ ikan

g. Pacar saya lebih suka ___________ air

h. Kamu ___________ apa untuk sarapan?

5. Translate into Indonesian

a. I eat rice.

b. We *(including)* drink iced coconut drink.

c. What do you eat?

d. What do you drink?

e. We *(excluding)* eat meatball soup often.

f. They sometimes eat fish.

g. She never drinks herbal drinks.

h. He always drinks water.

6. Translate into Indonesian

a. I never eat red meat. I don't like red meat because it is unhealthy.

b. I often eat fried chicken. I like fried chicken because it is crispy.

c. I drink fruit juice often. I love fruit juice because it is delicious and healthy.

d. I eat fried rice every day. I like fried rice a lot because it is very tasty.

e. I rarely eat vegetables. Vegetables are healthy but I don't like them because they are disgusting.

f. I never drink tea or coffee because I don't like the taste.

UNIT 12
Talking about food - Part 2
Likes/ Dislikes / Mealtimes

Grammar Time 9: Quantities
Grammar Time 10: The Suffix - NYA
Question Skills 2: Jobs / School Bag / Food

In this unit you will consolidate all that you learnt in the previous unit and learn how to say:
- What meals you eat every day and
- What you eat at each meal

You will revisit the following:
- Noun-to-adjective placement
- Pets, school

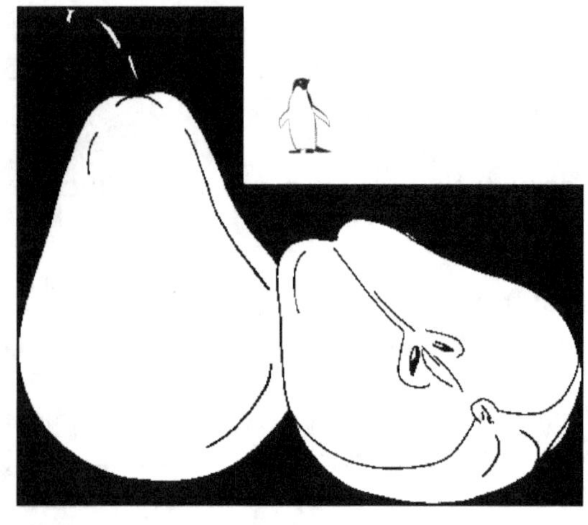

Unit 12 Talking about food: Part 2
Likes/ Dislikes /Mealtimes

Kamu makan apa untuk sarapan? *What do you eat for breakfast?*			
Apakah kamu suka ...? *Do you like ...?*			
Biasanya... *Usually*			
Kadang-kadang... *Sometimes*			
saya makan *I eat*	**air** *water*	**karena** *because*	**bergizi** *nutritious*
	apel *apple*		**saya menyukainya** *I like it*
saya minum *I drink*	**ayam panggang** *roast chicken*		**segar** *refreshing*
	bayam *spinach*		**sehat** *healthy*
saya makan camilan *I snack on*	**buah-buahan** *fruit*		**tidak begitu enak** *not very tasty*
	bubur *porridge*		
	cumi-cumi *squid*		**tidak sehat** *unhealthy*
untuk sarapan saya makan *for breakfast I eat*	**daging** *meat*		
	gado-gado *salad with peanut sauce*		
untuk makan siang saya makan *for lunch I eat*	**ikan** *fish*		
	ikan goreng *fried fish*	**karena rasanya** *because its taste is*	**empuk** *tender (of meat)*
	jus buah *fruit juice*		**enak** *tasty*
untuk makan malam saya makan *for dinner I eat*	**keju** *cheese*		**gurih** *crispy*
	kelapa *coconut*		**hambar** *bland*
	kentang goreng *fries*		**lezat** *delicious*
	kopi *coffee*		**manis** *sweet*
untuk pencuci mulut saya minum *for sweets I drink*	**lumpia** *spring rolls*		**menjijikkan** *disgusting*
	madu *honey*		**pahit** *bitter*
untuk pencuci mulut saya makan *for sweets I eat*	**nasi** *rice*		**pedas** *spicy*
	pisang *bananas*		
	rendang *beef curry*		
Saya sangat suka *I like a lot*	**roti bakar dengan selai** *jam toast* **sayur-sayuran** *vegetables*		
Saya sedikit suka *I like a bit*	**susu** *milk*		
	teh *tea*		
Saya suka *I like*	**tomat** *tomatoes*		
	udang *prawns*		
Saya tidak suka *I don't like*	**wortel** *carrots*		

amuUnit 12. Talking about food: Part 2 – Likes/Dislikes/Mealtimes: VOCABULARY

1. Match up

air	porridge
ikan	water
nasi	chicken satay
bubur	fish
sate ayam	spring roll
daging	honey
bayam	prawns
udang	coconut
madu	meat curry
lumpia	rice
rendang	fruit
kelapa	spinach
sayur-sayuran	vegetables
buah-buahan	meat

2. Complete with the missing words

a. Saya suka ___________________   *I like seafood*

b. Saya sangat suka _____________   *I really like beef curry*

c. Saya suka ___________________   *I like vegetables*

d. Saya suka ___________________   *I like coconut*

e. _______________ ini lezat   *This chicken is delicious*

f. _______________ ini empuk   *This meat is very tender*

g. Saya sangat suka _____________   *I like bananas a lot*

h. Saya suka ___________________   *I like spring rolls*

i. Saya tidak suka _______________   *I don't like fish*

3. Complete with the missing letters

a. a_ _   *water*

b. d_ _ _ ng *meat*

c. b_ _ _-b_ _ _ an *fruit*

d. ke_ _ _ a *coconut*

e. a _ _ _ *apple*

f. ken_ _ _ g *potato*

g. mak_ _ an l_ _ t *seafood*

h. l_ _ _ ia *spring roll*

i. m_ _ _ _ _ c_ _ _ _ _ _ _ *snack on*

j. i _ _ _ *fish*

k. em_ _ _ *tender*

l. n_ _ _ *rice*

m. es k_ _ _ *ice cream*

n. b_ b _ r *porridge*

o. wo_ _ _ l *carrot*

p. ba_ _ _ *good*

q. r _ _ _ *bread*

r. p_ _ _ _ _ *spicy*

4. Match up

biasanya	good
goreng	delicious
empuk	tender
enak	healthy
sehat	usually
baik	disgusting
lezat	fried
gurih	sweet
menjijikkan	crispy
manis	tasty
pahit	bitter

5. Sort the items below into the appropriate category

a. lezat	e. enak	i. apel	m. pahit	q. ikan	u. susu
b. manis	f. nanas	j. segar	n. daging	r. ayam	v. kelapa
c. keju	g. asin	k. menjijikkan	o. udang	s. gurih	w. wortel
d. hambar	h. tidak sehat	l. pisang	p. sehat	t. bayam	x. rendang

Buah-buahan	Sayur-sayuran	Kata Sifat	Ikan dan daging	Produk susu

Unit 12. Talking about food: Part 2 – Likes/Dislikes/Mealtimes: READING

Nama saya Risky. Apa yang saya makan? Biasanya saya tidak makan banyak untuk sarapan, hanya sebuah apel atau pisang dan kopi. Saya tidak suka kopi manis.

Setiap hari, biasanya saya makan hamburger dan kentang goreng untuk makan siang dan minum air atau jus buah. Hamburger tidak sehat, tetapi lezat. Saya suka jus buah. Sesudah sekolah saya makan dua potong roti bakar dengan selai dan mentega dan saya minum secangkir teh. Untuk makan malam saya makan banyak. Biasanya saya makan nasi, lumpia atau ayam panggang dengan sayuran dan sebuah pisang untuk pencuci mulut. Saya ingin makan keju, karena enak, tetapi ibu saya berkata bahwa tidak sehat. Dia tidak suka keju.

Nama saya Farah. Apa yang saya makan? Biasanya, saya tidak makan banyak untuk sarapan, hanya telur dan saya minum teh. Saya suka teh manis, dengan banyak gula. Kadang-kadang saya minum jus nanas. Untuk makan siang saya makan ayam panggang dengan sayuran dan saya minum air mineral. Saya makan banyak sayuran karena sehat dan enak. Saya ingin makan udang karena saya menyukainya.

Sesudah pulang sekolah, saya makan camilan roti dengan madu dan minum teh. Saya sangat suka madu karena manis, enak dan kaya akan vitamin. Untuk makan malam saya makan banyak. Biasanya saya makan nasi, rendang atau ikan goreng dengan sayuran dan untuk pencuci mulut segelas jus buah. Kadang-kadang saya makan ayam karena bergizi, tetapi saya kurang suka makan ayam karena rasanya tidak enak.

1. Find the Indonesian for the words below in Risky's text.

a. Breakfast : S____________

b. Tea: T____________

c. Sweet: M____________

d. Fries: K______G______

e. Lunch: M______ S______

f. Chicken: A____________

g. Roast: P____________

h. After: S____________

i. Cup: S____________

j. Jam: S____________

k. Vegetables: S____________

l. Healthy: S____________

m.Delicious: L____________

n. Dinner: M______M______

o. Tasty: E____________

p. Cheese: K____________

2. Complete the following sentences based on Farah's text

a. Usually at breakfast I only eat an _________ and a cup of ___________

b. I like __________ tea with a lot of _____________

c. For lunch I eat _______ _________ with _____________ and drink ___________ _____________

d. I eat a lot of vegetables because they are _____________ and tasty

e. After _____ as a snack I have ___________ with _______ and drink _________

f. At dinner I usually eat _____________, beef curry or _________ with ___________ and for sweets, a glass of ____________.

g. Sometimes I eat ____________

3. Find the Indonesian for the following in Risky's or Farah's text

a. I don't have much for breakfast

b. For lunch I eat

c. Roast chicken

d. I snack on

e. A glass of fruit juice

f. I would like to eat

g. A cup of tea

h. After school

i. Rice, beef curry or fish

j. Toast with jam

k. Burgers are not healthy

l. Very sweet

m. An apple or a banana

Unit 12. Talking about food: Part 2 – Likes/Dislikes/Mealtimes: READING 2

4. Who says this, Risky or Farah? Or both?

a. I would love to eat cheese – *Risky*

b. I like honey a lot

c. I like fruit juice

d. I don't eat much for breakfast

e. I would like to eat prawns

f. I have toast with jam and butter

g. I am crazy about burgers

h. Burgers are not healthy

i. At dinner I eat quite a bit

j. I drink mineral water

k. The mother hates cheese

l. Sometimes I drink pineapple juice

Nama saya Gunadi. Apa yang saya makan? Biasanya untuk sarapan saya makan banyak; pisang, bubur ayam, roti, dan secangkir kopi. Saya juga suka kopi manis.

Untuk makan siang, biasanya saya hanya makan nasi dengan ayam atau sayuran dan saya minum air mineral atau jus jeruk. Saya suka ayam karena sehat dan kaya akan protein. Kadang-kadang saya makan rendang. Saya suka rendang karena pedas dan bergizi.

Sesudah sekolah saya makan dua potong roti bakar dengan selai dan mentega dan saya minum secangkir teh.

Untuk makan malam saya makan banyak. Biasanya saya makan nasi, daging dengan sayuran dan es krim atau buah semangka untuk pencuci mulut. Saya ingin makan cokelat, karena enak, tetapi ibu berkata bahwa makan coklat tidak sehat.

---

5. Answer the following questions on Gunadi's text

a. How much does he eat at breakfast?

b. What does he eat? 3 things

c. How does he like his coffee?

d. What juice does he drink at lunch?

e. What does he have with rice?

f. Why does he like beef curry?

g. What does he put on toast in the afternoon?

h. Why doesn't his mother allow him to eat chocolate?

---

6. Find in Gunadi's text the following:

a. words for dessert, starting with P….M…:

b. a dessert starting with E:

c. a drink starting with T:

d. a type of meat dish starting with R:

e. a fruit starting with P:

f. a dairy product starting with M:

g. an adjective starting with P

h. a container starting with S:

i. a verb starting with M:

j. a fruit starting with S:

k. an adjective starting with B:

l. a meal starting with S:

Unit 12. Talking about food: Part 2 – Likes/Dislikes/Mealtimes: WRITING

1. Split sentences

Saya makan sate	dengan telur
Nasi goreng	selai
Roti dengan	ayam
Saya suka minum	pisang
Daging merah itu lezat	tetapi tidak sehat
Rendang	atau kopi
Buah favorit saya	jus buah
Saya minum teh	sangat pedas

2. Complete with the correct option

a. Saya suka ____________ laut, terutama cumi-cumi.

b. Biasanya, saya makan sate dengan _________.

c. Biasanya, untuk____________ saya makan sereal.

d. Selalu saya makan _________ dengan kakak saya.

e. Saya makan ikan dan salada______________.

f. Biasanya, saya ____________camilan kue.

g. Saya sangat suka madu karena sangat _________.

h. Kopi rasanya ____________, tetapi saya menyukainya.

i. Saya tidak ____________ susu, menjijikkan!

j. Buah mangga manis dan ______________.

hijau	nasi	makan	siang	pahit
sarapan	makanan	suka	manis	bergizi

3. Spot and correct the grammar and spelling mistakes note: in several cases a word is missing

a. Bisanya saya makan hamburger dengan kentang goreng

b. Saya minum air putih atau juz buah

c. Daging marah tidak sehat, tetapi saya menyukainya

d. Suka saya jus jeruk

e. Sepuluh sekolah saya makan roti dengan madu

f. Saya makan secangkir teh dengan susu

g. Saya suka madu karana rasanya manis dan bergizi

h. Untuk malam saya makan nasi dengan sayur-sayuran

i. Saya suka karena sayuran sehat

j. Ikan favorit saya ikan tuna. Sekali enak!

4. Complete the words

a. M______s_______ *lunch*

b. M______m______*dinner*

c. S____________*breakfast*

d. P____________*spicy*

e. L____________*delicious*

f. M____ c______ *snack on*

g. S____________*healthy*

6. Sentence level translation EN - IND

a. I like fruit juice a lot because it is sweet and refreshing

b. I don't like fish because it is disgusting

c. For dinner I eat spring rolls

d. I always drink tea with honey. I like it because it's sweet.

e. I like fish, but chicken is not tasty

5. Guided writing – write 3 short paragraphs in the first person using the details below

Person	Lunch	Location	With	After *(sesudah)*
Tono	Chicken and rice	The kitchen	Brother	Go to the beach
Arif	Burger	The dining room	Sister	Read a book
Aminah	Salad with peanut sauce	The garden	Mother	Listen to music

THE LANGUAGE GYM

Grammar Time 9: Quantities

Kamu menyiapkan apa untuk makan malam? *What are you preparing for dinner?*				
Kamu membeli apa di pasar swalayan? *What did you buy in the supermarket?*				
Dia *He/She* **Ibu saya** *My mother* **Kakak saya** *My older sibling* **Nenek saya** *My grandma* **Orang tua saya** *My parents* **Pemasak** *The chef* **Pembantu** *The housekeeper* **Penjual** *The seller* **Saya** *I*	**membeli** *buy/s* **menjual** *sell/s* **makan** *eat/s* **menyiapkan** *prepare/s* **memasak** *cook/s* **memesan** *order/s*	**beberapa** *a number of, several, a few* **banyak** *many*	**ayam panggang** *roast chickens* **bawang merah** *onions* **buncis** *beans* **ikan** *fish* **krupuk udang** *prawn crackers* **nanas** *pineapples* **pisang** *bananas* **telur** *eggs* **udang** *prawns* **wortel** *carrots*	**di pasar** *at the market* **di pasar swalayan** *at the supermarket* **di resep** *in the recipe* **sekali seminggu** *once a week* **setiap hari** *every day* **untuk sarapan** *for breakfast* **untuk makan siang** *for lunch* **untuk makan malam** *for dinner*
		telur-telur *eggs* **dua telur** *two eggs* **tiga pisang** *three bananas*		**untuk pesta** *for the party*
Ada *There are*	**dua** *two* **tiga** *three*	**telur** *eggs* **pisang** *bananas* **wortel** *carrots*		

Grammar Time 9. Quantities: TRANSLATION

1. Match the translations

a. Dia menjual beberapa ikan.

The housekeeper cooked many chickens.

b. Ibu saya menyiapkan dua telur untuk sarapan.

She cooked eggs.

c. Pembantu memasak banyak ayam.

The chef bought several onions.

d. Dia memasak telur-telur.

He sells a few fish.

e. Kakak perempuan saya makan dua pisang.

My mother prepared two eggs for breakfast.

f. Pemasak membeli beberapa bawang merah.

My sister ate two bananas.

Grammar Time 9. Quantities: TRANSLATION

2. Complete with the missing word

a. Dia makan ___________ *(several)* udang

b. Pemasak menyiapkan_______________ *(eggs)*

c. Pembantu membeli ________________ *(a few)* bawang merah

d. Ada ___________ telur di resep *(many)*

e. Dia memesan _______________ *(many)* ayam panggang

f. Saya membeli _______________ (three bananas) di pasar swalayan

g. Nenek memasak _______________(two fish) untuk makan malam.

4. Translate into English

a. Beberapa nanas dan dua buah pisang

b. Beberapa ayam panggang dan banyak telur

c. Banyak ikan dan udang

d. Beberapa telur untuk makan siang

e. Banyak wortel dan buncis

f. Nenek saya makan dua telur setiap hari

g. Dia menyiapkan beberapa telur untuk sarapan

5. Translate into Indonesian

a. A few eggs: ________________________________

b. Several prawns: ________________________________

c. Many chickens: ________________________________

d. Four onions: ________________________________

e. A few prawn crackers: ________________________

f. Many eggs: ___________________________

g. A number of pineapples: ___________________________

h. A few carrots and onions: ___________________________

3. Match the words

telur-telur	a number of
banyak	egg
banyak telur	two bananas
telur	many
dua buah pisang	eggs
beberapa	many bananas
banyak pisang	several bananas
beberapa pisang	many eggs

6. Translate into Indonesian

a. She buys several bananas at the market.

b. There are four eggs in the recipe.

c. My grandmother eats bananas every day and several fish once a week.

d. He sells many prawn crackers at the market every day.

e. The housekeeper buys eggs and several onions and carrots at the supermarket.

f. My parents eat a lot of fish for lunch every day but my brother and I eat only a few eggs.

g. My mother cooked a few roast chickens and many fish for the party.

Grammar Time 10: The Suffix -NYA

Bagaimana rasa makanan ini? *Describe the taste of this food?*
Bagaimana rasanya? *Describe the taste.*

Nasi goreng *fried rice* **Ayam goreng** *fried chicken* **Lumpia** *spring rolls* **Nasi uduk** *coconut rice* **Kue lapis** *layer cake* **Kopi** *coffee* **Buah lemon** *a lemon* **Sambal** *chili sauce* **Kecap manis** *sweet soy sauce* **Sate ayam** *chicken skewers*	**rasanya** *the taste is*	**asam** *sour* **asin** *salty* **lezat** *delicious* **enak** *tasty* **pahit** *bitter* **manis** *sweet* **pedas** *spicy*

Bagaimana rasa makanan ini? *Describe the taste of the food.*
Wah, enaknya pisang ini! *Wow, how tasty this banana is!*

Aduh *Oh no* **Waduh** *Oh dear* **Wah** *Wow*	**asam** *sour* **asin** *salty* **enak** *tasty* **lezat** *delicious* **manis** *sweet* **pahit** *bitter* **pedas** *spicy*	**-nya *** *how*	**ayam goreng** *fried chicken* **buah lemon** *a lemon* **kecap manis** *sweet soy sauce* **kopi** *coffee* **kue lapis** *layer cake* **lumpia** *spring rolls* **nasi goreng** *fried rice* **nasi uduk** *coconut rice* **sambal** *chili sauce* **sate ayam** *chicken skewers*	**ini!** *this* **itu!** *that*

Ini buku siapa?
Who's book is this ?

Ini buku dia. *This is his/her book.*
Ini bukunya.

Ini *this is* **Itu** *that is*	**buku latihan** *exercise book* **buku teks** *textbook* **kamus** *dictionary* **pena** *pen* **pensil** *pencil*	**siapa?** *who's*	**Ini** *This is* **Itu** *That is*	**buku latihan** *exercise book* **buku teks** *textbook* **kamus** *dictionary* **pena** *pen* **pensil** *pencil*	**-nya *** *his, her, their*

Siapa punya binatang peliharaan? *Who has pets?*
Anjingnya teman saya lima. *(The dogs of my friend are five.) My friend has five dogs.*

Anjing *dog* **Burung** *bird* **Kadal** *lizard* **Kelinci** *rabbit* **Kucing** *cat* **Kuda** *horse*	**-nya *** *his / her / their*	**keluarga kami** *our family* **keluarga teman saya** *my friend's family* **teman saya** *my friend* **tetangga saya** *my neighbour*	**satu** *one* **dua** *two* **tiga** *three* **empat** *four* **lima** *five* **banyak** *many*

**Author's note: Contrary to English sentence construction, Indonesian often uses 'object focus', i.e. the object of the sentence is at the beginning.*
*Remember to attach the suffix **-nya** to the end of the adjective or noun*
*e.g. **pedasnya** how spicy; **buku latihannya** his/her exercise book*

Grammar Time 10: The Suffix -NYA: DRILLS

1. Split sentences

Bagaimana	enak
Sambal	nasi goreng itu!
Wah enaknya	rasanya?
Ini kamus siapa? Ini	teman saya banyak
Kelincinya	bagaimana rasanya?
Rasanya lezat dan	dan pena birunya
Aduh pedasnya	kamusnya
Ini buku latihan	sambal ini!

2. Rewrite the phrase using -nya

anjing dia	
pena mereka	
kamus dia	
kuda dia	
kelinci mereka	
buku latihan dia	
binatang peliharaan dia	
binatang peliharaan keluarga dia	

3. Translate into English

a. Bagaimana rasanya nasi uduk?

b. Rasanya lezat.

c. Bagaimana rasanya kopi ini? Pahit!

d. Wah manisnya kue lapis ini!

e. Wah enaknya lumpia ini!

f. Waduh pedasnya sambal ini!

4. Broken words

a. Ba__aima__a ra__an__a a__a__ go__eng ?
Describe the taste of fried chicken

b. Wa__uh asa__n__a b__ __h l__mon i__ __!
Oh dear how sour is this lemon!

c. Ini pen__il-pen__il si__p__? Ini pen__il-pen__il__ __ __
Who's are these pencils? These are her pencils.

d. Kadal__ __ __ kel__ __rga ka__i b__ny__k
Our family has many lizards

e. K__ __ l__p__s rasa__ __a e__ __k tetapi tidak ma__i__.
The taste of layer cake is tasty but not sweet

5. Complete

a. Bagaimana ____________ sate ayam
Describe the taste of chicken skewers.

b. ____________ lezat *It tastes delicious*

c. Wah ________________ nasi uduk ini!
Wow how tasty is coconut rice!

d. Ini________ siapa? Ini ____________
Who's book is this? This is his book.

e. Keluarganya ________ dua anjing.
His family have two dogs.

6. Translate into Indonesian

a. Describe the taste

b. These prawns taste delicious

c. This coffee tastes sweet

d. My friend has five rabbits

e. The taste is sour

f. These are their dictionaries

g. Who's exercise book is this? This is her exercise book

Question Skills 2: Jobs/School bag/Food

1. Translate these questions into English

a. Kamu makan siang di mana?

b. Ibumu bekerja sebagai apa?

c. Ada apa di tas sekolahmu?

d. Apa makanan favoritmu?

e. Apa minuman favoritmu?

f. Berapa sering kamu makan daging?

g. Apakah kamu suka jus buah?

h. Mengapa kamu tidak makan sayuran?

i. Apakah kamu sering makan pencuci mulut?

j. Kamu ingin bekerja sebagai apa?

k. Bagaimana kakak perempuanmu?

l. Biasanya kamu makan sarapan dengan siapa?

2. Match the answers below to the questions in activity 1

1. Jus apel _____e_____

2. Dia pintar dan sangat lucu _______

3. Saya ingin menjadi tukang kebun _______

4. Ya. Saya menyukainya. Sangat segar. _______

5. Karena saya tidak menyukainya. _______

6. Nasi goreng _______

7. Ya. Hampir setiap hari. _______

8. Saya makan daging 2 kali seminggu. _______

9. Ada dua buku catatan dan buku harian _______

10. Ibu saya adalah seorang polisi. _______

11. Di kantin sekolah. _______

12. Sendiri saja _______

3. Provide the questions to the following answers

a. Saya tidak makan daging

b. Saya selalu makan sayuran karena sehat

c. Saya bekerja sebagai pemadam kebakaran

d. Saya suka buah-buahan karena enak dan sehat

e. Saya bermain sepak bola di sekolah

f. Saya sering makan daging merah

g. Saya makan dua porsi bakso sehari

h. Saya berasal dari Singapura

i. Saya tidak punya binatang peliharaan

j. Minuman favorit saya adalah jus apel

k. Bapak saya bekerja sebagai pengacara

l. Di kotak pensil saya hanya ada dua pensil

4. Complete

a. A_____ a____ d_ t_____ sekolahmu?

b. Ibumu b________ s________ a___?

c. A____ k____ m_________ makanan laut?

d. Daging a___ f_______ k____?

e. A______ k___ minum j_____b_____?

f. A______ k____ s______ m______ daging?

g. K____ b________ d______ mana?

h. A_______ k____ sudah makan sarapan?

UNIT 13
Talking about clothes and accessories I wear, how frequently and when

Grammar Time 11: ME- Verbs

Revision Quickie 3: Jobs, food, clothes and numbers 20-100

In this unit you will learn how to:

- Say what clothes you wear in various circumstances and places
- Describe various types of weather
- Give a wide range of words for clothing items and accessories
- Use a range of words for places in town
- Use a range of ME- verbs

You will revisit:
- Time markers
- Frequency markers
- Colours
- Self-introduction phrases
- Noun phrase word order

Talking about clothes

Kamu memakai apa kalau cuacanya ……….? *What do you wear when the weather is …..?*

Kamu memakai apa di …? *What do you wear at the …?*

Kalau cuacanya panas *When the weather is hot*	**saya memakai** *I wear*	**anting-anting** *earrings* **baju** *top* **baju hangat** *jumper* **baju kaus** *t-shirt*	**abu-abu** *grey* **biru** *blue* **biru muda** *light blue*
Kalau cuacanya dingin *When the weather is cold*	**saya tidak memakai** *I don't wear*	**baju olahraga** *tracksuit* **baju renang** *swimsuit* **celana panjang** *trousers*	**biru tua** *dark blue* **cokelat** *brown*
Kalau saya keluar dengan pacar saya *When I go out with my boyfriend/girlfriend*	**saya tidak pernah memakai** *I never wear*	**celana jins** *jeans* **celana pendek** *shorts* **cincin** *ring* **dasi** *tie* **gaun** *dress*	**emas** *gold* **hijau** *green* **hitam** *black*
Kalau saya keluar dengan orang tua *When I go out with my parents*	**saya jarang memakai** *I rarely wear*	**hijab** *head scarf* **ikat pinggang** *belt* **jam tangan** *watch* **jas** *coat* **jas hujan** *raincoat* **kalung** *necklace*	**jingga** *orange* **kuning** *yellow* **merah muda** *pink*
Kalau saya keluar dengan teman *When I go out with my friends*		**kaus kaki** *socks* **kebaya** *woman's trad. shirt* **kemeja** *shirt*	**merah** *red* **perak** *silver*
Kalau saya ke kantor *When I go to the office*	**saya selalu memakai** *I always wear*	**pakaian bermerek** *branded clothes* **pakaian olahraga** *sports clothes*	**putih** *white* **ungu** *purple*
Kalau saya bermain futbol aturan Australia *When I play Australian rules football*		**pakaian santai** *casual clothes* **pakaian tradisional** *traditional clothing* **peci** *trad. man's hat* **rok** *skirt*	
Kalau saya bermain olahraga *When I play sport*		**sandal** *sandals* **sandal jepit** *thongs* **sarung** *sarong*	
Di gym *At the gym*		**selendang** *scarf* **sepatu** *shoes*	
Di kelas fitnes *At fitness class*		**sepatu bot** *boots* **sepatu hak tinggi** *high heeled shoes*	
Di pantai *At the beach*			
Di pesta *At parties*			
Di rumah *At home*			
Di sekolah *At school*			
Biasanya *Usually*	**saya memakai** *I wear*	**sepatu kets** *sneakers* **seragam** *uniform* **setelan jas** *business suit* **topi** *hat*	

Unit 13. Talking about clothes: VOCABULARY BUILDING

1. Match up

anting-anting	hat
baju kaus	shoes
gaun	trousers
sepatu	shirt
celana panjang	t-shirt
kemeja	earrings
topi	dress

2. Translate into English

a. Saya memakai baju kaus hitam

b. Saya memakai jas abu-abu

c. Saya tidak memakai sepatu kets

d. Saya memakai topi biru

e. Saya tidak memakai jam tangan

f. Saya selalu memakai cincin

g. Saya memakai pakaian olahraga

h. Saya jarang memakai jas

i. Saya selalu memakai sandal

j. Biasanya saya memakai topi

k. Kakak saya selalu memakai celana jins

3. Complete with the missing word

a. Di rumah saya __________ ________ ________
At home I wear a T-shirt

b. Di sekolah saya memakai __________ ________
At school I wear a black uniform

c. Di gym saya _________ pakaian olahraga ________
At the gym I wear pink sports clothes

d. Di ________ saya memakai __________ __________
At the beach I wear a swimsuit

e. ____ pesta saya memakai _____________ hitam
At the party I wear a black dress

f. Saya jarang _________ sepatu ____ _________
I rarely wear high heel shoes

g. Saya tidak pernah _________ setelan jas *I never wear suits*

4. Anagrams clothes and accessories

a. poti	g. lecaan sijn
b. ajm gannat	h. yakbea
c. rusgan	i. sja jahun
d. gitnna-gitnna	j. gaseram
e. patseu	k. kapaain
f. juab suak	l. jemkae

5. Associations – match each body part below with the words in the box

a. Kepala *(head)* – e.g. **topi**

b. Kaki *(feet)* –

c. Kaki *(legs)* -

d. Leher *(neck)* –

e. Badan *(upper body)* –

f. Telinga *(ears)* –

g. Tangan *(hand)* –

selendang	dasi	sepatu	sepatu bot
jas	kemeja	kaus kaki	**topi**
anting-anting	celana jins	rok	cincin
jam tangan	peci	kalung	baju kaus

6. Complete

a. Saya memakai sepatu b_____ *I wear boots*

b. Di r______________   *At home*

c. Saya punya j____ t______ *I have a watch*

d. Saya memakai d____ merah *I wear a red tie*

e. Saya memakai s_____ jas biru *I wear a blue suit*

f. Kakak saya memakai s_________ tradisional
My older brother wears a traditional sarong

g. Dia selalu memakai g_________ h_______
She always wears black dresses

Unit 13. Talking about clothes: READING

Nama saya Sinta. Saya berasal dari Indonesia. Saya berumur lima belas tahun. Saya sangat sportif, jadi saya memiliki banyak pakaian olahraga. Saya lebih suka pakaian berkualitas baik tetapi tidak terlalu mahal. Biasanya saya memakai baju olahraga di rumah. Saya memiliki empat atau lima baju olahraga dengan warna dan gaya yang berbeda. Kalau saya keluar dengan pacar saya, saya memakai anting-anting, kalung, gaun merah atau hitam dan sepatu hak tinggi.

Nama saya Renaud. Saya berasal dari Prancis dan umur saya tiga belas tahun. Saya suka membeli pakaian, terutama sepatu. Saya memiliki banyak sepatu kets bermerek. Kalau cuacanya dingin, saya biasanya memakai baju hangat dan celana panjang hitam atau ungu. Kadang-kadang saya memakai baju olahraga. Kalau cuacanya panas saya memakai baju tanpa lengan, celana jins dan sepatu kets. Di rumah, saya punya seekor kuda bernama Napoleon.

Nama saya Gerda. Saya berasal dari Jerman dan berumur dua belas tahun. Saya selalu membeli pakaian dari toko pakaian Zara. Saya suka pakaian bagus tetapi tidak terlalu mahal. Saya tidak suka pakaian bermerek. Saya selalu memakai baju olahraga seperti baju kaus, dan sepatu kets. Kalau cuacanya dingin saya memakai baju olahraga. Kalau cuacanya panas saya memakai baju kaus dan celana pendek.

Nama saya Matt. Saya berasal dari Australia. Umur saya empat belas tahun. Ketika saya pergi ke sekolah saya memakai kemeja, celana panjang dan sepatu. Biasanya di rumah, saya memakai baju kaus dan celana jins. Saya punya banyak baju kaus dan jins. Kalau saya pergi ke gym saya memakai baju kaus, celana pendek dan sepatu kets. Ketika saya pergi ke mal bersama teman-teman saya, saya memakai jas, kemeja, celana panjang hitam atau abu-abu, dan sepatu hitam.

1. Find the Indonesian in Sinta's text

a. I am from

b. Sporty

c. Many

d. Good quality clothes

e. Tracksuit

f. When I go out

g. With my boyfriend

h. Earrings

i. A red or black dress

j. High heel shoes

2. Find the Indonesian in Matt's text

a. When I go

b. I wear a shirt

c. T-shirt and jeans

d. At home

e. Gym

f. With my friends

g. A coat

h. Black trousers

i. sneakers

j. Usually

3. Complete the following statements about Renaud

a. He is _________ years old

b. He likes buying _________

c. He has many branded _________

d. When it's cold he wears a _________ and _________ or
_________ _________

e. Sometimes he wears a_________

4. Answer the questions about Gerda (in Indonesian)

a. Siapa namanya?

b. Dia berasal dari mana?

c. Berapa umurnya?

d. Dia suka apa?

e. Dia membeli pakaian dari mana?

f. Kalau cuacanya dingin, dia memakai apa?

g. Kalau cuacanya panas, dia memakai apa?

5. Find Someone Who...

a. ...loves branded clothes

b. ...is from Germany

c. ...wears t-shirts in the gym

d. ...wears earrings when she goes out with her boyfriend

e. ...has four or five different tracksuits

f. ...has a lot of T-shirts and jeans at home

g. ...is very sporty

h. ...wears grey or black trousers at the shopping mall

104

Unit 13. Talking about clothes: WRITING

1. Split sentences

Di	memakai baju kaus dan celana pendek
Kalau cuacanya	rumah saya memakai
Di gym saya	saya memakai setelan jas
Kalau cuacanya panas saya	dingin saya memakai selendang
Di pesta saya memakai kebaya	memakai baju renang di pantai
Kalau saya ke kantor	dan sarung
Saya memakai gaun	pakaian tradisional
Kadang-kadang saya memakai	hitam

2. Complete with the correct option

a. _________ keluar dengan ________ saya memakai pakaian santai

b. Di sekolah saya _________ seragam biru

c. Di kelas fitnes saya memakai ___________ kets

d. Di pantai saya memakai pakaian _____________

e. Kalau _________ panas saya memakai ______ kaus

f. Di rumah saya memakai baju ____________

g. Kalau cuacanya sangat dingin saya memakai_________

h. Saya ________ pernah memakai setelan jas

jas	pacar	olahraga	memakai	kalau
sepatu	tidak	cuacanya	renang	baju

3. Spot and correct the grammar and spelling mistakes note: in several cases a word is missing

a. Kalau saya keluar orang tua, saya memakai gawn indah

b. Di rumah saya mepakai baju olahraga

c. Saya punya banyak sepatu-sepatu

d. Adik saya salalu memakai jins

e. Di sekolah saya seragam

f. Saya tidak peduli dengan pakian bermerek

g. Kalau saya pergi ke mal, saya biasanya memakai santai, yaitu jins dan baju kaus.

h. Saya selalu memakai sepatu kest

4. Complete the words

a. R_______________ *skirt*

b. S_________J________ *suit*

c. A_______ - a________ *earrings*

d. C______ P_________ *trousers*

e. S_______________ *shoes*

f. S_______________ *scarf*

g. P_______________ *clothing*

5. Guided writing – write 3 short paragraphs in the first person ['I'] using the details below

Person	Lives	Always wears	Never wears	Doesn't wear
Anisa	Jakarta	Blue headscarf	Shorts	Earrings
Jackie	Sydney	White T-shirts	Coats	Watches
Julius	Singapore	Jeans	Suits	Ties

6. Describe this person in Indonesian

Name: John

Lives in: London

Age : 20

Pet: A black spider

Hair: Blond

Eyes: Green

Always wears: A suit

Never wears: Jeans

At the gym wears: An Adidas tracksuit

THE LANGUAGE GYM

Grammar Time 11: ME- Verbs

		baju *blouse/top*	abu-abu *grey*
Saya *I (formal)*	***memakai** *wear*	baju hangat *jumper*	**biru** *blue*
	membeli *buys*	baju kaus *t-shirt*	**cokelat** *brown*
Aku *I (informal)*	**membuat** *makes*	celana *trousers*	**emas** *gold*
		dasi *tie*	**hijau** *green*
Anda *You (form)*	**memiliki** *own/have*	gaun *dress*	**hitam** *black*
	meminjam *borrow/s*	ikat pinggang *belt*	**jingga** *orange*
Kamu *You (inf)*	**mempunyai** *own /s*	jam tangan *watch*	**kuning** *yellow*
	mencuci *washes*	jas *jacket*	**merah** *red*
Dia *S/he*		kalung *necklace*	**pelangi** *rainbow*
	menjahit *sews*	kemeja *shirt*	**perak** *silver*
Kita *We (inc. listener)*	**menjual** *sells*	mantel *coat*	**putih** *white*
	****memperbaiki** *repairs*	pakaian olahraga *sports clothes*	**ungu** *purple*
Kami *We (ex. listener)*		baju renang *swimsuit*	
		pakaian tradisional *traditional clothes*	**anggun** *elegant*
Anda semua *You all*		rok *a skirt*	**bergaya** *fashionable*
		syal *scarf*	**bermerek** *branded*
Mereka *They*		seragam *uniform*	**gaul** *stylish*
		setelan jas *business suit*	**jelek** *ugly*
		topi *hat/cap*	**mahal** *expensive*
			murah *cheap*

Author's note: A base word can be changed into a verb by adding a ME- prefix according first letter of the base word:

me-	*l, m, n, r, y, w*	lihat →melihat	to see	*Underlined letters are dropped
mem-	**p, b, f, v*	pakai →memakai	to wear	***suffixes -KAN and -I
men-	*t, d, j, c, z*	tulis →menulis	to write	also added to these base words
meng-	*k, h, g, a, e, i, o, u*	kerja →mengerjakan***	to do	
meny-	*s*	suka →menyukai***	to like	

** The prefix **MEMPER-** and suffix **-I** has been added to the base word **baik**

Grammar Time 11. ME- Verbs: TRANSLATION

1. Complete with the missing pronoun according to the word in the bracket.

a. _________ tidak pernah memakai rok (I)

b. _________ memakai baju apa? (you, informal)

c. Adik meminjam banyak pakaian ____ (my)

d. Orang tua _______memakai baju bermerek (her)

e. Guru seni______ memakai baju pelangi (his)

f. _________ memakai sepatu kets bermerek (They)

g. Di sekolah ____ memakai seragam (we, excl.)

h. _________ punya banyak jins (He)

i. _________ memakai pakaian apa? (you all)

j. Ibu ______ punya banyak pakaian (my)

k. ____ selalu memakai gaun bergaya (She)

l. Kalau dingin ______memakai syal (we, incl)

Grammar Time 11. ME- Verbs: TRANSLATION

2. Complete with the missing ME- verb

a. Ibu saya____________ banyak pakaian bermerek *My mother buys a lot of branded clothes*

b. Saudara laki-laki saya juga __________ baju kaus *My brothers also wear T-shirts*

c. Biasanya kakak perempuan saya ______ jinsnya *Usually my sister repairs her jeans*

d. Guru-guru saya selalu ____________ setelan jas *My teachers always wear suits*

e. Pacar saya ______________ banyak anting-anting *My girlfriend makes many earrings*

f. Dia __________________ baju kaus hitam *She washed the black T-shirt*

g. Orang tua saya ____ _____ banyak pakaian olahraga *My parents don't wear a lot of sporty clothes*

h. Sepupu saya tidak ___________ banyak pakaian *My cousins don't have many clothes*

3. Write the base word of these ME- verbs

membeli	
memakai	
mencuci	
menjual	
membuat	
menjahit	
memiliki	
memperbaiki	
meminjam	

4. Match the phrases

a. meminjam dasi	owns branded sneakers
b. mencuci rok merah	sells rings
c. memiliki sepatu kets bermerek	sews a blue shirt
d. menjual cincin	buys fashionable jeans
e. membuat pakaian	borrows a tie
f. membeli jins bergaya	repairs a necklace
g. memperbaiki kalung	washes a red skirt
h. menjahit baju biru	makes clothes

5. Translate into English

a. Saya tidak pernah membuat anting-anting

b. Saya selalu mencuci jins baru saya

c. Kami tidak membeli gaun mahal

d. Dia memiliki banyak sepatu

e. Mereka menjual banyak sepatu bermerek

f. Mereka selalu memakai sepatu kets

g. Apakah kamu membuat kemeja baru itu?

h. Di mal ada toko yang memperbaiki pakaian

6. Translate into Indonesian

a. Do you make hats?

b. We have many shoes

c. I don't own an elegant dress

d. My father sells suits and ties

e. My mother sews dresses

f. I always wash my clothes

g. You are buying what clothes?

h. They never wear uniforms

i. She wore a red tracksuit

j. She sews beautiful clothes

Revision Quickie 3: Jobs, food, clothes and numbers 20-100

1. Complete (numbers)

a. 100 ser
b. 90 se
c. 30 ti
d. 50 li
e. 80 de
f. 60 en
g. 40 em

2. Translate into English (food and clothes)

a. baju renang
b. minuman
c. ayam
d. rok
e. babi
f. air
g. daging
h. udang
i. ikan
j. selendang
k. sepatu
l. sayuran
m. jus
n. makan malam

3. Write in a word for each letter in the categories below as shown in the example *(there is no obvious word for the greyed out boxes!)*

HURUF	Pakaian	Makanan dan Minuman	Angka	Pekerjaan
T	topi	tempe	tujuh belas	tukang becak
S				
D				
R				
A				

4. Match up

memakai	to drink
saya punya	breakfast
saya memiliki	to live in
makan malam	to work
ada	I have
minum	dinner
sarapan	there is/are
bekerja	I eat
tidak punya	my name is
tinggal di	I own
saya makan	to wear
nama saya	do not have

5. Translate into English

a. Saya jarang memakai rok

b. Saya selalu makan roti bakar dengan madu

c. Saya bekerja sebagai karyawan

d. Saya sering minum kopi

e. Saya tidak suka minuman panas

f. Saya selalu makan telur untuk sarapan

g. Ibu saya adalah seorang pengusaha

h. Saya tidak mempunyai banyak pakaian bermerek

i. Saya tidak makan banyak, hanya selada

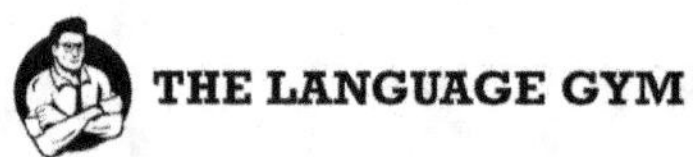

UNIT 14
Saying what I and others do in our free time

Grammar Time 12: Adverbs of Frequency (Part 2) & BER- Verbs (Part 3)

In this unit you will learn how to say:

- What activities you do using the verbs 'bermain' (play) and 'pergi ke' (go to)
- Other free time activities
- How often you do an activity

You will revisit:
- Time and frequency markers
- Expressing likes/dislikes
- Adjectives and pronouns
- Pets

UNIT 14
Saying what I (and others) do
in our free time

Kalau ada waktu luang, kamu melakukan apa? *If you have free time, what do you do?*

Dua kali seminggu saya *Twice a week I*	**bermain** *play*	**catur** *chess* **bola basket** *basketball* **kartu** *cards* **komputer** *the computer* **olahraga** *sport* **sepak bola** *soccer* **tenis** *tennis*	**bersama keluarga saya** *with my family* **bersama pacar saya** *with my boy/girlfriend* **bersama sahabat saya** *with my close friend* **bersama teman saya** *with my friends* **sendiri saja** *alone*

Full table reproduction:

Dua kali seminggu saya *Twice a week I*

Kalau ada waktu luang saya *When I have free time I*

Kalau cuacanya* buruk saya *When the weather is bad I*

Kalau cuacanya* cerah saya *When the weather is good/fine I*

Pada akhir minggu saya *On the weekend I*

Pada akhir pekan saya *On the weekend I*

Saya kadang-kadang *I sometimes*

Sekali seminggu saya *Once a week I*

Setiap hari saya *Every day I*

---

bermain *play*
- **catur** *chess*
- **bola basket** *basketball*
- **kartu** *cards*
- **komputer** *the computer*
- **olahraga** *sport*
- **sepak bola** *soccer*
- **tenis** *tennis*

berenang go *swimming*
mengangkat besi *weight lifting*
memancing go *fishing*
memanjat tebing go *rock climbing*
mengecek email *check emails*
mengecek media sosial *check social media*
mendaki *hiking*
mendengarkan musik *listen to music*
menonton televisi *watch television*
naik sepeda *go cycling*

membaca *read*
- **buku** *books*
- **komik** *comics*
- **majalah** *magazines*
- **surat kabar** *newspapers*

pergi ke *go to*
- **bioskop** *the cinema*
- **gym** *the gym*
- **kolam renang** *the pool*
- **mal** *the mall*
- **pantai** *the beach*
- **pesta** *a party*
- **restoran** *a restaurant*
- **rumah teman saya** *my friend's house*
- **taman** *the park*
- **taman bersepeda** *bike park*

bersama keluarga saya *with my family*

bersama pacar saya *with my boy/girlfriend*

bersama sahabat saya *with my close friend*

bersama teman saya *with my friends*

sendiri saja *alone*

---

*Author's note: -nya is optional in this phrase

Unit 14. Free time: VOCABULARY BUILDING – Part 1 Activities

1. Match up

Saya bermain catur	I check emails
Saya membaca buku	I play chess
Saya mengecek email	I play basketball
Saya bermain kartu	I go hiking
Saya naik sepeda	I go swimming
Saya berenang	I go cycling
Saya mendaki	I read books
Saya bermain bola basket	I play cards

2. Complete with the missing word

a. Saya bermain ____________   *I play chess*

b. Saya bermain ___________   *I play soccer*

c. Saya ____________ kartu   *I play cards*

d. Saya __________ sepeda   *I go cycling*

e. Saya bermain___________   *I play basketball*

f. Saya pergi ke ___________   *I go to a party*

g. Saya _________ surat kabar   *I read newspapers*

h. Saya __________________   *I go rock climbing*

i. Saya ________ ke bioskop   *I go to the cinema*

j. Saya tidak mengerjakan ______   *I don't do homework*

bermain	memanjat tebing	pergi	pesta	PR
naik	sepak bola	membaca	bola basket	catur

3. Translate into English

a. Saya naik sepeda setiap hari

b. Saya pergi ke taman

c. Dua kali seminggu saya mendaki

d. Saya mendengarkan music sendiri saja

e. Kalau cuacanya buruk saya bermain kartu atau catur

f. Kalau ada waktu luang saya bermain bola basket

g. Saya pergi ke pesta bersama teman

h. Saya pergi ke rumah teman saya

i. Saya pergi ke pantai setiap hari

j. Sekali seminggu saya memancing

k. Kalau cuacanya cerah saya bermain golf

4. Broken words

a. Saya men________________ musik *I listen to music*

b. Saya be__________________   *I go swimming*

c. Saya me________________   *I go fishing*

d. Saya na___________ sepeda   *I go cycling*

e. Saya ber___________ catur   *I play chess*

f. Saya pergi ke res___________   *I go to a restaurant*

g. Saya bermain ka___________   *I play cards*

h. Saya meng_________ media sosial *I check social media*

5. 'Belum pernah' or 'Sudah pernah' according to whether you have done these activities

a. Mendaki   ____________

b. Naik sepeda   ____________

c. Bermain catur ____________

d. Bermain kartu ____________

e. Berenang   ____________

f. Memancing   ____________

g. Bermain tenis ____________

h. Mengangkat besi __________

6. Bad translation – spot any translation errors and fix them

a. Saya pergi ke mal : *I walk to the mall*

b. Saya suka bermain kartu : *I like playing chess*

c. Setiap hari saya mengecek email: *Every week I check emails*

d. Kalau cuacanya baik saya memancing : *When the weather is nice I go hiking*

e. Sekali seminggu saya naik sepeda : *I go cycling every day*

f. Saya bermain catur dengan teman saya : *I play chess with my dad*

g. Saya sering mendaki : *I never go hiking*

h. Saya menonton televisi sendiri saja : *I go fishing alone*

THE LANGUAGE GYM

Unit 14. Free time: READING

Nama saya Tom Weidner. Saya orang Jerman. Kalau ada waktu luang, saya bermain banyak olahraga. Olahraga favorit saya adalah memanjat tebing. Saya mendaki setiap hari. Kalau cuaca buruk saya tinggal di rumah dan bermain catur atau kartu. Saya juga sangat suka bermain video game dan saya sering bermain PlayStation.

Nama saya Verónica Palacin. Saya orang Spanyol, dari Madrid. Saya berambut merah dan keriting, tetapi saya tidak terlalu sportif. Saya lebih suka membaca buku, bermain kartu atau catur, dan mendengarkan musik. Namun, kalau cuacanya cerah, saya kadang-kadang pergi ke taman atau bermain tenis dengan adik laki-laki saya. Saya tidak suka pergi ke gym atau kolam renang. Saya tidak suka berenang karena saya tidak suka air.

Nama saya Olga. Saya dari Jerman. Kalau ada waktu luang, saya sangat suka membaca buku, majalah dan surat kabar. Saya juga suka bermain kartu dan catur. Saya tidak terlalu sportif tetapi saya kadang-kadang pergi ke gym dan mengangkat besi. Juga, pada akhir pekan, kalau cuacanya cerah, saya pergi ke pantai dengan anjing saya. Namanya Buddy dan dia dachshund yang kecil dan berwarna cokelat.

Nama saya Ronan. Saya orang Prancis. Saya suka naik sepeda setiap hari bersama teman-teman saya. Ini aktivitas favorit saya. Saya kadang-kadang mendaki, berlari santai atau berjalan-jalan di kota. Saya tidak suka tenis atau sepak bola. Juga saya jarang membaca tetapi saya suka membaca buku komik. Dua kali seminggu saya pergi ke mal bersama teman saya, Julien. Saya suka mendengarkan musik.

1. Find the Indonesian for the following in Tom's text

a. I do a lot of sport

b. My favourite sport

c. Climbing

d. Every day

e. When the weather is bad

f. I play chess

g. Also

h. I play on the Playstation

2. Find the Indonesian in Ronan's text for

a. I like to go cycling

b. with my friends

c. sometimes

d. don't like tennis

e. I go to the mall

f. I go climbing

g. with my friend, Julien

3. Complete the following statements about Verónica

a. She is from ________________

b. She is not very ____________

c. She plays cards or _____________

d. When the weather is nice she goes ______________

e. She also plays tennis with her____________________

f. She doesn't enjoy going to the gym or the ___________

4. List 8 details about Olga

1.

2.

3.

4.

5.

6.

7.

8.

5. Find Someone Who...

a. ...enjoys reading newspapers

b. ...doesn't like swimming

c. ...does a lot of sport

d. ...does weight lifting

e. ...goes to the mall twice a week

Unit 14. Free time: TRANSLATION

1. Gapped translation

a. Saya pergi ke pesta: *I _____________ parties*

b. Saya bermain Playstation: *I __________Playstation*

c. Saya tidak bermain tenis: *I __________ play tennis*

d. Saya bermain ____________: *I play chess*

e. Saya _________ kartu: *I play cards*

f. Dua kali seminggu saya naik sepeda: ___________ *I go cycling*

g. Saya pergi ke kolam renang: *I go to the _____________*

h. Kalau cuacanya _________ saya mendaki: *When the weather is good, I go hiking*

2. Translate to English

a. Pergi ke

b. Bermain

c. Kalau cuacanya buruk

d. Ke rumah teman saya

e. Sekali seminggu

f. Setiap hari

g. Saya memanjat tebing

h. Mendengarkan musik

i. Saya memancing

3. Translate into English

a. Saya tidak pernah memancing dengan bapak saya

b. Saya bermain kartu bersama adik laki-laki saya

c. Saya pergi ke mal bersama ibu saya

d. Saya kadang-kadang bermain catur bersama teman saya

e. Saya pergi ke pesta setiap hari Sabtu

f. Saya tidak pernah bermain Playstation bersama kakak saya

4. Translate into Indonesian

a. *Cinema*: B

b. *Rock Climbing*: M   t

c. *Basketball*: B   b

d. *Fishing*: M

e. *Weight lifting*: M   b

f. *Party*: P

g. *Chess*: C

h. *Cards*: K

i. *Hiking*: M

j. *Soccer*: S   b

5. Translate into Indonesian

a. I go fishing

b. I play chess

c. I rock climb

d. I swim

e. I check emails

f. I do weights

g. I go to parties

h. I watch television

i. I read magazines

j. I listen to music

Unit 14. Free time: WRITING

1. Split sentences

a. Saya tidak	kolam renang
b. Saya bermain catur	berolahraga
c. Saya pergi ke restoran setiap	pernah memanjat tebing
d. Saya berenang di	komputer
e. Saya sering bermain	musik setiap hari
f. Saya banyak	dengan teman saya Joni
g. Saya mendengarkan	gym
h. Saya mengangkat besi di	minggu

2. Complete the sentences

a. Saya ____________ pernah berlari santai

b. Kadang-kadang saya _____________ catur

c. Saya mendaki kalau ada waktu _________

d. Saya sering memancing _________ teman saya

e. Saya _________ tenis

f. Saya pergi ___ bioskop dengan sahabat saya

g. Kalau ada __________ luang …

h. Saya ___________ ke gym

i. Saya selalu ___________________ PR

3. Spot and correct mistakes (note: in some cases a word is missing)

a. Saya bermain tennis:

b. Saya bemain catur:

c. Saya pergi rumah teman saya:

d. Saya kadang-kadang bermain majalah:

e. Saya mengerjakan pekerjaan ramah saya:

f. Pada ahkir pekan:

g. Saya sering besi mengangkat:

4. Complete the words

a. Cat_________________

b. Bo_____ b___________

c. Ola_________________

d. Rest______________

e. Bios_______________

f. Se_______ bo_________

g. Ka________- ka________

5. Write a paragraph for each of the people below in the first person singular (I):

Name	Sport I do	How often	Who with	Where	Why I like it (menyukainya)
Dian	Hiking	Every day	With my boyfriend	In the countryside	It's fun
Kristiono	Weight-lifting	Often	With my friend James	At home	It's healthy
Arif	Listen to music	When the weather is nice	Alone	In the park	It's stress relieving

Grammar Time 12: Adverbs of Frequency (Part 2) & BER- Verbs (Part 3)

Seberapa sering kamu melakukan kegiatan ini pada waktu luang? *How often do you do these activities in your free time?*				
Saya *I (formal)* **Aku** *I (informal)* **Dia** *S/he* **Kita** *We (inc. listener)* **Kami** *We (ex. listener)* **Mereka** *They* **Teman saya dan saya** *My friend and I* **Sahabat saya** *My close friend* **Adik saya** *My younger sibling* **Kakak saya** *My older sibling*	**belum/tidak pernah** *not ever, never (not yet)* **jarang** *rarely* **kadang-kadang** *sometimes* **selalu** *always* **sering** *often*	**bermain** *play, plays*	**bola basket** *basketball* **bola voli** *volleyball* **bulu tangkis** *badminton* **futbal aturan Australia** *Australian rules football* **sepak bola** *soccer*	**bersama keluarga saya** *with my family* **bersama pacar saya** *with my boy/girlfriend* **bersama sahabat saya** *with my close friend* **bersama teman** *with friends* **sendiri saja** *alone*
		berbelanja *go shopping* **berenang** *go swimming* **berjalan-jalan** *walk around* **berlibur** *go on holidays* **berkuda** *go horse riding* **berlari** *go running* **berlari santai** *go jogging* **berolahraga** *play sport* **bersepeda** *go cycling* **bertamasya** *go sightseeing*		
		pergi *goes* **berjalan kaki** *walks* **naik mobil** *drive /s*	**ke** *to*	**bioskop** *cinema* **gereja** *church* **kolam renang** *pool* **mal** *shopping mall* **masjid** *mosque* **perpustakaan** *library* **restoran** *restaurant* **skatepark** *skatepark* **taman bersepeda** *bike park*

Grammar Time 12: Adverbs (Part 2) & BER- Verbs (Part 3): TRANSLATION

1. Match up

Saya	He/she
Kamu	We
Dia	You
Kita	I
Aku	They
Mereka	I (informal)

2. Match the phrases

a. kadang-kadang bermain	always does
b. jarang pergi ke	not yet ridden a bike
c. selalu mengerjakan	often goes to
d. belum bersepeda	never ridden a horse
e. berenang setiap hari	sometimes plays
f. sering pergi ke	always swims
g. tidak pernah berkuda	rarely goes to
h. selalu berenang	swims every day

3. Translate

a. I often play:

b. You never go:

c. She sometimes does:

d. We often play:

e. She goes to:

f. They rarely do:

g. He never plays:

h. You and I sometimes go to:

i. He rarely goes to:

4. Complete with the verb PERGI or BERMAIN

a. Saya _____________ bola basket

b. Dia_____________ sepak bola setiap hari

c. Saya sering _____________ ke kolam renang

d. Saya jarang_____________ kartu

e. Saya _____________ ke mal sekali seminggu

f. Setiap hari mereka_____________ ke gym

g. Dia sering_____________ ke rumah temannya

h. Mereka tidak pernah_____________ bola voli

i. Saya_____________ ke stadion bersama bapak saya

5. Spot and correct the translation errors

a. Saya ke taman bersepeda *You go to the bike park*

b. Kamu pergi ke gereja *You go to the garage*

c. Saya pergi ke mal
They go to the shopping mall

d. Saya tidak pernah pergi ke rumah Marta
We never go to Marta's house

e. Mereka pergi ke bioskop sekali seminggu
She goes to the cinema once a week

6. Complete with the correct pronoun

a. _______ pergi ke restoran   *I go to the restaurant*

b. _______ naik mobil ke taman *They drive to the park*

c. _______ pergi ke pantai   *We (incl.)go to the beach*

d. _________ ke kolam renang *They go to the pool*

e. _________mau pergi ke mana? *Where do you want to go?*

Grammar Time 12: Adverbs (Part 2) & BER- Verbs (Part 3): TRANSLATION

7. Complete

a. Kita ________________ kolam renang   *always go to*

b. Saya dan ibu ______________ catur   *sometimes play*

c. Mereka ________ berlibur   *rarely go on holidays*

d. Kakak saya bermain tenis __________   *twice a week*

e. Dia ________________ bulu tangkis   *never plays*

f. Teman saya bermain Playstation________   *every day*

g. Saya ______________ pekerjaan rumah   *sometimes do*

h. Kalau cuacanya cerah dia ______ ke pantai   *always*

8. Complete with a BER- verb

a. Saya selalu _______ sepak bola   *play*

b. Dia sering ________ di pantai   *swims*

c. Kami selalu ____________   *play sport*

d. Saya _______ di mal bersama teman saya   *go shopping*

e. Kakak saya suka ___________   *running*

f. Kami jarang _________ bola voli *play*

g. Kami sering ___-__ di mal *walk around*

h. Saya belum pernah __________   *ridden a horse*

i. Bapak saya selalu _________ di taman   *goes cycling*

j. Saya jarang _______ santai *go jogging*

k. Dia sering ____________ di mal   *goes shopping*

l. Kami kadang-kadang ____ bulu tangkis   *play*

m. Saya dan adik ______ sekali seminggu   *go swimming*

9. Translate into English

a. Saya belum pernah bermain sepak bola

b. Saya selalu bermain bola basket

c. Kami tidak pernah berenang di pantai

d. Mereka jarang bersepeda ke perpustakaan

e. Kalau cuacanya cerah mereka berjalan kaki ke taman

f. Saya belum pernah bermain futbal aturan Australia

g. Kalau cuacanya buruk saya berolahraga di gym

10. Translate into Indonesian

a. We never go to the swimming pool

b. He rarely plays sport

c. She plays basketball every day

d. When the weather is fine, I always jog

e. I sometimes go to the bike park

f. I often go to the skatepark

g. My father and I often go to the library

h. My sister plays badminton twice a week

i. I walk to the mosque once a week

j. When the weather is bad I play basketball at the gym

k. They always do their homework

l. I often go to church with my family

UNIT 15
Talking about weather and free time

Grammar Time 13: YANG - *the one* or *which*

Revision Quickie 4: Clothes / Free Time / Weather

Question Skills 3: Clothes / Free Time / Weather

In this unit you will learn how to say:
- What free-time activities you do in different types of Weather
- Where you do them **and** who with
- Words for places in town

You will also learn how to ask and answer questions about:
- Clothes
- Free time
- Weather

You will revisit:
- Sports and hobbies
- Pets
- Places in town
- Clothes
- Family members
- Numbers from 1 to 100

Kamu melakukan apa pada akhir minggu? *What do you do on the week-end?*
Kalau cuacanya …. kamu melakukan apa? *If the weather is …. what do you do?*

Kadang-kadang *Sometimes* **Kalau ada waktu** *If there is time* **Pada akhir minggu/pekan** *At the weekends* **Pada hari kerja** *On weekdays* *__Pada saat__ bersalju** *When it snows*	**saya bermain** *I play* **teman saya Sari bermain** *my friend Sari plays*	**catur** *chess* **kartu** *cards* **bola basket** *basketball* **sepak bola** *soccer* **ski** *skiing* **tenis** *tennis* **bersama teman saya** *with my friends* **bersama temannya** *with his/her friends*
****Pada saat cuac<u>anya</u> berangin** *When it is windy* **Pada saat ada badai guntur** *When there are thunderstorms* **Pada saat cuacanya berkabut** *When it is foggy*	**saya** *I* **teman saya Ketut** *my friend Ketut*	**berenang** *goes swimming* **berkuda** *go horse riding* **berlari santai** *goes jogging* **berolahraga** *play sport* **bersepeda** *go cycling* **memancing** *go fishing* **memanjat tebing** *go rock climbing* **mendaki** *go hiking* **mengerjakan PR** *does homework*
Pada saat cuacanya buruk *When the weather is bad* **Pada saat cuacanya cerah** *When the weather is clear/fine* **Pada saat cuacanya dingin** *When it is cold* **Pada saat cuacanya lembab** *When it is humid* **Pada saat cuacanya panas** *When it is hot*	*****saya <u>pergi</u> ke** *I go to* **teman saya pergi ke** *my friend goes to*	**gym** *the gym* **kolam renang** *the pool* **lapangan olahraga** *the sports field* **luar kota** *the countryside* **mal** *the mall* **pantai** *the beach* **pegunungan** *the mountains* **pesta** *the party* **rumah teman saya** *my friend's house* **rumah temannya** *his/her friend's house* **taman** *the park*

Pada saat hujan *When it rains* **Pada saat langit cerah** *When the sky is clear/sunny* **Pada saat langit berawan** *When the sky is cloudy*	**saya** *I* **dia** *he/she* **Ketut** **Sari** **mereka** *they*	**berada di** *stays at*	**kamar saya** *my room* **kamarnya** *his/her room* **rumah saya** *my home* **rumahnya** *his/her home*

Author's notes:
* **Pada saat** *At the moment/time when and* **Kalau** *When/If, are interchangeable in all of these weather phrases*
** *Remember that the* **-nya** *suffix is optional in these phrases i.e.* **cuaca** *or* **cuacanya** *the weather*
*** *When using the phrase* **pergi ke**, *the word* **pergi** *can be omitted and is understood: for example,* **Saya pergi ke mal** *becomes* **Saya ke mal** *I go to the mall.*

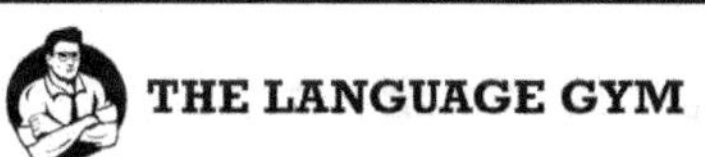

Unit 15. Talking about weather and free time: VOCABULARY BUILDING 1

1. Match up

Pada saat	It's cold
Dingin	It's hot
Panas	Clear skies
Cuacanya cerah	When it is
Cuacanya buruk	It's good weather
Langit cerah	It's raining
Ada hujan	It's bad weather

2. Complete with the missing word

a. Pada saat cuaca____________ *When it's bad weather*

b. Pada saat __________dan ____________
When it rains and is cold

c. Pada saat langit _________ dan ___________
When the sky is clear and hot

d. Pada saat ada _____________ saya berada di rumah
When there are thunderstorms I stay at home

e. Pada saat cuaca____________ saya pergi ke taman
When it's good weather I go to the park

f. Pada saat __________ saya bermain ski di gunung
When it snows I go skiing on the mountain

g. Pada saat cuaca ______ teman saya berada di rumahnya
When the weather is bad my friend stays at home

h. Saya suka cuaca _______ *I like it when it's sunny*

3. Translate into English

a. Pada saat cuaca dingin

b. Pada saat hujan

c. Langit cerah

d. Pada saat cuaca panas

e. Pada saat bersalju

f. Pada saat cuacanya cerah

g. Pada saat berkabut

h. Saya bermain tenis

i. Saya bermain ski

j. Pada saat cuaca buruk

4. Anagrams: weather

a. nignid	e. herac	i. tubaerkb
b. aansp	f. kuurb	j. wanareb
c. jusla	g. dabai turung	k. karih kenap
d. juahn	h. ninarbeg	l. albbme

5. Associations – match each weather word below with the clothes/activities in the box

a. Cuaca buruk: badai guntur, angin, hujan –

b. Cuaca cerah: langit cerah dan panas–

c. Salju turun dan dingin –

sepatu bot salju	di rumah	bermain ski	di pantai
jas hujan	celana pendek	menonton televisi	topi
di gunung	mantel	baju hangat	berenang

6. Complete the translation

a. Cuaca __________ *It's clear weather*

b. Saya berada di_________ *I stay at home*

c. Pada saat ___________ *When it rains*

d. Saya ____________ cuaca panas
I like it when it's hot

e. Saya_________ ke pantai *I go to the beach*

f. Pada saat ___________ *When it is windy*

g. Pada saat ________ cerah...
When the skies are clear

h. Pada saat cuaca _____________
When it is cloudy

Unit 15. Talking about weather and free time: VOCABULARY BUILDING 2

1. Match these phrases

Bermain tenis	I go to a party
Bermain kartu	In her bedroom
Saya berkuda	He goes fishing
Saya ke pesta	Play tennis
Dia memancing	I go horse riding
Di kamar tidurnya	Play cards
Berada di rumah	Go swimming
Berenang	Stay at home

2. Complete with the missing word

a. Saya berada _____ kamar tidur saya *I stay in my bedroom*

b. Teman saya pergi ___ pantai *My friend goes to the beach*

c. Saya ________ ke rumah ________ *I go to my friend's house*

d. Saya ke pusat ________________ *I go to the sports centre*

e. Saya__________mengerjakan PR pada hari kerja
I always do my homework on weekdays

f. Saya suka akhir ___________ *I like the weekends*

g. Saya bermain bersama______saya *I play with my friends*

h. Teman saya Iva selalu _______ ke ________ temannya
My friend Iva always goes to her friend's house

i. Saya selalu ___________ *I always go hiking*

3. Translate into English

a. Rumah teman saya

b. Saya berenang

c. Langit cerah

d. Saya memanjat tebing

e. Dia mendaki

f. Pergi ke pusat olahraga

g. Pergi ke kolam renang

h. Saya berolahraga

4. Anagrams: activities

a. barerli ntsaai

b. rebangen

c. jaberlan-lajan

d. dukareb

e. labo skabte

f. pesak labo

g. utrak

h. rucat

i. lanberbeja

j. seberdape

k. ginnamcem

l. rolaahgaber

5. Broken words

a. S______b________s_____b____ bersama t____-t____ saya
I play soccer with my friends

b. B______ s________ G______ b____________ k________
My aunt Grace plays cards

c. S____ p________ k__ r________ t________ s______
I go to my friend's house

d. J________ p________ k__ p______ o____________
Joni goes to the sports centre

e. S___ b____________ b__________s______ s______
I go horse riding with my cousin

f. T_____ s______ b_____ d__ r______nya dan m______ PR
My friend stays at her home and does homework

6. Complete the translations

a. Saya mengerjakan __ *I do homework*

b. Dia _______ di rumah *He stays at home*

c. Dia __________ *He goes swimming*

d. Saya _____ ke bioskop *I go to the cinema*

e. ______ke perpustakaan *I go to the library*

f. Saya _______ di gym *I play sports at gym*

g. Saya __________ *I do climbing*

h. Saya _________ ____ di ____________
I go skiing in the mountains

i. Di _________ saya *In my room*

Unit 15. Talking about weather and free time: READING

Nama saya Gino. Saya berasal dari Italia. Saya berumur sebelas tahun. Saya sangat atletik, jadi saya suka kalau cuacanya cerah karena saya selalu pergi ke taman bersama teman saya dan bermain sepak bola. Juga, kalau panas saya selalu pergi ke pantai dengan anjing saya. Dia kecil dan hitam. Saya memakai baju renang, sandal dan topi ketika saya pergi ke pantai.

Nama saya Chloe. Saya dari Prancis. Umur saya delapan belas tahun. Pada saat cuaca panas dan cerah, saya pergi ke kolam renang dan berenang. Saya juga memancing dengan bapak saya di perahunya. Memancing agak membosankan tetapi saya suka mengobrol dengan bapak. Pada malam hari saya pergi ke kota dengan teman-teman saya. Ketika saya pergi ke klub saya biasanya memakai baju kaus dan jins. Nama teman saya Sofia. Dia baik hati dan cerdas. Kalau cuaca buruk dan ada hujan, dia selalu berada di rumahnya dan mengerjakan pekerjaan rumahnya.

Nama saya Isabel. Saya berasal dari Roma, di Italia. Umur saya lima belas tahun. Saya suka membeli baju kaus dan tas. Saya suka kalau ada badai guntur. Saya berada di rumah dengan kakak laki-laki saya dan bermain video game atau kartu dengan dia. Badai guntur sangat indah dan mengherankan. Saya tidak suka cuaca dingin karena saya tidak suka memakai jas dan syal. Saya punya anjing, kucing, dan burung nuri yang bisa berbahasa Italia!

Nama saya Anna. Saya berasal dari Brazil. Saya berumur dua belas tahun. Saya suka bernyanyi pada waktu luang. Kalau cuaca dingin saya pergi ke mal bersama teman. Saya memakai mantel, syal, dan sepatu bot. Saya suka cuaca dingin! Film favorit saya adalah Frozen 2. Pada saat cuaca panas saya berada di rumah karena saya tidak menyukai cuaca panas. Saya tidak pernah pergi ke pantai. Saya benci pantai!

1. Find the Indonesian for the following in Gino's text

a. I am from

b. I am 11

c. I like

d. when

e. it is sunny

f. I go to the park

g. with my dog

h. small and black

i. a swimsuit

2. Find the Indonesian for the following in Chloe's text

a. when it's hot

b. it's clear

c. I go swimming

d. I go fishing

e. a bit boring

f. I go to a club

g. a t-shirt

h. my friend's name is

i. stays

j. in her house

3. Complete the following statements about Isabel

a. She is ________ years old

b. She likes to buy __________ and ___________

c. She likes it when there are ________

d. When it's stormy she plays _________ or _________ with her _________ brother

e. Isabel does not like _________ weather

f. Her pet can ___________ Italian

4. In Indonesian answer the questions below about Anna

a. Dia berasal dari mana?

b. Berapa umurnya?

c. Dia melakukan apa pada waktu luangnya?

d. Dia suka cuaca apa?

e. Dia melakukan apa saat cuaca panas?

f. Apakah dia suka cuaca panas?

g. Apa film favorit Anna?

5. Find Someone Who...

a. ...likes to go fishing
b. ...is from France
c. ...likes cold weather
d. ...has three pets at home
e. ...thinks that storms are pretty
f. ...wears jeans to go out
g. ...goes to the beach with an animal
h. ...never goes to the beach
i. ...owns a boat

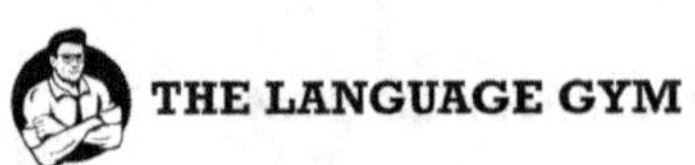

Unit 15. Talking about weather and free time: WRITING

1. Split sentences

a. Saya suka cuaca	saya pergi ke pantai
b. Saya tidak	jas dan syal
c. Pada saat cuaca panas	saya pergi ke taman
d. Kalau sangat dingin saya pakai	suka hujan
e. Badai guntur	saya bermain ski
f. Pada saat cuaca buruk	saya berada di rumah
g. Pada saat cuaca cerah	dingin
h. Pada saat bersalju	sangat indah

2. Complete with the correct option

a. ___________ cuaca dingin saya memakai syal. Saya tidak___________!

b. Pada___________ pekan saya mengerjakan PR.

c. Pada saat _________ buruk saya _________ di rumah.

d. Pada saat cuaca _______ saya tidak pergi ke ________

e. Pada saat cuaca __________ saya pergi ke pantai.

f. Pada saat cuaca _______ saya mendaki gunung.

g. Pada saat cuaca buruk teman saya Harto berada di rumah______ .

panas	cuaca	berada	gunung	cerah
suka	akhir	kalau	berkabut	nya

3. Spot and correct the grammar and spelling mistakes note: in several cases a word is missing

a. Pada saat berangin saya bergi ke gym bersama teman saya

b. Pada saat berawan teman saya Joni bermain tennis

c. Saya suka badai karana sangat indah

d. Pada saat cuaca buruk teman saya berada rumah

e. Pada saat berkabut saya tidak bermain sepak

f. Pada akhir pekan saya pergi ke pantia dengan anjing saya

g. Pada saat cerah saya pargi ke luar kota dan memakai kaus putih

h. Saya selalu memakai spatu kets kalau saya bermain bola sepak

4. Complete the words

a. D___________ *cold*

b. P___________ *hot*

c. B___________ *cloudy*

d. P____s______ *when*

e. B____g______ *thunderstorms*

f. B___________ *windy*

g. B___________ *foggy*

6. Describe this person in Indonesian using the 3rd person

Name: Nyoman

Lives in: Denpasar

Age : 13

Pet: A white bird

Weather: Humid and good weather

Always: Goes to the countryside and goes hiking

Never: Stays at home and does homework

5. Guided writing – write 3 short paragraphs in the first person I using the details below

Person	Lives	Weather	Activity	With
Hendri	Medan	Good weather	Go to the park	Family
Ketut	Bali	Hot and humid	Go to the beach	Friends
Julie	Melbourne	Cold and rainy	Stay home	Older sister

THE LANGUAGE GYM

Grammar Time 13: YANG – *The One* or *Which* - Making Plans

Pada akhir pekan/ minggu *On the weekend* **Pada hari Minggu** *On Sunday* **Pada hari Senin** *On Monday* **Pada hari Selasa** *On Tuesday* **Pada hari Rabu** *On Wednesday* **Pada hari Kamis** *On Thurdsay* **Pada hari Jumat** *On Friday* **Pada hari Sabtu** *On Saturday*	**saya** *I* **kita** *we*	**akan** *will*	**menonton** *to watch* **bermain** *to play* **pergi ke** *go to*	**film** *a film* **olahraga** *sport* **bioskop** *cinema* **kolam renang** *swimming pool* **mal** *shopping mall* **pantai** *beach* **pesta** *party* **taman** *park* **toko** *shop*	**yang mana?** *which one*

Mungkin *Maybe* **Tentu saja** *Of course*	**yang paling baik** *the best* **yang paling dekat** *the closest* **yang paling terkenal** *the most popular* **bermain sepak bola** *play soccer* **bermain bola basket** *play basketball* **bermain bulu tangkis** *play badminton*

Naik *Travel by/Go by*	**mobil** *car* **bus** *bus* **kereta api** *train*	**yang mana?** *which one/whose*	**Yang** *The one which is*	**punya saya** *owned by me* **punya teman saya** *my friend's* **punya ibu saya** *my mum's*
			Yang *The one which is*	**nomor dua belas** *number 12* **dari pusat kota** *from the city centre*

Kita akan bertemu pada jam berapa? *We will meet at what time?*

Bagaimana kalau *How about*	***jam** *at (the time)*	**tujuh** *7 o'clock*			**pagi** *6am-11am* **siang** *11am-4pm* **sore** *4pm-6pm* **malam** *6pm-6am*
		setengah dua *half past one*			
		tiga *3* **empat** *4*	**lewat** *past* **kurang** *less*	**seperempat** *a quarter* **dua puluh menit** *20 minutes*	

Author's note:

***Jam** or **pukul** can be used to identify time, however when **jam** follows a number it is then referring to *hours*, e.g. **jam empat** – *four o'clock* **empat jam** – *four hours*

****setengah** *half*, when referring to a time phrase **setengah** means *half <u>TO</u> the next hour*, rather than half past the previous hour as in English, **setengah tiga** is *half past two (half to three)*

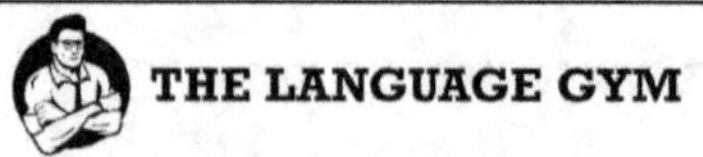

Grammar Time 13: YANG - Making Plans: TRANSLATION

1. Gapped translation

a. *On Saturday we will go to which shopping mall?* Pada ___ Sabtu kita ___ pergi ___ mal ___mana?

b. *Maybe the closest one?* Mungkin yang ______ dekat

c. *Which train will we take?* ______ api _____ mana?

d. *The train from the city centre* Kereta _____ dari ______ kota

e. *We will meet at what time? Two o'clock in the afternoon.* Kita akan ____ pada ___ berapa?___ jam ____ siang

2. Match the meanings of these phrases

Indonesian	English
a. mobil yang mana	which swimming pool
b. kolam renang yang mana	which train
c. kereta api yang mana	which sport
d. kota yang mana	which car
e. olahraga yang mana	which town

3. Translate into English

a. taman yang mana?

b. mobil yang mana?

c. yang paling baik

d. yang paling dekat

e. pantai yang mana?

f. kota yang mana?

g. kereta api yang mana?

h. bermain olahraga yang mana?

i. menonton film yang mana?

4. Complete the words

a. Pa__ h_____ S_____ k__ aka__   *On Tuesday we will*

b. Per_ k_ pan___ y___ m____   *Go to which beach*

c. N____ ker____ a__ y_____ m____   *Go by which train*

d. Berm____ ola______ y__ m_____   *Play which sport*

e. Te__ s__ y___ p__b____   *Of course the best one*

f. K_____ r_____ y___ m_____   *Which swimming pool*

g. P___ a__ p___ k___ a___   *On the weekend we will*

5. Split sentences

a. Mungkin	setengah tujuh
b. Naik bus	dari pusat kota
c. Pada jam	yang mana?
d. Kita akan pergi	olahraga yang mana?
e. Kereta api	ke toko yang mana?
f. Kita akan bermain	yang paling dekat

6. Translate into Indonesian

a. Which beach?

b. Maybe the best one

c. Go to which shopping centre?

d. We will play which sport?

e. On the weekend we will watch which film?

f. Which train would you travel by?

Revision Quickie 4: Clothes /Free time/ Weather

1. Activities - Match

Saya mengerjakan PR	I go to church
Saya berolahraga	I go to the swimming pool
Saya bermain bola voli	I go to the gym
Saya bermain kartu	I go shopping at the mall
Saya pergi ke gereja	I do homework
Saya pergi ke kolam renang	I go swimming
Saya ke gym	I do rock climbing
Saya berbelanja di mal	I play sport
Saya berenang	I go horse-riding
Saya berkuda	I go to the beach
Saya pergi ke pantai	I play cards
Saya memanjat tebing	I play volleyball

2. Weather – Complete

a. Cuaca di_ _ _ _ _

b. Cuaca pa_ _ _

c. Cuaca c_ _ _ _ _

d. Cuaca berk_ _ _ _ _

e. Cuaca ba_ _

f. Cuaca b_ _ _ _ _

g. Cuaca beran_ _ _

h. Cuaca bera_ _ _

i. Pada saat h_ _ _ _ _

3. Fill in the gaps in Indonesian

a. Kalau cuaca d______, saya memakai m____________   *When it is cold I wear a coat*

b. Pada saat cuaca b_______ saya____________ di rumah   *When the weather is bad I stay at home*

c. Pada saat cuaca c_____ saya pergi ke p_________   *When it is sunny I go to the beach*

d. Pada saat saya ke gym, saya m______baju o_______   *When I go to the gym I wear a tracksuit*

e. Kalau cuaca p_________ saya pergi k__ k______ r_______   *When it is hot I go to the swimming pool*

f. Pada akhir minggu saya m_________ p________ r_______   *At the week-end I do my homework*

g. Kalau ada w_________ l__________   *When I have free time*

h. Saya m____________ t____________   *I go rock climbing*

4. Translate into Indonesian

a. When it is hot:

b. When it is cold:

c. I play basketball:

d. I do my homework:

e. I go rock climbing:

f. When I have free time:

g. I go to the swimming-pool:

h. I go to the gym:

5. Translate to Indonesian

a. I wear a coat

b. We wear a uniform

c. They play basketball

d. She goes rock climbing

e. He has free time

f. They go swimming

g. My parents play sport

h. She often plays soccer

Question Skills 3: Clothes/Free time/Weather

1. Translate into English

a. Kalau cuaca dingin kamu memakai apa?

b. Bagaimana cuaca di tempat tinggal kamu?

c. Kamu melakukan apa kalau ada waktu luang?

d. Apakah kamu berolahraga?

e. Seberapa sering kamu bermain bola basket?

f. Mengapa kamu tidak suka bermain sepak bola?

g. Di mana kamu mendaki?

h. Yang mana olahraga favoritmu?

2. Complete with the missing question word:

a. ____________ kamu tinggal?

b. __________ kamu berolahraga?

c. Kamu lebih suka olahraga _________?

d. ____________ kamu berenang?

e. __________ kamu membeli sepatumu?

f. Kamu suka melakukan _____ pada waktu luang.

g. Kamu bermain tenis bersama __________ ?

h. Kamu sering berkuda bersama ________ ?

i. _________ kita akan bermain sepak bola?

3. Split questions

a. Kamu melakukan apa	mendaki?
b. Bersama siapa	ke mana?
c. Mengapa kamu	pada waktu luang?
d. Di mana kamu	banyak pakaian baru?
e. Yang mana	kamu bermain catur?
f. Kamu mau pergi	kalau cuaca dingin?
g. Apakah kamu punya	olahraga favoritmu?
h. Kamu memakai apa	tidak suka tenis?

4. Translate into Indonesian

a. What?

b. Where?

c. How?

d. When?

e. Why?

f. How much?

g. How many times?

h. From where?

i. Which one?

5. Write the questions to these answers

a. Kalau dingin saya memakai mantel

b. Pada akhir pekan saya berolahraga

c. Saya pergi ke gym jam lima sore

d. Saya punya dua baju olahraga

e. Saya bermain tenis bersama bapak atau kakak

f. Saya berenang di kolam dekat rumah saya

g. Saya jarang mendaki

6. Translate into Indonesian

a. Where do you play tennis?

b. What do you do when you have free time?

c. How many shoes do you have?

d. What is your favourite hobby?

e. Do you play sport often?

f. At what time do you do your homework?

UNIT 16
Talking about my daily routine

Revision Quickie 5: Clothes / Food / Free Time / Descriptions

In this unit you will learn how to say:

- What you do every day
- At what time you do it
- Sequencing events/actions (e.g. using 'then', 'finally')

You will revisit:
- Numbers
- Free time activities
- Nationalities
- Clothes
- Hair and eyes
- Food
- Jobs

Talking about my daily routine

Bagaimana kebiasaan sehari-hari kamu? *Describe your daily routine.*		
Sekitar pukul... *At around...*	**Pada pukul...** *At .... o'clock*	
...satu *1*	saya makan malam *I have dinner* saya makan siang *I have lunch* saya sarapan *I have breakfast*	**akhirnya...** *finally*
...lima *5*		**dan biasanya...** *and usually*
...enam *6*	**pagi** *in the morning* — **saya bangun** *I get up* **saya berangkat dari rumah** *I leave my house*	**kemudian...***then*
...delapan lewat lima *8.05*	**siang** *in the mid morning (10am-3pm)* — **saya beristirahat** *I rest* **saya bermain komputer** *I play on the computer*	**sesudah itu...** **setelah itu ...** *after that*
...delapan lewat sepuluh *8.10*	**saya berpakaian** *I get dressed*	**sebelumnya...** *before that*
...delapan lewat seperempat *8.15*	**saya bersantai** *I relax*	
...delapan lewat dua puluh *8.20*	**sore** *in the afternoon* — **saya mandi** *I wash/shower* **saya mendengarkan musik** *I listen to music*	
...delapan lewat dua puluh lima *8.25*	**saya mengecek email** *I check emails*	
...*setengah sembilan *8.30*	**malam** *in the evening* — **saya mengemasi tas sekolah** *I pack my school bag*	
...delapan kurang dua puluh lima *8.35*	**saya mengerjakan PR** *I do my homework*	
...sembilan kurang dua puluh *8.40*	**saya menggosok gigi** *I brush my teeth*	
...sembilan kurang seperempat *8.45*	**saya menonton televisi** *I watch television*	
...sembilan kurang sepuluh *8.50*	**saya naik bus ke sekolah** *I go to school by bus*	
...sembilan kurang lima *8.55*	**saya pergi ke sekolah** *I go to school*	
Pada tengah hari *At midday* **Pada tengah malam** *At midnight*	**saya pulang** *I go home* **saya tidur** *I go to sleep*	

Author's Note: *There are alternatives when describing clock times*

    a.   **jam** *or* **pukul** *precedes the hour,* **jam lima** *(five o'clock) or* **pukul enam** *(six o'clock)*

    b.   **lebih** *(more) or* **lewat** *(past) can both be used to express the "after the hour" times*

'half past' times are half <u>to</u> the next hour, i.e. **jam setengah sembilan** *8:30 is half <u>to</u> nine*

Unit 16. Talking about my daily routine: VOCAB BUILDING (Part 1)

1. Match up

Saya bangun	I eat lunch
Saya pergi ke sekolah	I eat dinner
Saya tidur	I get up
Saya makan siang	I have a shower
Saya makan malam	I relax
Saya mandi	I go to school
Saya bersantai	I go home
Saya pulang	I go to sleep

2. Translate into English

a. Saya bangun pada pukul enam pagi

b. Saya tidur pada pukul sebelas malam

c. Saya makan siang pada tengah hari

d. Saya makan sarapan pada pukul enam pagi

e. Saya pulang pada pukul setengah empat sore

f. Saya makan malam sekitar pukul delapan malam

g. Saya menonton televisi

h. Saya mendengarkan musik

i. Saya berangkat dari rumah pada pukul tujuh pagi

3. Complete with the missing words

a. Saya _______ ke sekolah   *I go to school*

b. Saya___________ rumah   *I leave the house*

c. Saya ___________   *I wash*

d. Saya___________ televisi   *I watch television*

e. Saya___________ PR   *I do my homework*

f. Saya_______________ musik   *I listen to music*

g. Saya___________komputer   *I play on the computer*

h. Saya _____ ______ pada jam satu   *I have lunch at 1 o'clock*

4. Complete with the missing letters

a. Saya ____santai   *I relaxed*

b. Saya __ulang   *I go home*

c. Men_engarkan musik   *Listen to music*

d. Saya makan _arapan   *I eat breakfast*

e. Saya makan _alam   *I eat dinner*

f. Saya ber_ekolah   *I go to school*

g. Saya _angun   *I get up*

h. Saya __idur   *I go to sleep*

i. Saya makan _iang   *I have lunch*

5. Faulty translation – spot and correct any English translation mistakes. Not all translations are wrong.

a. Saya beristirahat sesudah itu: *I shower after that*

b. Saya tidur pada tengah malam: *I go to sleep at noon*

c. Saya mengerjakan PR saya: *I do your homework*

d. Saya makan malam: *I eat lunch*

e. Saya pergi ke sekolah: *I go home from school*

f. Saya pulang: *I leave the house*

g. Saya menonton televisi: *I watch television*

h. Saya berangkat dari rumah: *I leave school*

i. Saya menggosok gigi: *I wash my hands*

6. Translate the following times into Indonesian *(add pagi / siang / sore / malam where appropriate)*

a. At 6.30 a.m.

b. At 7.30 a.m.

c. At 8.20 p.m.

d. At midday

e. At 9.20 a.m.

f. At 11.00 p.m.

g. At midnight

h. At 5.15 p.m.

Unit 16. Talking about my daily routine: VOCAB BUILDING (Part 2)

1. Complete the table

Saya tidur	
	I brush my teeth
Saya bangun	
	I go home
Saya mengemasi tas	
Saya makan siang	
	I eat dinner
Saya mendengarkan musik	
	I leave my house
Saya mandi	
Saya bersantai	
	I do my homework
Saya berpakaian	

2. Complete the sentences using the words in the table

a. Pada pukul__________tujuh   *At six thirty*

b. Sekitar ________ lima   *At around 5.00*

c. Pada pukul delapan ________ *At 8.00 a.m.*

d. Pada tengah ________   *At noon*

e. Pada pukul _____lewat seperempat *At 11.15*

f. Pada pukul tiga____ dua puluh *At 2.40*

g. Pada tengah__________   *At midnight*

h. _______ pukul empat   *At about 4.00*

i. _____ pukul tujuh   *At 7.00*

j. Pada pukul delapan kurang ___ *At 7.55*

lima	setengah	sekitar	pagi	hari
sebelas	pada	kurang	pukul	malam

3. Translate into English (numerical)

a. Pada pukul setengah sembilan ___*At 8.30*___

b. Pukul sembilan lebih seperempat__________

c. Pada jam sepuluh kurang sepuluh__________

d. Pada tengah hari__________________

e. Pada tengah malam______________

f. Pada jam sebelas kurang lima______________

g. Pada pukul dua belas lebih dua puluh ______

4. Complete

a. Pada p_____ s________ e__________   *At 5.30*

b. Pada j___ d______ l_____ s______   *At 8.15*

c. Pada t_________ h______   *At midday*

d. Pada pukul d_______ k______ s_____   *At 7.45*

e. Pada t________ m_______   *At midnight*

f. Pada p___ s________ d____b_____   *At 11.30*

g. Sekitar p_____ s______   *At about 1.00*

5. Translate the following into Indonesian

a. I go to school at around 8am

b. I go home at around 3pm

c. I eat dinner at 7.30pm

d. I do my homework at around 5.30pm

e. I eat breakfast at 6.45am

f. I go to sleep at midnight

g. I eat lunch at midday

Unit 16. Talking about my daily routine: READING (Part 1)

Nama saya Hiroto. Saya orang Jepang. Kebiasaan sehari-hari saya sangat sederhana. Biasanya saya bangun pada pukul enam. Lalu saya mandi dan berpakaian. Saya makan sarapan bersama bapak dan adik laki-laki saya. Kemudian saya menggosok gigi dan menyisir rambut. Sekitar pukul setengah delapan saya berangkat dari rumah ke sekolah naik sepeda. Saya pulang sekitar pukul empat. Kemudian saya bersantai. Biasanya saya menonton TV. Jadi, saya pergi ke taman bersama teman-teman saya sampai pukul enam. Dari pukul enam sampai setengah tujuh saya mengerjakan PR saya. Kemudian, pada pukul delapan, saya makan malam bersama keluarga. Saya tidak makan banyak, hamburger saja. Kemudian, saya menonton film di televisi dan, sekitar pukul sebelas, saya tidur.

Nama saya Gregorio. Saya orang Meksiko. Kebiasaan sehari-hari saya sangat sederhana. Biasanya saya bangun pada pukul enam lewat seperempat. Kemudian saya mandi dan makan sarapan bersama kedua saudara laki-laki saya. Setelah itu, saya menggosok gigi dan mengemasi tas sekolah saya. Sekitar pukul tujuh saya berjalan kaki ke sekolah. Saya pulang sekitar pukul setengah empat. Biasanya saya berselancar di Internet, menonton serial di Netflix atau mengobrol dengan teman-teman saya di Whatsapp atau Snapchat. Dari pukul lima sampai enam, saya mengerjakan PR saya. Kemudian, pada pukul setengah tujuh, saya makan malam bersama keluarga saya. Kami makan nasi atau selada. Kemudian, saya menonton televisi dan, pada pukul setengah dua belas, saya tidur.

Nama saya Andreas. Saya orang Jerman. Kebiasaan sehari-hari saya sangat sederhana. Biasanya saya bangun pagi, sekitar pukul lima. Saya berlari santai dan kemudian saya mandi dan berpakaian. Kemudian, sekitar pukul setengah enam, saya makan buah untuk sarapan bersama ibu dan saudara perempuan saya. Saya menggosok gigi dan mengemasi tas sekolah. Sekitar pukul tujuh lewat seperempat saya pergi ke sekolah. Saya pulang sekitar pukul setengah empat. Kemudian saya bersantai. Biasanya saya menonton sinetron di televisi atau mengobrol dengan teman-teman saya di Internet. Dari pukul enam sampai delapan saya mengerjakan PR saya. Kemudian, pada jam delapan lewat seperempat, saya makan malam bersama keluarga saya. Saya tidak makan banyak. Kemudian saya bermain PlayStation sampai tengah malam. Akhirnya, saya tidur.

1. Answer the following questions about Hiroto

a. Where is he from?

b. At what time does he get up?

c. Who does he have breakfast with?

d. At what time does he leave the house?

e. Until what time does he stay at the park?

f. How does he go to school?

2. Find the Indonesian for the phrases below in Hiroto's text

a. At around eleven

b. With my friends

c. I go by bike

d. I go to the park

e. I shower and get dressed

f. I don't eat much

g. From six to half past seven

h. I do my homework

3. Complete the statements below about Andreas

a. He gets up at _______________________________

b. He goes home from school at _______________

c. For breakfast he eats _______________________

d. He eats breakfast with ______________________

e. After getting up he ________________ and then showers

f. Usually he ____________________________ until midnight

g. After breakfast he brushes his teeth and then

____.

4. Find the Indonesian for the following phrases/sentences in Gregorio's text

a. I am Mexican
b. I shower
c. With my two brothers
d. I pack my school bag
e. I eat rice or salad
f. I surf the Internet
g. I eat dinner

Unit 16. Talking about my daily routine: READING (Part 2)

Nama saya Liling. Saya berumur dua belas tahun. Saya orang Cina. Kebiasaan sehari-hari saya sangat sederhana. Biasanya saya bangun sekitar pukul setengah enam dan saya mandi dan berpakaian. Setelah itu, saya makan sarapan dengan ibu dan saudara laki-laki saya, Li Wei. Kemudian saya menggosok gigi dan mengemasi tas sekolah. Sekitar pukul setengah tujuh saya pergi ke sekolah. Saya pulang sekitar pukul empat. Kemudian saya beristirahat sebentar. Biasanya saya menonton TV, mendengarkan musik atau membaca komik favorit saya. Dari pukul enam sampai setengah tujuh saya mengerjakan PR saya. Pada pukul delapan, saya makan malam bersama keluarga. Saya tidak makan banyak. Kemudian, saya menonton film di televisi dan, sekitar pukul sebelas, saya tidur.

Nama saya Kim, saya orang Inggris. Umur saya lima belas tahun. Kebiasaan sehari-hari saya sangat sederhana. Biasanya saya bangun pagi, sekitar pukul setengah enam. Saya berlari santai dan kemudian saya mandi dan berpakaian. Kemudian, sekitar pukul tujuh, saya makan sarapan bersama ibu dan saudara tiri saya. Sesudah itu saya menggosok gigi dan mengemasi tas sekolah. Kemudian, sekitar pukul setengah tujuh saya pergi ke sekolah. Saya pulang sekitar pukul tiga. Saya beristirahat sebentar. Kemudian saya mendengarkan musik atau mengobrol dengan teman-teman saya di Internet. Dari pukul enam sampai delapan saya mengerjakan PR. Pada pukul delapan lewat seperempat, saya makan malam bersama keluarga saya. Kemudian saya menonton film di televisi sampai tengah malam. Akhirnya, saya tidur.

Nama saya Anna. Saya orang Italia. Kebiasaan sehari-hari saya sangat sederhana. Biasanya saya bangun pukul enam lewat seperempat. Kemudian saya mandi dan makan sarapan dengan kakak perempuan. Setelah itu, saya menggosok gigi dan mengemasi tas sekolah. Sekitar pukul tujuh saya pergi ke sekolah naik bus. Saya pulang sekitar pukul setengah dua. Kemudian saya beristirahat sebentar. Biasanya saya mengecek media sosial, menonton televisi atau membaca majalah. Dari pukul lima sampai tujuh, saya mengerjakan PR. Kemudian, pada pukul delapan, saya makan malam bersama keluarga. Biasanya buah-buahan atau sayur-sayuran. Setelah itu, saya membaca novel dan, sekitar pukul setengah sebelas, saya tidur.

1. Find the Indonesian phrases in Liling's text

a. I am Chinese

b. My daily routine

c. I shower

d. Very simple

e. At around 6.30

f. I don't eat much

g. I watch television

h. I go to school

i. I do my homework

j. From six to half past six

2. Translate these phrases in Kim's text

a. I am English

b. Usually

c. At around 5.30

d. With my mum and stepsister

e. I go home

f. I eat dinner with my family

g. I rest a bit

h. I brush my teeth

3. Answer the following questions on Anna's text

a. What nationality is Anna?

b. At what time does she get up?

c. What three things does she do after school?

d. How does she go to school?

e. Who does she have breakfast with?

f. At what time does she go to sleep?

g. What does she eat for dinner?

h. What does she read before going to sleep?

4. Find Someone Who…

a. …has breakfast with their older sister

b. …reads novel at night

c. …reads fashion magazines

d. …gets up at 5.30am

e. …eats breakfast with their brother and mother

f. …chats with their friends on the internet after school

g. …does exercise in the morning

Unit 16. Talking about my daily routine: WRITING

1. Split sentences

a. Saya pergi ke sekolah	televisi
b. Saya pulang	pekerjaan rumah
c. Saya mengerjakan	naik bus
d. Saya menonton	ke rumah
e. Saya bermain	tengah malam
f. Saya bangun	dari rumah
g. Saya tidur sekitar	sekitar pukul enam
h. Saya berangkat	komputer

2. Complete with the correct option

a. Saya bangun pada _________________ enam pagi

b. Saya _________________ pekerjaan rumah

c. Saya _________________ televisi

d. Saya bermain _________________

e. Saya _________________ pada tengah malam

f. Saya _________________ dari sekolah

g. Saya berangkat dari _________________

h. Saya pergi ke sekolah _________________ bus

pulang	tidur	pukul	naik
menonton	mengerjakan	rumah	komputer

3. Spot and correct the grammar and spelling mistakes in several cases a word is missing

a. Saya pergi ke sekolah dengan sepeda

b. Saya bangun jam setengah tujuh

c. Saya pergi sekolah pada jam delapan

d. Saya palang

e. Saya pergi ke sekolah niak bus

f. Saya tidur sekitar jam sabalas

g. Saya makan malam pada jam tengah tujuh

h. Saya mengerjakan perkerjaan ramah saya pada pukul lima

4. Complete the words

a. sep_________________ *quarter*

b. set_________________ *half*

c. pada p_________ s_________ *at 10*

d. s_________________ *at around*

e. pada p_______ d_________ *at 8 o'clock*

f. d_________ p_____________ *twenty*

g. k_________________ *then*

h. saya m_________s_______ *I eat lunch*

i. saya p_________________ *I go home*

j. saya b_________________ *I play*

5. Guided writing – write 3 short paragraphs in the first person using the details below

Person	Gets up	Showers	Goes to school	Comes back home	Watches TV	Has dinner	Goes to sleep
Agus	6.30am	7.00am	8.05am	3.30pm	6.00pm	8.10pm	11.10pm
Santi	6.40am	7.10am	7.40am	4.00pm	6.30pm	8.15pm	12.00pm
Dian	7.15am	7.30am	8.00am	3.15pm	6.40pm	8.20pm	11.30pm

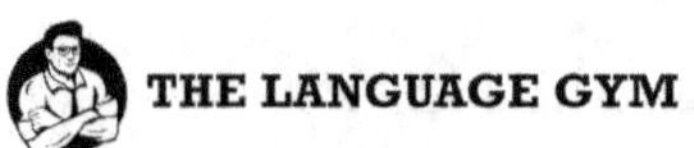

Revision Quickie 5: Clothes / Food / Free Time / Describing people

1. Clothes – Match up

Syal (1)	A hat
Setelan jas	A skirt
Topi	A dress
Dasi	A shirt
Rok	A T-shirt
Gaun	Jeans
Baju kaus	A suit
Kemeja	Socks
Jins	Trousers
Kaus kaki	A scarf (1)
Celana panjang	A tie

2. Food – Provide a word for each of the cues below

e.g. A fruit starting with **M**	mangga
a. A vegetable starting with **K**	
b. A dairy product starting with **S**	
c. A cereal starting with **N**	
d. A drink starting with **J**	
e. A drink made using lemons **J L**	
f. A sweet treat starting with **P**	
g. A fruit starting with **N**	

3. Complete the translations below

a. Shoes: *sep________________*

b. Hat: *to________________*

c. Hair: *ra________________*

d. Curly: *ker________________*

e. Purple: *un________________*

f. Milk: *su________________*

g. Water: *a________________*

h. Drink: *mi________________*

i. Job: *pe________________*

k. Clothes: *pa________________*

4. Clothes, Colours, Food, Jobs – Categories

Pakaian	Warna	Makanan	Pekerjaan

kemeja	biru	pramugari	sopir
daging	hijau	pengacara	ayam
sepatu	memasak	susu	dasi
jeruk	topi	nasi	merah

5. Match questions and answers

a. Pekerjaan favoritmu yang mana?	Baju olahraga
b. Kamu lebih suka warna apa?	Guru Seni
c. Kamu tidak suka daging apa?	Pengacara
d. Kamu memakai baju apa ke gym?	Catur
e. Guru favoritmu yang mana?	Biru
f. Minuman favoritmu yang mana?	Babi
g. Hobi favoritmu yang mana?	Jus buah

6. (Free time) Complete with *pergi* or *bermain* as appropriate

a. Saya tidak ______________ bulu tangkis

b. Saya jarang ______________ bola basket

c. Saya sering ______________ ke gym

d. Saya______________ ke mal setiap hari

e. Saya selalu ______________ Playstation

f. Saya tidak __________ ke kolam renang hari ini

7. Complete with the missing verb, choosing from the list below

a. Saya________________ banyak jus buah.

b. Dia _________________ televisi.

c. Sesudah ________ PR saya __________ ke gym.

d. Saya ___________ di gunung.

e. Untuk sarapan saya tidak _______ banyak. Hanya sebuah apel.

f. Kakak saya _________ sebagai insinyur. Dia __________ di Jakarta.

g. Saya ____ ____ menonton kartun tetapi saya ____ ____ menonton serial di Netflix

h. Setiap hari saya _________ sekitar pukul enam dan ________

bekerja	bangun	menonton	lebih suka
mandi	minum	mendaki	tidak suka
pergi	makan	tinggal	mengerjakan

8. Time markers – Translate

a. Belum pernah:

b. Kadang-kadang:

c. Selalu:

d. Setiap hari:

e. Jarang:

f. Sekali seminggu:

9. Split sentences (Relationships)

a. Saya dekat dengan	ibu saya
b. Saya tidak	kakek-nenek saya
c. Orang tua	bertengkar dengan …
d. Saya cinta	dekat dengan ibu
e. Kakak laki-laki saya	matematika saya streng
f. Guru	karena dia pemurah
g. Pacar saya sangat	ramah dan cantik
h. Saya suka paman	hati
i. Saya tidak akrab	saya sangat baik
j. Pacar saya baik	dengan adik saya

10. Complete the translation

a. Kakak saya ________________________________
My brother is a firefighter

b. Saya tidak _______________. Saya _________________
I don't work. I am a student

c. Kadang-kadang saya_________________ ke bioskop
I sometimes go to the cinema

d. Saya tidak pernah ____________________ televisi
I never watch television

e. Saya tidak ____________ __________ pacar saya
I don't quarrel with my boyfriend

f. Orang tua saya ______________________________
My parents are strict

g. Saya tidak pernah ____________ ______________
I never go jogging

11. Translate into Indonesian

a. I play tennis every day

b. I sometimes wear a jacket

c. I often go to the gym

d. I don't watch cartoons

e. I get up at around 6 a.m.

f. I shower twice a day

UNIT 17
Describing my house:
- indicating where it is located
- saying what I like/dislike about it

Grammar Time 14: Prepositions Di + Ke + Dari
Grammar Time 15: Interrogatives

In this unit you will learn how to say in Indonesian:

- Where your house/apartment is located
- What your favourite room is
- What you like to do in each room
- Check understanding using question tags

You will revisit:
- Adjectives to describe places
- Frequency markers
- Places
- Prepositions

Bagaimana rumahmu? *Describe your home.*
Apakah kamu tinggal di rumah atau di apartemen? *Do you live in a house or an apartment?*
Rumah atau apartemen kamu terletak di mana? *Where is your house or apartment located?*
Ada berapa kamar di rumahmu? *How many rooms are in your house?*

| **Saya tinggal di** *I live in* | **apartemen yang** *flat which is*

 rumah yang *house which is* | **baru** *new*
 besar *big*
 jelek *ugly*
 kecil *small*
 mewah *luxurious*
 modern *modern*
 sederhana *simple*
 tua *old* | **di daerah permukiman** *in a residential area*
 di desa *in a village*
 di kota *in the city*
 di pantai *on the coast*
 di pedesaan *in the countryside*
 di pegunungan *in the mountains*
 di pinggiran kota *on the outskirts of town*
 di pusat kota *in the city centre* |

| **Di rumah saya** *In my house*

 Di apartemen saya *In my house* | **ada** *there are* | satu 1   lima 5 <br> dua 2   enam 6 <br> tiga 3   tujuh 7 <br> empat 4   delapan 8 | **kamar** *rooms*
 kamar tidur *bedrooms*
 kamar mandi *bathrooms* |

Ada *There is* **Juga ada** *Also there is* **Kamar favorit saya adalah** *My favourite room is*	**dapur** *kitchen* **kamar kecil** *toilet* **ruang keluarga** *family room* **ruang kerja** *study* **ruang makan** *dining room* **kamar mandi** *bathroom* **kamar tidur** *bedroom* **kolam renang** *swimming pool* *****ruang tamu** *living room* **taman** *garden* **teras** *terrace*
Saya *I* **Saya suka** *I like* **Saya selalu** *I always*	**belajar di** *study in* **bersantai di** *relax in* **mengerjakan PR saya di** *do my homework in* **mandi di** *shower in*

Author's note:
Kamar *or* **ruang? Taman** *or* **kebun?** *There are subtle differences between the use of these words.*
As homes are becoming more open plan, the terms for rooms are adapting. **Kamar** *is generally an enclosed space, while* **ruang** *is a more open space or combined space e.g.* **dapur + ruang makan** *kitchen/dining room;* **ruang keluarga + ruang makan** *family room/dining room.*
Taman *is a home garden while* **kebun** *is a productive garden.*
*****Ruang tamu** *lit.* guest room *– this space is a formal sitting or lounge room where you receive visitors and serve refreshments.*

Unit 17. Describing my house: VOCABULARY BUILDING (PART 1)

1. Match up

saya tinggal di	a flat
rumah	new
apartemen	residential
besar	area
baru	I live in
pedesaan	a house
daerah	big
permukiman	countryside

3. Complete with the missing words

a. Saya tinggal ___ pantai *I live on the coast*

b. Saya suka _________ saya *I like my house*

c. Saya_______ di rumah yang tua tetapi
_________ *I live in an old but pretty house*

d. Saya suka _____________ di teras
I like to relax on the terrace

e. _________saya di ___________ kota
My house is on the outskirts

f. Saya tidak pernah ___________ di taman!
I never shower in the garden!

2. Translate into English

a. Saya tinggal di rumah yang tua dan kecil

b. Saya tinggal di apartemen yang besar dan baru

c. Apartemen saya di pinggiran kota

d. Rumah saya di pedesaan

e. Kamar favorit saya adalah kamar tidur saya

f. Saya suka dapur

g. Saya suka mengerjakan PR saya di ruang kerja

h. Saya mandi di kamar mandi

i. Saya suka bersantai di taman

4. Complete the words (about 'rumah')

a. r____________	*house*	g. p____________	*coast*
b. j____________	*ugly*	h. p______k______	*outskirts*
c. b____________	*new*	i. p____________	*centre*
d. t____________	*old*	j. t____________	*garden*
e. b____________	*big*	k. t____________	*terrace*
f. d____________	*in*	l. k________ saya	*my room*

5. Classify the words/phrases below in the table below

a. **selalu**	i. besar
b. bersantai	j. kadang-kadang
c. tidak pernah	k. ruang makan
d. baik	l. pedesaan
e. baru	m. kecil
f. pegunungan	n. mengerjakan
g. belajar	o. pantai
h. kamar tidur	p. tinggal

Time phrases	Nouns	Verbs	Adjectives
a.			

6. Translate into Indonesian

a. I live in an old flat

b. I live in a new house

c. In the town centre

d. I like to relax in the family room

e. I always shower in the bathroom

f. I live in a residential area

g. My favourite room is the kitchen

Unit 17. Describing my house: VOCABULARY BUILDING (PART 2)

1. Complete the phrase

tinggal di	pantai
rumah yang	permukiman
di	apartemen
apartemen	tua dan indah
di pusat	baru
daerah	bersantai
saya selalu	kota
saya suka	mandi

3. Translate into English

a. Saya tinggal di rumah yang kecil

b. Rumah itu di pantai

c. Apartemen yang besar tetapi jelek

d. Itu di daerah permukiman

e. Di rumah saya ada lima kamar

f. Saya suka bekerja di ruang makan

g. Saya suka bersantai

h. Saya tinggal di rumah di pantai

i. Saya tinggal di pinggiran kota

2. Complete with the missing word

a. Saya tidak suka _______________   *I don't like to work*

b. Yang kecil tetapi_____________   *It is small but luxurious*

c. Yang di ________________ kota   *It is in the town centre*

d. Yang di ________________ kota   *It is on the outskirts*

e. Saya tinggal di ______ yang besar   *I live in a big house*

f. Di ______________ permukiman   *In a residential area*

g. ________________ favorit saya   *My favourite room*

h. Saya bersantai di ______________   *I relax in the terrace*

i. Saya belajar di kamar________saya   *I study in my bedroom*

j. ________________ empat kamar   *There are four rooms*

daerah	bekerja	pinggiran	pusat	teras
rumah	tidur	mewah	kamar	ada

4. Broken words

a. Saya suka ber________________   *I like to relax*

b. Saya tinggal di peg____________   *I live in the mountains*

c. Pusat k____________   *The city centre*

d. Saya tidak p________ m_______...   *I never shower…*

e. … di t_____________   *…in the garden*

f. Kamar f_____s______ adalah...   *My favourite room is…*

g. k_______ _______ saya   *my bedroom*

5. Anagrams

a. adurp   _____________

b. danim   _____________

c. mrauh   _____________

d. maark   _____________

e. kamra dtiru   _____________

f. arugn matu   _____________

g. patearenm   _____________

h. karam ndmai   _____________

i. runga arkegalu _____________

j. etasr   _____________

6. Bad translation: spot and fix the translation errors

a. Saya tinggal di rumah di pantai *I live in a flat on the coast*

b. Kamar favorit saya adalah dapur
My favourite room is the dining room

c. Saya suka bersantai di kamar tidur saya
I like to work out in my bedroom

d. Saya tinggal di apartemen di daerah permukiman
I live in a house in a residential area

e. Saya suka rumah saya karena besar dan mewah
I don't like my house because it is big and ugly

f. Saya belajar di ruang keluarga *I study in the dining room*

g. Di rumah saya ada empat kamar
In my house there are fourteen rooms

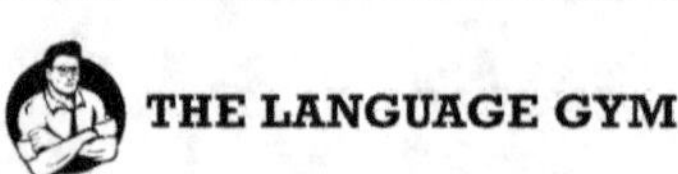

Unit 17. Describing my house: READING

Nama saya Ketut. Saya dari Bali. Saya tinggal di rumah besar yang indah di pantai. Di rumah saya ada sepuluh kamar dan kamar favorit saya adalah dapur. Saya suka memasak di dapur bersama ibu saya. Saya selalu bangun, mandi di kamar mandi, dan kemudian berpakaian di kamar tidur saya. Teman saya Putu tinggal di rumah kecil di pegunungan. Putu sangat lucu dan rajin. Dia tidak suka rumahnya karena terlalu kecil.

Nama saya Mahmud. Saya orang Indonesia dan saya tinggal di rumah yang sangat tua tetapi sangat bagus di pedesaan. Saya suka rumah saya! Di rumah saya ada lima kamar tetapi kamar favorit saya adalah ruang keluarga. Sesudah pulang dari sekolah saya suka bersantai di ruang keluarga dan menonton televisi bersama kakak perempuan saya. Saya tidak suka kamar mandi karena kadang-kadang ada tikus di sana!

Nama saya Matius. Saya dari Papua. Saya selalu bangun pada jam lima pagi karena saya tinggal jauh dari sekolah, di pinggiran kota. Saya tinggal di rumah yang sangat tua dan sedikit jelek, tetapi saya menyukainya. Saya suka bersantai di kamar tidur saya. Kadang-kadang saya membaca buku dan mendengarkan musik di Spotify. Kamar tidur saya adalah kamar favorit saya.

Nama saya Ismail dan saya berasal dari Padang, di Sumatra. Rumah saya di pusat kota, dan saya tinggal di dekat pantai. Dengan keluarga saya, saya berbicara bahasa Minang dan bahasa Indonesia; Bahasa Minang adalah bahasa yang sangat tua dan indah.

Saya tinggal di rumah kecil, yang baru dan sangat bagus. Ada enam kamar dan saya juga punya taman yang besar. Kura-kura saya tinggal di taman. Namanya Bejo. Kamar favorit saya di rumah saya adalah ruang makan karena saya sangat suka makan.

Saya suka bersantai di kamar tidur saya. Saya selalu menonton kartun dan serial di Netflix. Saya juga suka bekerja di sini, misalnya kalau ada pekerjaan rumah.

1. Answer the following questions about Ketut

a. Where is he from?

b. What is his house like?

c. How many rooms are there in his house?

d. Which is his favourite room?

e. Where does he get dressed?

f. Where does Putu live?

g. Does he like his house? (Why?)

2. Find the Indonesian for the phrases below in Ismail's text

a. my house is in the city centre

b. I live near…

c. I speak Minang and Indonesian

d. I also have a big garden

e. I really like to eat

f. he lives in the garden

g. I like to relax

h. I like to work here

3. Find the Indonesian for the following phrases/sentences in Matius's text

a. I am from Papua

b. I always wake up at 5

c. I live far from school

d. I live in a very old house

e. …and a bit ugly

f. … but I like it

g. Sometimes I read books

4. Find Someone Who…

a. …lives far from school

b. …speaks two languages

c. …has a big house

d. …sometimes finds 'unwanted guests' in the bathroom

e. …has a big pet that lives outside the house

f. …listens to music on a streaming platform

g. …is a foodie (loves food)

h. …has a friend that doesn't like their own house

Unit 17. Describing my house: TRANSLATION

1. Gapped translation

a. Saya tinggal di pinggiran kota *I live on the* _____________

b. Rumah saya sangat besar tetapi agak jelek

My house is _____________ *big but quite* _____________________

c. Terletak di pegunungan *It is located in the* _____________

d. Saya tinggal di ____________ ____________

I live in the city centre

e. Di rumah saya _________ lima kamar tidur

In my house there are five bedrooms

f. Saya tidak begitu suka _____________ karena _______

I don't really like the kitchen because it's ugly

2. Translate to English

a. pantai

b. ruang keluarga

c. tinggal di

d. pusat

e. kota

f. kamar favorit saya

g. saya suka bersantai

h. kamar tidur saya

i. ruang tamu

3. Translate into English

a. Saya tinggal di apartemen yang kecil dan jelek

b. Rumah saya modern tetapi cukup sederhana

c. Apartemen saya sudah tua tetapi saya sangat menyukainya

d. Saya tinggal di rumah di pantai

e. Di rumah saya ada lima kamar

f. Kamar favorit saya adalah kamar tidur saya

4. Translate into Indonesian

a. Big: B_____________

b. Small: K_____________

c. Outskirts: P_____________

d. Coast: P_____________

e. Area: D_____________

f. Residential: P_____________

g. Ugly: J_____________

h. Room: R_____________

i. There are: A_____________

j. Old: T_____________

5. Translate into Indonesian

a. I live in a small house

b. In the city centre

c. In my house there are...

d. Seven rooms

e. My favourite room is...

f. The living room

g. I like to relax in my bedroom

h. And I like to work in the study

i. I live in a small and old flat

j. In a residential area

Grammar Time 14: Basic Prepositions Di + Ke + Dari

Saya *I* Dia *He/She* Teman saya *My friend* Mereka *They*	**mengerjakan PR** *do homework* **membaca** *read* **makan** *eat* **minum** *drink* **bekerja** *work* **bersantai** *relax* **mengobrol** *chat*	***sambil** *while* **sesudah** *after* **sebelum** *before*	**belajar** *study* **membaca** *reading* **menonton TV** *watching TV* **bermain komputer** *playing the computer* **mengobrol** *chat*	**di** *in*	**ruang keluarga** *the family room* **ruang makan** *the dining room* **kantor** *the office* **halaman rumah** *back/front yard* **perpustakaan** *library* **teras** *terrace*

Di *In*	**keluarga saya** *my family* **rumah saya** *my house* **apartemen saya** *my apartment* **kota saya** *my town* **desa saya** *my village* **daerah saya** *my area*	**ada** *there is/are*	**empat** *4* **enam** *6* **delapan** *8* **banyak** *many*	**orang** *people* **kamar** *rooms* **kamar tidur** *bedrooms* **kolam renang** *pools* **taman** *parks*

Saya *I* Dia *He/She* Sahabat saya *My close friend* Teman saya *My friend* Mereka *They* Orang tua saya *My parents*	**naik** *go by, travel by*	**bus** *bus* **kereta api** *train* **mobil** *car* **pesawat** *plane* **sepeda motor** *motor bike* **taksi** *taxi* **Gojek** *ride share*	**dari** *from*	**kota** *city* **rumah saya** *my house* **kota Sydney** *the city of Sydney* **pusat kota** *the city centre* **daerah pemukiman** *residential area* **desa** *village*	**ke** *to*	**pantai the** *beach* **pinggiran kota** *the city outskirts* **kota Jakarta** *the city of Jakarta* **kota Melbourne** *Melbourne* **kantor** *the office* **rumah teman saya** *my friend's house* **sekolah** *school* **toko** *shop*
	tinggal *live/s*		**di** *in*		**di** *in*	**kota Jakarta** *the city of Jakarta* **ibu kota** *the capital city*

berasal *originates*	**dari** *from*	**negera Jepang** *the country Japan* **kota Adelaide** *the city of Adelaide*	**tetapi sekarang** *but now*	**tinggal** *lives*	**di** *in*	**negera Australia** **kota Melbourne**

Author's note:

*** sambil** – while*: *one person is doing two actions at the same time, it can be placed at the beginning of the sentence or between the two actions.*

Grammar Time 14: Basic Prepositions Di + Ke + Dari: TRANSLATION

1. Match up

dari rumah saya	in the capital city
tinggal di	originates from
di ibu kota	from my house
berasal dari	from the Philippines
ke kantor	lives in
dari negera Filipina	to the office

3. Broken words

a. Bapak saya tin________ d__ kota Jakarta.

Ibu saya tin________ d___ negara Malaysia.

b. Kamu beras__ d________ m________?

c. Saya na___ bus k__ pu____ kota

d. Dia memb _______ d__ taman

e. Mere__ bersan______ d______ teras

f. D__ rum____ sa_____ ada emp_____

kamar tid____

g. Orang t_____ sa____ beras___ d_______

negara Singapura

5. Complete the translation

a. Orang tua ______tinggal ________ desa
   My parents live in the village

b. Saya _________ komputer ______ kamar

____
   I play on the computer in the bedroom

c. Saya _________ gojek ________ kantor
   I go by ride share to the office

d. Mereka _________ sesudah belajar ______
perpustakaan
   They relax after studying in the library

e. Mereka berasal _______mana?
   Where do they come from?

2. Complete with the correct preposition, 'di', 'ke' or 'dari'

a. ________ rumah saya ada empat kamar tidur

In my house there are four bedrooms

b. Dia berasal ________ mana? *Where does she come from?*

c. Mereka naik gojek_________ pusat kota

They took a ride share from the city centre

d. Saya tinggal ________ ibu kota

I live in the capital city

e. ________ kota saya ada banyak taman

In my town there are many parks

f. Saya naik mobil _________ rumah saya ______pantai

I went by car from my house to the beach

g. Teman saya belajar sambil menonton TV _______
ruang keluarga
My friend studies while watching TV in the family room

4. Translate into English

a. Di daerah saya ada banyak kolam renang

b. Dia berasal dari negara Jepang

c. Sahabat saya naik taksi ke pusat kota

d. Di keluarga saya ada empat orang

e. Dia makan sambil belajar di ruang keluarga

f. Saya naik bus dari kota ke pantai

6. Translate into Indonesian

a. My parents and I live in a small house

b. They chat while studying in the library

c. My close friend goes by train from the city centre to the beach

d. She relaxes while reading in the garden

e. I do my homework after watching TV in the study

f. He comes from Indonesia but now lives in Australia

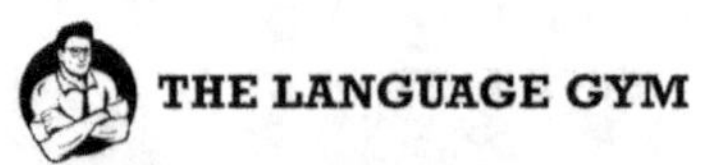

Grammar Time 15: Negative Indicators
Tidak, bukan, belum; jangan

Saya *I (formal)* **Aku** *I (informal)* **Anda** *you (form)* **Kamu** *you (inf)* **Dia** *s/he* **Mereka** *they* **Teman Anda** *your friend* **Bapak Anda** *your dad* **Kakak saya** *My older sibling* **Kakek saya** *My grandpa* **Sepupu saya** *My cousin* **Teman saya <u>Alia</u>** *My friend <u>Alia</u>* **Pak Anton** *Mr Anton* **Ibu Indah** *Ms Indah* **Orang yang** *People who*	**tidak *** *is not/ does not*	**makan nasi** *eat rice* **suka tempat ini** *like that place* **minum kopi panas** *drink hot coffee* **naik bus ke sekolah** *go to school by bus* **punya kucing** *have a cat* **lebih tinggi daripada dia** *taller than him/her*
	bukan* *is not*	**seorang dokter gigi** *a dentist* **seorang guru melainkan seorang pengacara** *a teacher but a lawyer* **orang Indonesia** *an Indonesian person* **guru Seni saya** *my Art teacher* **ibu Irfan** *Irfan's mother*
	belum* *not (yet)*	**bermain sepak takraw** *played takraw* **masak untuk sarapan** *cooked breakfast* **pernah ke negara Indonesia** *ever been to Indonesia* **menjadi insinyur** *become an engineer* **membaca buku itu** *read that book* **memanaskan motor** *warmed up the engine*

bermain sepak bola, *plays soccer* **guru Bahasa Inggris,** *is an English teacher* **seorang montir,** *is a mechanic* **tinggal di rumah itu,** *lives in that house*	**bukan? **** **ya?**

Jangan *****Don't/Not**	**berisik!** *be noisy* **berjalan di rumput!** *walk on the grass* **besok, bagaimana kalau minggu depan?** *tomorrow, how about next week* **ganggu konsentrasi saya!** *disturb my concentration* **makan makanan pedas!** *eat spicy food* **malas!** *be lazy* **marah!** *be angry* **pergi sendirian** *go alone*

Author's note:
* Use **Tidak** to negate verbs, adjectives or adverbs. **Apakah kamu <u>suka</u> buah durian? Tidak, saya <u>tidak</u> <u>suka</u> buah durian** *Do you <u>like</u> durian? No, I <u>don't like</u> durian.*
Bukan negates nouns or pronouns. **Ini <u>bukumu</u>? Bukan.** *Is this <u>your</u> <u>book</u>? No.*
Belum has the sense that it is possible that one day this could occur but hasn't yet.
Using **bukan and **ya** as question tags **Anda guru, bukan?** *You're a teacher aren't you?*
*****Jangan** literally means *do not* and is a request or a polite command.

Grammar Time 15 : Negative Indicators: TRANSLATION

1. Match up

belum	no (adjectives)
bukan	no (verbs)
tidak	do not
tidak	not yet
jangan	no (nouns)

2. Match up these question phrases/sentences.

Tidak makan malam	Don't like this place
Tidak suka tempat ini	Not my food
Bukan makanan saya	Didn't eat dinner
Bukan rumah saya	Has not read yet
Belum membaca	Hasn't warmed up the engine
Belum memanaskan motor	Don't disturb him
Jangan ganggu dia	Not my house

3. Complete with the missing word: BUKAN, TIDAK or BELUM

a. Saya ____________ bermain sepak takraw.

b. Kami ____________ minum kopi panas di kantin sekolah hari ini

c. Teman saya ____________ pernah ke Indonesia

d. Ibu dan bapak ____________ makan sarapan setiap hari

e. Bapak ____________ suka makan buah durian

f. Sepupu saya ____________ naik bus ke sekolah

g. Pak Anton ____________ guru Bahasa Indonesia saya

h. Apakah ini tas sekolahmu? __________

4. Complete with the correct option.

a. __________ makan di restoran mewah

b. Bapak _______ pernah makan nasi dengan sambal di warung Pak Ali

c. __________ marah!

d. Mereka __________ minum teh panas di kantin sekolah setiap hari

e. Anda semua_______ pergi ke kantor besok

f. Ibu dan bapak __________ makan sarapan

g. Bapak __________ memanaskan motor lagi

h. Saya __________ menjadi penyanyi terkenal

i. Ibu Indah __________ibu Irfan

j. ______________ganggu dia

Tidak	Bukan	Belum	Jangan

5. Draw a line between each word and translate the sentence into English

a. T e m a n k a m u s e o r a n g g u r u B a h a s a I n g g r i s b u k a n ?

b. K a k e k s a y a b e l u m p e r n a h k e i b u k o t a I n d o n e s i a

c. M e r e k a t i d a k s u k a t e m p a t i t i k a r e n a s a n g a b e r i s i k

d. B a p a k s a y a b u k a n s e o r a n g m o n t i r d i a s e o r a n g i n s i n y u r

e. M e r e k a b e r m a i n s e p a k b o l a d i s e k o l a h s e t i a p m i n g g u b u k a n ?

Saying what I do at home, how often, when and where

Grammar Time 16: Compound Prepositions

In this unit you will learn how to provide a more detailed account of your daily activities building on the vocabulary learnt in the previous unit.

You will learn how to say in Indonesian:
- Where things are located

You will revisit:
- Time markers
- Parts of the house
- Description of people and places
- Telling the time
- Nationalities
- ME- and BER- verbs

Unit 18
Saying what I do at home, how often, when and where

Bagaimana kebiasaan sehari-hari kamu? *Describe your daily routine.*		

Kira-kira jam …saya *At around … o'clock I*	**berangkat dari rumah** *leave the house*	
Pada jam … saya *At … o'clock I*	**bersantai** *relax*	**di dapur** *in the kitchen*
	bermain Playstation *play Playstation*	**di garasi** *in the garage*
Saya sering *I often*	**berpakaian** *get dressed*	**di ruang keluarga** *in the family room*
	berselancar di Internet *surf the Internet*	**di ruang kerja** *in the study*
Kadang-kadang saya *Sometimes I*	**makan sarapan** *eat breakfast*	**di ruang makan** *in the dining room*
	makan malam *eat dinner*	**di kamar mandi** *in the bathroom*
Kalau ada waktu saya *When I have time I*	**mandi** *shower/wash*	**di kamar tidur adik laki-laki saya** *in my brother's bedroom*
	membaca komik *read comics*	**di kamar tidur orang tua saya** *in my parents' bedroom*
	membaca majalah *read magazines*	**di kamar tidur saya** *in my bedroom*
Dua kali seminggu saya *Twice a week I*	**membereskan** *tidy up*	**di ruang mainan** *in the games room*
	mendengarkan musik *listen to music*	**di taman** *in the garden*
	mengerjakan pekerjaan rumah saya *do my homework*	**di teras** *on the terrace*
Saya tidak pernah *I have never*	**menggosok gigi** *brush my teeth*	**larut malam** *late at night*
	mengobrol dengan ibu *chat with my mum*	**pagi-pagi** *very early in the morning*
Biasanya saya *Usually I*	**mengobrol di Skype** *chat on Skype*	
	mengunggah foto ke Instagram *upload pics to Instagram*	
Saya selalu *I always*	**menonton film** *watch films*	
	mengunduh serial di Netflix *download a series on Netflix*	
Setiap hari saya *Every day I*	**menonton televisi** *watch television*	
	menonton video TikTok *watch TikTok videos*	
	menyiapkan makanan *prepare food*	
	naik sepeda *ride my bike*	

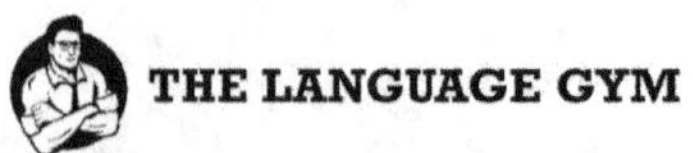

Unit 18. Saying what I do at home: VOCABULARY BUILDING (PART 1)

1. Match up

membaca komik	chat with
menonton film	brush teeth
menyiapkan makanan	watch movies
membaca majalah	prepare food
berpakaian	read magazines
mengobrol dengan	shower
menggosok gigi	get dressed
mandi	read comics

2. Complete with the missing words

a. Saya _______________ *I get dressed*

b. Saya ___________ komik *I read comics*

c. Saya membaca _______ *I read magazines*

d. Saya ___________ gigi *I brush my teeth*

e. Saya ___________ *I shower*

f. Saya_________ makanan *I prepare food*

g. Saya _____ di Internet *I surf the Internet*

h. Saya ___________ musik *I listen to music*

i. Saya_________ foto di Instagram
I upload photos onto Instagram

3. Translate into English

a. Biasanya saya mandi kira-kira pukul tujuh pagi

b. Saya tidak pernah menyiapkan makanan

c. Biasanya saya membaca majalah di teras

d. Kira-kira jam tujuh pagi saya makan sarapan di ruang makan

e. Kadang-kadang saya mengobrol dengan ibu di dapur

f. Kadang-kadang saya makan sarapan di dapur

g. Kadang-kadang saya bermain Playstation bersama adik di ruang mainan

h. Saya selalu berangkat dari rumah pada jam delapan pagi

4. Complete the words

a. M___________ *shower* g. B____________*get dressed*

b. M___________ *read* h. B____________ *play*

c. N___________ *chat* i. B____________ *leave*

d. M___________ *prepare* j. M____________ *do*

e. M___________ *upload* k. N____________ *ride*

f. M___________ *brush* l. M____________ *watch*

5. Classify the words/phrases below in the table below

a. **kira-kira jam enam** i. menggosok gigi
b. selalu j. kadang-kadang
c. tidak pernah k. setiap hari
d. kamar tidur l. mendengarkan musik
e. menonton televisi m. membaca komik
f. bermain Playstation n. naik sepeda
g. mandi o. dua kali seminggu
h. mengunggah di Instagram p. mengobrol di Skype

Time phrases	Rooms in the house	Things you do in the bathroom	Free-time activities
a.			

6. Fill in the table with what activities you do in which room

Bermain Playstation	di kamar tidur saya
Menonton televisi	
Mandi	
Mengerjakan PR	
Menggosok gigi	
Bersantai	
Menyiapkan makanan	

Unit 18. Saying what I do at home: VOCABULARY BUILDING (PART 2)

7. Complete the table

English	Indonesian
Get dressed	
Shower/wash	
	Mengerjakan PR
Upload photos	
	Berangkat dari rumah
	Mengobrol dengan kakak laki-laki saya
Relax	

8. Multiple choice quiz

	A	B	C
Tidak pernah	always	never	sometimes
Kadang-kadang	sometimes	always	never
Kamar tidur	bedroom	lounge	garden
Menggosok	shave	brush	go out
Mandi	shower	go out	rest
Bersantai	go out	watch	relax
Taman	garden	garage	kitchen
Dapur	bedroom	lounge	kitchen
Bermain	rest	play	prepare
Menonton	watch	read	play
Berangkat	go out	leave	read
Selalu	always	never	every day

9. Anagrams: unscramble & translate

(Example) kTaid nherPa – *Tidak pernah - never*

a. ruDpa

b. rBeatnkga

c. beMmcaa

d. elSual

e. enMggunahg tofo

f. idanM

10. Broken words

a. Da________________	*Kitchen*
b. Tidak p___________	*Never*
c. Kad______________	*Sometimes*
d. Se______________	*Always*
e. Ser______________	*Often*
f. K________________	*Comics*
g. K______t______ saya	*My bedroom*
h. Sa_____ b__________	*I leave*
i. Sa_____ m_________	*I chat*

11. Complete based on the translation

a. K__-k__ j___ s______ d_____, s__ m______ g____
At around seven thirty, I brush my teeth

b. K__-k___ p_____ d_____ l_____ seperempat, s__ makan
s______ *At around a quarter past eight I have breakfast*

c. K___- k______ s____ m________ m__________
Sometimes I prepare the food

d. S______ s______ m_________ t_______ sambil
m_____s_______ *I always watch TV while having breakfast*

e. B_________, s___ b____ d__ r_____ pada p___ setengah
s______ *Usually, I leave the house at eight thirty*

f. S____ j________m_________k______ *I rarely read comics*

g. K________-k_______ pada p______ l______ s_____
m__________ p______________ r________ s_______
At around five I do my homework

12. Gap-fill from memory

a. Kadang-kadang saya ________ komik

b. Saya selalu _________ gigi sesudah makan

c. Saya______ serial di Netflix setiap hari

d. Saya tidak pernah _________ majalah

e. Saya tidak pernah _________ PR saya

f. Saya sering ________ foto di Instagram

g. Pada akhir minggu saya______ sepeda

h. Saya pulang kira-kira ______ tujuh

i. Saya sering ___________ musik

Unit 18. Saying what I do at home: READING

Nama saya Fabián. Saya berasal dari Gibraltar. Saya punya anjing. Saya selalu bangun pagi-pagi, jam lima lewat seperempat. Kemudian saya pergi ke gym. Saya mandi ketika saya pulang. Kakak saya Joe sangat malas dan tidak aktif. Dia bangun jam tujuh. Joe tidak pernah bermain sepak bola, dan dia tidak pernah berolahraga. Karena itu dia gemuk. Pada sore hari, saya membaca komik di kamar saya atau mendengarkan musik. Ketika saya pulang, saya mengerjakan PR di ruang keluarga bersama ibu saya. Saya menyukainya karena dia sangat cerdas dan selalu membantu saya. Akhirnya, saya tidur pada jam sembilan, di kamar saya, tentu saja.

Nama saya Valentino. Saya orang Italia. Saya selalu bangun pagi-pagi, sekitar jam setengah enam. Kemudian saya mandi dan menggosok gigi di kamar mandi. Saya tidak makan sarapan tetapi adik perempuan saya Valeria makan sereal untuk sarapan di ruang makan bersama bapak. Saya berjalan kaki ke sekolah. Saya pulang kira-kira jam setengah empat dan kemudian saya bersantai. Biasanya saya menonton TV di ruang keluarga. Kemudian saya berselancar di Internet, menonton serial di Netflix, atau menonton video TikTok di kamar tidur saya. Sesudah itu saya makan malam. Ibu selalu menyiapkan makanan yang sehat untuk saya. Saya tidur larut malam, sekitar jam sepuluh.

Nama saya Evie dan saya tinggal di Prancis di desa kecil. Setiap hari saya bangun pada jam lima pagi. Kemudian saya mandi dan makan sarapan di teras kalau cuacanya cerah. Saya berangkat rumah pada pukul tujuh dan pergi ke sekolah naik kuda. Ketika saya pulang, kadang-kadang saya mengobrol di Skype dengan teman saya di kota London. Kemudian saya naik kuda saya di taman dengan dua anjing saya. Kadang-kadang saya menonton kartun dan mengunggah foto ke Instagram di kamar tidur adik laki-laki saya. Dia bernama Samuel dan dia mengunggah video TikTok tarian barunya. Saya sangat menyukai saudara saya karena dia sangat lucu dan aktif. Dia pandai menari! Saya selalu mengobrol dengannya dan juga kami suka bermain catur. Samuel adalah sahabat terbaik di dunia.

1. Answer the following questions about Fabián

a. Where is he from?

b. What animal does he have?

c. What does he do after he wakes up?

d. Why is Joe fat?

e. Where does he do his homework on weekdays?

f. Who helps him with his homework?

g. Where does he go to sleep?

2. Find the Indonesian for the phrases below in Evie's text

a. I wake up

b. then I shower

c. I go to school

d. by horse

e. I chat on Skype

f. upload photos to Instagram

g. his new dances

h. I always chat

3. Find the Indonesian for the following phrases in Valentino's text

a. I am Italian

b. I wake up early

c. I don't eat breakfast

d. Valeria eats cereal

e. In the dining room

f. In the family room

g. I watch TikTok videos

4. Find Someone Who

a. ...wakes up earliest

b. ...gets helps with their homework from a family member

c. ...likes to watch videos of people dancing

d. ...has nothing for breakfast

e. ...has a really lazy brother

f. ...always prepares healthy food

g. ...has a family member that is their best friend

h. ...goes to school in an unusual way

Unit 18. Saying what I do at home: WRITING

1. Split sentences and phrases

Saya mengobrol dengan	makanan
Saya bersantai di	pagi-pagi
Menyiapkan	ibu saya
Mengunggah foto	kamar tidur saya
Mengerjakan	gigi
Bangun	di Instagram
Bermain	komputer
Menggosok	pekerjaan rumah

2. Complete with the correct option

a. Saya bangun pada jam enam ____________

b. Saya bermain sepak bola di ____________

c. Saya menonton televisi di ____________

d. Saya mendengarkan musik di ____________

e. Saya menyiapkan ____________ dengan bapak

f. Saya menggosok ____________

g. Saya suka ________ kartun

h. Saya ________ ke sekolah naik kuda

ruang keluarga	menonton	gigi	pergi
kamar tidur	makanan	pagi	halaman

3. Spot and correct the grammar and spelling mistakes note: in some cases a word is missing

a. saya mandi kamar mandi

b. saya sarapan di dapar

c. di kamar tidor saya

d. bermain computer

e. berangkat rumah pada pukul delepan

f. mergerjakan pekerjaan rumah

g. menanton serial di Netflix

h. pergi sekolah naik kuda

i. kamar tidur adik laki saya

4. Complete the words

a. saya m_____ s_________ *I have breakfast*

b. d__________ *the kitchen*

c. k______ t______ saya *my bedroom*

d. g________ *the garage*

e. b________ dari r______ *leave the house*

f. di r_____ k_____ *in the family room*

g. di r_____ m_____ *in the dining room*

h. di k______ m______ *in the bathroom*

i. s_____ m___________ f_____ d___
k_____ t______ a____ l___-l_____ s____
I watch films in my younger brother's bedroom

5. Guided writing – write 3 short paragraphs in the first person (I) using the details below

Person	Wakes up	Showers	Has breakfast	Goes to school	Evening activity 1	Evening activity 2
Gunardi	6.15	In bathroom	Kitchen	With brother	Watch TV in family room	Prepare food in the kitchen
Mahmud	7.30	In bathroom	Dining room	With mother	Read book in bedroom	Talk to family on Skype
Sari	6.45	In bathroom	Living room	With Uncle	Listen to music in garden	Upload photos to instagram

Grammar Time 16: Compound Prepositions

Ada *There is* Tidak ada *There isn't*		buku dan majalah *books and magazines* HP *mobile phone* kotak pensil *pencil case* makanan dan minuman *food and drink* pakaian *clothes* piring dan mangkok *plates and bowls* tas sekolah *school bag*	di atas *on top of/ above* di bawah *under* di belakang *behind* di dalam *inside* di dekat *near* di depan *in front of* di luar *outside* di samping *next to* di sekitar *around*	segelas air putih *a glass of water* meja *table* meja makan *dining table* meja tulis *desk* jendela *window* kulkas *refrigerator* komputer *computer* kursi *chair* lemari *cupboard* lemari buku *bookcase* pintu *door* secangkir kopi *a cup of coffee* secangkir teh *a cup of tea* tas *bag* tas sekolah *school bag*		
Saya *I* Aku *I (inf)* Anda *You (form)* Kamu *You (inf)* Dia *S/he* Mereka *They* Teman saya *My friend* Bapak Anda *Your father* Kakak saya *My older sibling* Kakek saya *My grandpa* Sepupu saya *My cousin* Teman saya Alia *My friend Alia*	meletakkan *put (placed)* memasukkan *put (something into)* melihat *saw*					
			di antara *between*	lampu *light* buku *book* komputer *computer* jendela *window*	dan *and*	surat kabar *newspaper* pintu *door*

THE LANGUAGE GYM

Grammar Time 16. Compound Prepositions: TRANSLATION

Prepositions of Place

di atas	on top of, above
di bawah	under
di belakang	behind
di depan	in front of
di dekat	near
di dalam	inside
di samping	next to
di sekitar	around
di antara	between

1. Complete the table of prepositions

Indonesian	English
	inside
di dekat	
	in front of
di luar	
	around
di bawah	
	behind
di atas	
	between

2. Complete with the appropriate preposition

a. Pakaian ada ___________________ kursi

The clothes are on top of the chair

b. Saya naik sepeda _____________ taman

I ride my bike around the garden

c. Ada banyak majalah _____________ meja

There are many magazines under the table

d. Biasanya dia memarkir mobilnya _____________ rumah

Usually he parks the car in front of the house

e. Iva memasukkkan HP _____________ tasnya

Iva put her mobile phone inside her bag

f. Ada teras _______________ garasi

There is a terrace behind the garage

g. Saya sering bersantai _____________ kolam renang

I often relax next to the swimming pool

h. Kamar mandinya _____________ ruang makan

The bathroom is near the dining room

3. Match the phrases

a. di antara rumah	*behind the table*
b. di sekitar kota	*under the chair*
c. di atas tempat tidur	*in front of the computer*
d. di belakang meja	*next to the garage*
e. di depan komputer	*around the city*
f. di samping garasi	*between the houses*
g. di bawah kursi	*on top of the bed*

4. Translate into English

a. Ada seekor kucing hitam di belakang kursi

b. Ada banyak buku di dalam lemari buku itu

c. Dia meletakkan makanan di atas meja makan

d. Tidak ada komputer di dekat tempat tidurnya

5. Translate into Indonesian

a. There is a computer on the desk

b. He placed the books inside his schoolbag

c. The car is in front of the house

d. The swimming pool is between the house and the garage

UNIT 19
My holiday plans
(Talking about future plans for holidays)

Revision Quickie 6: Daily routine / House /Home Life / Holidays

Question Skills 4: Daily routine / House /Home Life / Holidays

In this unit you will learn how to talk about:

- What you intend to do on future holidays
- Where you are going to go
- Where you are going to stay
- Who you are going to travel with
- How it will be
- Means of transport

You will revisit:
- The verb 'pergi ke'
- Free-time activities
- Previously seen adjectives

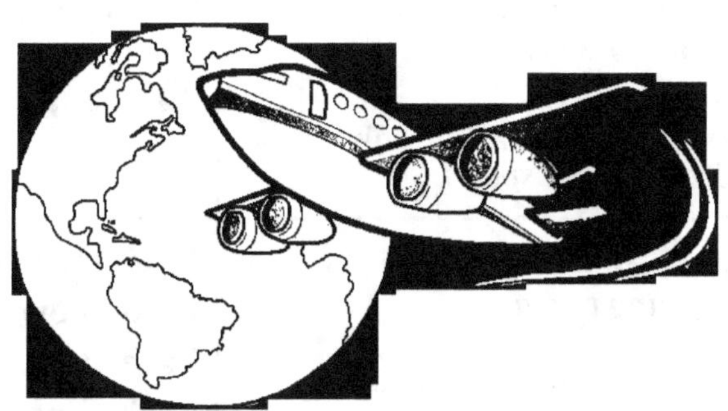

UNIT 19
My holiday plans

Kamu akan pergi ke mana pada liburan? *Where will you go during the holidays?*			
Musim panas ini….. *This summer….* **Pada liburan yang akan datang…** *In the coming holidays…*			
…saya akan pergi ke *I am going to go to* **…saya akan berlibur ke** *I am going to go on holiday to* **…kami akan berlibur ke** *we are going to go on holiday to*	**Bali** **Kalimantan** **Jakarta** **Singapura** **Sydney**	**naik bus** *by bus* **naik kapal laut** *by boat* **naik kereta api** *by train* **naik pesawat** *by plane* **naik mobil** *by car*	**Itu akan luar biasa** *It will be awesome*
Saya akan menghabiskan waktu *I will spend* **Kami akan menghabiskan waktu** *We will spend*	**seminggu** *one week* **dua minggu** *two weeks*	**di sana** *there* **bersama keluarga saya** *with my family*	**Itu akan membosankan!** *It will be boring*
Saya akan menginap di *I am going to stay in* **Kami akan menginap di** *We are going to stay in*	**hotel murah** *a cheap hotel* **hotel mewah** *a luxury hotel* **karavan** *a caravan* **perkemahan** *a campsite* **rumah keluarga saya** *my family's house*		**Itu akan membuat saya santai!** *It will be relaxing*
Saya akan *I am going* **Saya ingin** *I would like* **Saya tidak akan** *I will not* **Kami akan** *We are going* **Kami ingin** *We would like* **…untuk** *in order to*	**berbelanja** *to go shopping* **berdansa** *to dance* **berjemur** *to sunbathe* **bermain ukelele** *to play the ukulele* **berolahraga** *to play sport* **berpesta** *to go to a party* **bersantai** *to relax* **bersepeda** *to go biking* **bertamasya** *to go sightseeing* **bertemu dengan teman-teman** *to meet with friends* **makan dan tidur** *to eat and sleep* **makan makanan lezat** *to eat delicious food* **membeli oleh-oleh** *to buy souvenirs* **mengunjungi tempat wisata** *visit tourist places* **menyelam** *to go diving* **pergi ke pantai** *to go to the beach* **pergi ke pusat kota** *to go the city centre*		**Itu akan menarik sekali!** *It will be very interesting* **Itu akan menyenangkan!** *It will be fun*

Unit 19. My holiday plans: VOCABULARY BUILDING

1. Match up

saya akan pergi	I'm going to go
menghabiskan	a campsite
saya akan menginap	to spend
hotel murah	it will be awesome
perkemahan	I'm going to stay
saya ingin	to buy
berbelanja	a cheap hotel
luar biasa	I would like to

2. Complete with the missing word/s

a. Makan dan ______________ *To eat and sleep*

b. Saya akan ______________ *I am going to relax*

c. Saya __________ pergi ke… *I would like to go to…*

d. __________ dengan teman-teman *To meet with friends*

e. ____ ____ menginap di… *I am going to stay in…*

f. ____ ____ membosankan *It will be boring*

g. Kami akan ______ ______ *We are going to spend…*

h. Saya akan naik __________ *I'm going to travel by plane*

i. Saya akan ______ ____ dua minggu di sana bersama __________ saya

I am going to spend two weeks there with my family

3. Translate into English

a. Musim panas ini saya akan pergi ke Bali

b. Saya akan menghabiskan waktu tiga minggu

c. Saya akan pergi ke Sydney naik pesawat

d. Kami akan berbelanja

e. Saya ingin pergi ke pusat kota

f. Saya akan bertamasya dengan teman saya

g. Kita ingin makan dan tidur

h. Saya akan bersantai setiap hari

i. Saya akan berolahraga dengan adik saya

4. Broken words

a. Mak______ dan tid________ *To eat and sleep*

b. Kami akan bert__________ *We are going to sightsee*

c. Saya ak__ mengh________ *I am going to spend*

d. Saya i________ pergi ke… *I would like to go to…*

e. Pergi ke p______________ *To go to the beach*

f. Untuk ber______________ *In order to go biking*

g. Untuk ber______________ *In order to sunbathe*

h. Itu akan mem____ saya s____ *It will be relaxing*

5. 'Pergi', 'Bermain', 'Ber-' or 'Me-'?

a. ____________ beli

b. ____________ ke pusat kota

c. ____________ tamasya

d. ____________ sepak bola

e. ____________ (s)elam

f. ____________ ke pesta

g. ____________ sepeda

h. ____________ olahraga

i. ____________ catur

j. ____________ ke pantai

6. Bad translation – spot any translation errors and fix them

a. Musim panas ini kami akan…: *Last summer I will…*

b. Saya akan pergi ke Singapura bersama bapak saya : *I am going to go to Singapore with my mother*

c. Saya akan makan dan tidur: *I am going to drink and sleep*

d. Saya ingin bersantai banyak: *I would like to relax a bit*

e. Kami akan menginap di hotel: *I am going to stay in a hotel*

f. Saya akan menghabiskan waktu dua minggu di sana: *I am going to spend one week here*

g. Kami akan naik kereta api dan pesawat: *I am going to travel by train and boat*

h. Saya akan menginap di rumah keluarga saya: *We are going to stay in my family's house*

Unit 19. My holiday plans: READING (Part 1)

Nama saya Hugo. Saya dari Barcelona tetapi saya tinggal di Madrid. Musim panas ini saya akan berlibur ke selatan Spanyol, ke Cádiz. Saya akan naik mobil dengan pacar saya Alex. Kami akan menghabiskan waktu empat minggu di sana dan kami akan pergi ke pantai setiap hari. Kami juga akan makan makanan lezat. Saya tidak akan bertamasya karena sangat membosankan. Saya lebih suka berjemur di pantai.

Nama saya Deryk dan saya dari Kanada. Kami berempat di keluarga saya. Orang favorit saya adalah istri saya, Anna. Musim panas ini kami akan berlibur ke Inggris dan kemudian ke Quebec, Kanada. Saya akan bersantai dan membaca buku di Inggris dan kemudian bermain ski dan menghabiskan waktu dengan teman-teman saya di pegunungan Kanada. Anna akan naik sepeda dan makan makanan lezat, seperti poutine (mirip dengan kentang goreng dengan keju). Itu akan luar biasa!

Nama saya Dina. Saya orang Italia, dari Venesia. Musim panas ini saya akan berlibur ke Meksiko naik pesawat. Saya akan menghabiskan waktu dua minggu di sana, sendirian, dan saya akan tinggal di karavan di pantai. Saya akan mengunjungi monumen, museum dan galeri seni. Saya tidak suka olahraga, tetapi saya suka budaya. Itu akan menarik sekali.

Nama saya Diana. Saya dari Polandia tetapi saya tinggal di Cina. Musim panas ini saya akan berlibur ke Meksiko dengan teman saya Olivia. Saya akan naik kapal laut karena saya punya banyak waktu. Saya akan menghabiskan waktu lima minggu di sana dan saya akan menginap di hotel mewah. Saya suka menari, jadi saya akan menari setiap hari. Saya juga akan makan banyak dan tidur banyak. Saya tidak akan pergi ke museum karena sangat membosankan.

1. Find the Indonesian for the following in Hugo's text

a. I am from…

b. But I live in…

c. I am going to travel by…

d. With my girlfriend…

e. We are going to spend…

f. Every day…

g. I am not going to…

h. I prefer to sunbathe…

2. Find the Indonesian for the following in Diana's text

a. by boat…

b. I have a lot of time…

c. I am going to spend…

d. I like to dance…

e. so/therefore…

f. also…

g. it is very boring

3. Complete the following statements about Deryk

a. He is from _______________

b. His favourite person is _____________

c. They will travel to ____________ and ______________

d. Deryk is going to ______________ and _____________

e. Anna is going to ______________ and ______________

f. "Poutine" is made up of ___________ and ___________

4. List any 8 details about Dina in English

1.

2.

3.

4.

5.

6.

7.

8.

5. Find Someone Who…

a. …likes to travel by boat for long periods

b. …loves learning about culture

c. …prefers the beach to going sightseeing

d. …has opposite interests to Dina

e. …is going to travel by car

Unit 19. My holiday plans: READING (Part 2)

Nama saya Monty. Saya dari Ambon. Saya punya kura-kura di rumah. Kura-kura ini sangat lambat dan sangat gemuk tetapi saya menyukainya. Dia teman terbaik saya. Pada liburan saya akan pergi ke pulau Jawa bersama keluarga saya. Saya akan naik pesawat dan kemudian naik mobil. Kami akan menghabiskan waktu tiga minggu di Yogyakarta dan kami akan menginap di hotel mewah. Itu akan sangat menyenangkan! Kemudian kami akan naik mobil ke Magelang dan kami akan melihat monumen terkenal, Candi Borobudur (candi Budha dari zaman dahulu). Saya akan makan makanan lezat. Saya juga akan berbelanja setiap hari dan membeli pakaian baru.

Nama saya Fredy. Saya dari Banda Aceh, di pulau Sumatra. Musim panas ini saya akan berlibur ke kota Yogyakarta di selatan pulau Jawa, bersama saudara laki-laki saya Idris. Kami akan naik pesawat dan kami akan menghabiskan waktu dua minggu di sana. Di Solo kita akan mengunjungi tempat yang sangat istimewa dan terkenal keraton Surakarta. Itu akan sangat menarik dan menyenangkan. Juga, kami akan mendaki Gunung Bromo. Ini akan sulit tetapi sangat luar biasa. Saya ingin bersantai dan bermain musik. Saya suka menyanyi dan saudara saya Idris sangat suka bermain gitar. Grup favorit kami adalah Queen. Musik favorit saya musik rok.

Nama saya Serafina dan saya tinggal di Bandung, di selatan pulau Jawa. Pada liburan saya akan pergi ke Jakarta, di utara pulau Jawa. Saya akan naik mobil dan kemudian kereta api. Saya akan menghabiskan waktu dua minggu di sana dan saya akan menginap di hotel murah. Di Jakarta saya ingin mengunjungi monumen yang sangat terkenal, namanya Masjid Istiqlal. Masjid itu yang sangat besar dan indah, yang dibangun pada tahun 1978. Saya juga akan pergi ke pantai. Pantai Jakarta agak jelek jadi saya akan naik kapal ke kepulauan dekat Jakarta yang bernama Kepulauan Seribu. Pantai di sana sangat spektakuler! Saya punya teman yang bernama Alicia. Dia tinggal di kepulauan ini. Kami akan mengobrol di pantai dan menyelam bersama. Ini akan menyenangkan dan membuat saya santai.

1. Answer the following questions about Monty

a. Where is she from?

b. What animal does she have?

c. Who will she go on holiday with?

d. Where will they stay?

e. How will they get to Yogyakarta?

f. What is Borobodur?

g. What will she do every day?

2. Find the Indo in Serafina's text

a. In the holidays

b. And then

c. Which is called

d. A mosque

e. Built in

f. A bit ugly

g. The beach there

h. Dive together

3. Find the Indonesian for the following phrases/sentences in Fredy's text

a. My brother Idris

b. The Surakarta palace

c. It will be very interesting and fun

d. It will be tough

e. I would like to relax

f. To play the guitar

g. Our favourite group

h. Rock music

4. Find Someone Who...

a. ...is going to travel north

b. ...has a brother who is a musician

c. ...has a slow moving pet

d. ...is going to be hiking in the mountains

e. ...is going to visit a Muslim place of worship

f. ...is going to visit a famous palace

g. ...is going to visit the oldest historical site

h. ...is planning to relax on the beach

Unit 19. My holiday plans: TRANSLATION/WRITING

1. Gapped translation

a. Saya akan _______________   *I am going to go on holiday*

b. Saya akan naik ____________   *I am going to travel by car*

c. Kami akan _______________waktu satu minggu ___ _______
   We are going to spend one week there

d. ________ ________ menginap di hotel _______________
   I am going to stay in a cheap hotel

e. Kami ______ makan dan __________ setiap _______
   We are going to eat and sleep every day

f. Kalau cuaca ___________ saya akan pergi ke ___________
   When the weather is nice I am going to go to the beach

g. Saya akan _______________   *I am going to go shopping*

2. Translate to English

a. Makan

b. Membeli

c. Bersantai

d. Tempat wisata

e. Pergi ke pantai

f. Setiap hari

g. Naik pesawat

h. Menyelam

i. Pergi ke pusat kota

3. Spot and correct the grammar and spelling mistakes note: in several cases a word is missing

a. Saya akan olahraga

b. Saya akan waktu satu minggu di sana

c. Saya akan menginap mewah hotel

d. Kami akan meninap di hotel

e. Saya ingin bermain sepak

f. Kami pusat kota ke

g. Saya akan pergi pantai

h. Saya akan bermain teman

4. Categories: Positive or Negative?
Write P or N

a. Akan menyenangkan: __**P**__

b. Akan membosankan: ______

c. Akan baik: ______

d. Akan santai: ______

e. Akan menarik: ______

f. Akan sangat buruk: ______

g. Akan rajin: ______

h. Akan menjijikkan: ______

i. Akan mengagumkan: ______

j. Akan mengesankan: ______

5. Translate into Indonesian

a. I am going to relax

b. I am going to go diving

c. We are going to go to the beach

d. I am going to sunbathe

e. I would like to go sightseeing

f. I am going to stay in...

g. ...a cheap hotel

h. We are going to spend two weeks

i. I am going to go by plane

j. It will be fun

Revision Quickie 6: Daily Routine/House/Home life/Holidays

1. Match-up

Di sekitar	In the garden
Di ruang tamu	In the living room
Di dapur	In my bedroom
Di rumah saya	In my house
Di taman	In the guest room
Di kamar tidur saya	In the dining room
Di ruang makan	In the bathroom
Di kamar mandi	In the kitchen
Di ruang keluarga	Around

2. Complete with the missing letters

a. Saya ma_____	*I shower*
b. Saya ba_____	*I get up*
c. Saya men____ televisi	*I watch television*
d. Saya mem___ komik	*I read comics*
e. Saya ber_____ dari rumah	*I leave home*
f. Saya ti_______ di sekolah	*I arrive at school*
g. Saya na_____ bus	*I catch the bus*
h. Saya berp________	*I get dressed*
i Saya makan sar_______	*I eat breakfast*

3. Spot and correct any of the sentences below which do not make sense

a. Saya mandi di lemari es

b. Saya makan di kamar mandi

c. Saya menyiapkan makanan di kamar tidur saya

d. Saya mencuci rambut di kamar duduk

e. Saya pergi ke kamar tidur naik bus

f. Saya bermain tenis meja dengan anjing saya

g. Sofanya ada di dapur

h. Saya menonton TV di kompor

i. Saya tidur di lemari

j. Saya mengunduh tas dari Netflix

4. Split sentences

Saya menonton	naik bus
Saya mendengarkan	makan sereal
Saya membaca	televisi
Saya ke sekolah	kopi
Untuk sarapan saya	musik
Saya akan ke Jepang	komik
Saya minum	PR saya
Saya mengunggah	naik pesawat
Saya mengerjakan	foto ke Instagram
Saya mengemasi	kartu
Saya bekerja di	tas saya
Saya bermain	komputer

5. Match the opposites

Baik	Sakit
Ramah	Jahat
Mudah	Indah
Menyenangkan	Tidak ramah
Sehat	Sulit
Jelek	Membosankan
Mahal	Cepat
Lambat	Tinggi
Sering	Murah
Tidak pernah	Jarang
Rendah	Selalu

Revision Quickie 6. Daily Routine/House/Home life/Holidays

6. Complete with the missing words

a. Saya akan ke Jepang _______ pesawat

b. Saya akan berlibur ____ orang tua saya

c. Saya tidak pernah_______ sepak bola

d. Agus ____________ kriket

e. Saya menginap di _________ mewah

f. Saya ke taman dua _________ seminggu

g. Saya berselancar ___ Internet

h. Saya mengunggah foto ____ Instagram

7. Draw a line in between each word

a. Sayasangatsukabermainbolabasket

b. Sayamenontontvdanmendengarkanmusik

c. Padawaktuluangsayabermainvideogame

d. SayaakankeBandungnaikmobil

e. Sayaakanmenginapdihotelmewah

f. Setiappagisayaakanpergikepantai

g. SayaakanberbelanjapadahariSabtu

h. SayatidakpernahmengerjakanPRsaya

8. Spot the translation mistakes and correct them

a. Saya bangun pagi-pagi: *I go to sleep early*

b. Saya suka sekali bola basket: *I hate basketball*

c. Saya akan pergi ke kolam renang: *I am going to go to the beach*

d. Kami ingin berbelanja setiap hari: *We want to play sport every day*

e. Saya akan berenang: *I am going to run*

f. Saya akan naik mobil: *I am going to travel by plane*

g. Saya akan menginap di hotel mewah: *I am going to stay in a cheap hotel*

h. Saya akan menonton film: *I am going to watch a series*

9. Translate into English:

a. Saya naik pesawat

b. Saya akan pergi

c. Saya akan menginap

d. Saya mandi

e. Saya menonton film

f. Saya membersihkan kamar tidur

g. Saya makan sayuran

h. Saya makan telur untuk sarapan

i. Saya tidak akan membeli oleh-oleh

j. Saya bekerja di komputer

10. Translate into Indonesian

a. I shower then I eat breakfast

b. Tomorrow I am going to go to Japan

c. I tidy up my bedroom every day

d. I never play basketball

e. I wake up early

f. I eat a lot for breakfast

g. I am going to go to Jakarta by car

h. In my free time I play chess and read books

i. I spend many hours on the Internet

11. Translate into Indonesian

a. have dinner: M_ _ _ _ _ m _ _ _ _ _

b. to watch: M_ _ o _ _ _ _ _

c. to do: M_ l _ _ _ k _ _

d. to clean: M_ _ b_ _ s _ _ k _ _

e. to read: M_ _b_ _ _

f. to work: M_ _ _ e _ _ _ _ _ _ _

g. to relax: B_ _s _ _ _ _ _ _

h. to tidy up: M_ _ b_ _ e _k _ _ _

i. to travel by: N_ _ _ _

Question Skills 4: Daily routine/House/Home life/Holidays

1. Complete the questions with the correct option

a. Jam_______________kamu bangun?

b. Kamu ingin melakukan _____ pada waktu luang?

c. Sesudah tamat sekolah kamu mau menjadi ______?

d. ______ jam kamu menghabiskan waktu di komputer?

e. Kamu bermain Playstation dengan _______________ ?

f. _________________ kamu tidak berolahraga?

g. Kamu akan pergi_____________ pada Jumat malam?

h. Kamar_____________________ kamar favoritmu?

ke mana	apa	berapa	apa
mengapa	yang mana	berapa	siapa

2. Split questions

Kamu melakukan apa pada	kamu mau bermain sepak bola dengan kami?
Kamu makan apa	seminggu kamu pergi ke gym?
Apakah	kamu pulang?
Dengan siapa	berlari santai?
Jam berapa	untuk sarapan?
Berapa kali	kamu bermain catur?
Di mana kamu	waktu luang?
Bagaimana	orang tua di rumah?
Apakah dia membantu	rumahmu?

3. Match each statement below to one of the questions included in activity 1 above

a. Dua atau tiga jam

b. Saya menghabiskan waktu luang bermain di komputer

c. Dengan adik saya

d. Sekitar pukul enam pagi

e. Saya akan pergi de pesta dengan sahabat saya

f. Saya mau menjadi guru

g. Karena saya malas dan tidak ada cukup waktu

h. Kamar tidur, tentu saja

4. Translate into Indonesian

a. Who?

b. When?

c. Who with?

d. Why?

e. How many?

f. How much?

g. Which ones?

h. Where to?

i. Do you do...?

j. Can you...?

k. Where is...?

l. How many hours?

m. How many people?

5. Translate

a. Where is your room?

b. Where do you go after school?

c. What do you do in your free time?

d. Until what time do you study?

e. How long do you spend on the Internet?

f. What is your favourite sport?

g. Who does he help in the house?

VOCABULARY TESTS

On the following pages you will find one vocabulary test for every unit in the book. You could set them as class assessments or as homework at the end of a unit. Students could also use them to practice independently.

1a. Translate the following sentences (worth one point each) into Indonesian

What is your name?	
My name is Ketut	
How old are you?	
I am five years old	
I am seven years old	
I am nine years old	
I am ten years old	
I am eleven years old	
I am twelve years old	
I am thirteen years old	
Score	**/10**

1b. Translate the following sentences (worth two points each) into Indonesian

What is your brother called?	
What is your sister called?	
My brother is called Made	
My sister is fourteen years old	
My brother is fifteen years old	
I don't have any siblings	
My name is Jono and I am Indonesian	
I have a brother who is called Idris	
I live in the capital city of Indonesia	
I live in the capital city of the Philippines	
Score	**/20**

1a. Translate the following sentences/phrases (worth one point each) into Indonesian

My name is Sari	
I am eleven years old	
I am fifteen years old	
I am eighteen years old	
On the 3rd May	
On the 4th April	
On the 5th June	
On the 6th September	
On the 10th October	
On the 8th July	
Score	**/10**

1b. Translate the following sentences (worth two points each) into Indonesian

I am 17. My birthday is on 21st June	
My brother is called Amir. He is 19	
My sister is called Maya. She is 22	
My brother's birthday is on 23rd March	
My name is Idris. I am 15. My birthday is on 27th July	
My name is Dona. I am 18. My birthday is on 30th June	
When is your birthday?	
Is your birthday in October or November?	
My brother is called Wayan. His birthday is on 31st January	
Is your birthday in May or June?	
Score	**/20**

1a. Translate the following sentences/phrases (worth one point each) into Indonesian

Black hair	
Dark brown (black) eyes	
Blond hair	
Blue eyes	
My name is Gede	
I am 12 years old	
I have long hair	
I have short hair	
I have green eyes	
I have brown eyes	
Score	**/10**

1b. Translate the following sentences (worth two points each) into Indonesian

I have grey hair and grey eyes	
I have red straight hair	
I have curly white hair	
I have brown hair and brown eyes	
I wear glasses and have short hair	
I don't wear glasses and I have a beard	
My brother has blond hair and has a moustache	
My brother is 22 years old and has a short hair	
Do you wear glasses?	
My sister has blue eyes and wavy black hair	
Score	**/20**

1a. Translate the following phrases (worth one point each) into Indonesian

My name is	
I am from	
I live in	
In a house	
In a modern building	
In an old building	
On the outskirts	
In the city centre	
On the coast	
In Jakarta	
Score	**/10**

1b. Translate the following sentences (worth two points each) into Indonesian

My brother is called Ketut	
My sister is called Aminah	
I live in an old building	
I live in a modern building	
I live in a luxurious house on the coast	
I live in an ugly house in the city centre	
I am from Medan but live in the city centre of Jakarta	
I am 15 years old and I am Indonesian	
I am Japanese, from Tokyo but I live in Kuala Lumpur, in Malaysia	
I live in a small flat in the countryside	
Score	**/20**

1a. Translate the following phrases (worth one point each) into Indonesian

My younger brother	
My older brother	
My older sister	
My younger sister	
My father	
My mother	
My uncle	
My auntie	
My male cousin	
My female cousin	
Score	**/10**

1b. Translate the following sentences (worth two points each) into Indonesian

In my family there are four people	
My father, my mother and two brothers	
I don't get along with my older brother	
My older sister is 22	
My younger sister is 16	
My grandfather is 78	
My grandmother is 67	
My uncle is 54	
My auntie is 44	
My female cousin is 17	
Score	**/20**

1a. Translate the following words (worth one point each) into Indonesian

Tall	
Short	
Ugly	
Handsome	
Generous	
Boring	
Intelligent	
Lazy	
Good	
Pretty	
Score	**/10**

1b. Translate the following sentences (worth two points each) into Indonesian

My mother is strict and boring	
My father is stubborn and unfriendly	
My older sister is intelligent and hard-working	
My younger sister is sporty	
In my family there are five people	
I get along with my older sister because she is nice	
I don't get along with my younger sister because she is annoying	
I love my grandparents because they are funny and generous	
What are your parents like?	
My uncle and auntie are fifty years old and I don't get along with them	
Score	**/20**

1a. Translate the following words (worth one point each) into Indonesian

A horse	
A rabbit	
A dog	
A turtle	
A bird	
A parrot	
A duck	
A guinea pig	
A cat	
A mouse	
Score	**/10**

1b. Translate the following sentences (worth three points each) into Indonesian

I have a white horse	
I have a green turtle	
At home we have two fish	
My sister has a spider	
I don't have pets	
My friend Lukas has a blue bird	
My cat is very fat	
I have a snake that is called Adam	
My duck is funny and noisy	
How many pets do you have at home?	
Score	**/30**

1a. Translate the following sentences (worth one point each) into Indonesian

He is a cook	
He is a journalist	
She is a waitress	
She is a nurse	
He is a househusband	
She is a doctor	
He is a teacher	
She is a businesswoman	
He is a hairdresser	
She is a farmer	
Score	**/10**

1b. Translate the following sentences (worth three points each) into Indonesian

My uncle is a cook	
My mother is a nurse	
My grandparents don't work	
My sister works as a teacher	
My auntie is an actress	
My cousin is a student	
My father is a lawyer	
He doesn't like his job because it is hard	
He likes his job because it is rewarding	
He hates his job because it is stressful	
Score	**/30**

THE LANGUAGE GYM

1a. Translate the following sentences (worth two points each) into Indonesian

He is taller than me	
He is more generous than her	
She is less fat than him	
He is slimmer than her	
She is better looking than him	
She is more talkative than me	
I am more funny than him	
My dog is less noisy	
My rabbit is more fun	
She is as talkative as me	
Score	/20

1b. Translate the following sentences (worth 3 points each) into Indonesian

My brother is stronger than me	
My mother is shorter than my father	
My uncle is more handsome than my father	
My older sister is more talkative than my younger sister	
My sister and I are taller than my cousins	
My grandfather is less strict than my grandmother	
My friend Pia is more friendly than my friend Fenti	
My duck is more noisy than my rabbit	
My cat is fatter than my dog	
My mouse is faster than my turtle	
Score	/30

1a. Translate the following sentences (worth one point each) into Indonesian

I have a pen	
I have a ruler	
I have an eraser	
In my bag	
In my pencil case	
My friend Amir	
Ismail has	
I don't have	
A purple exercise book	
A yellow pencil sharpener	
Score	**/10**

1b. Translate the following sentences (worth three points each) into Indonesian

In my schoolbag I have four books	
I have a yellow pencil case	
I have a red schoolbag	
I don't have a black felt tip pen	
There are two blue pens	
My friend Dian has a pencil sharpener	
Do you guys have an eraser?	
Do you have a red pen?	
Is there a ruler in your pencil case?	
What is there in your schoolbag?	
Score	**/30**

1a. Translate the following sentences (worth three points each) into Indonesian

I don't like milk	
I really like meat	
I don't really like fish	
I don't like chicken	
Fruit is healthy	
Meat curry is spicy	
I prefer vegetables	
Eggs are disgusting	
Fried rice is delicious	
Lollies are unhealthy	
Score	**/30**

1b. Translate the following sentences (worth five points each) into Indonesian

I love chicken satay because it is delicious	
I like bananas a lot because they are healthy	
I don't like red meat because it is unhealthy	
I don't like bread because it is unhealthy	
I really like fish with rice	
I like coffee a bit because it is bitter	
I like fruit because it is healthy and tasty	
I like meat curry with rice	
I like eggs because they are nutritious	
I prefer fried rice because it is tasty	
Score	**/50**

1a. Translate the following sentences/phrases (worth one point each) into Indonesian

For breakfast	
I have lunch	
I snack on	
I have dinner	
It tastes delicious	
It tastes bland	
It tastes disgusting	
It tastes refreshing	
Healthy	
It tastes sweet	
Score	**/10**

1b. Translate the following sentences (worth three points each) into Indonesian

I eat eggs and drink coffee for breakfast	
I have seafood for lunch	
I never have dinner	
For snack I have two bananas	
Usually for breakfast I eat fruit	
I really like meat because it is tasty	
Sometimes I eat cheese	
For dinner I eat roast chicken	
I eat meat and fish because it is nutritious	
For sweets I drink fruit juice	
Score	**/30**

1a. Translate the following phrases (worth two points each) into Indonesian

Red skirt	
Blue suit	
Green scarf	
Black trousers	
White shirt	
Brown hat	
Yellow T-shirt	
Blue jeans	
Purple tie	
Grey shoes	
Score	/20

1b. Translate the following sentences (worth three points each) into Indonesian

I often wear traditional clothing	
At home I wear a blue tracksuit	
At school we wear a green uniform	
At the beach I wear a red swimsuit	
My sister always wears jeans	
My brother never wears a watch	
My mother wears branded clothes	
I very rarely wear a suit	
My girlfriend wears an elegant dress	
My brother always wears sneakers	
Score	/30

1a. Translate the following sentences (worth two points each) into Indonesian

I do my homework	
I play soccer	
I go rock climbing	
I go cycling	
I do weightlifting	
I go to the swimming pool	
I play sport	
I listen to music	
I play tennis	
I go to the beach	
Score	**/20**

1b. Translate the following sentences (worth five points each) into Indonesian

I never play basketball because it is boring	
I play PlayStation with my friends	
My father and I sometimes go fishing	
My brother and I go to the gym every day	
I do weights and go swimming every day	
When the weather is nice, we go hiking	
When the weather is bad, I play chess	
My father goes swimming at the weekend	
My younger brother goes to the bike park	
In my free time, I go rock climbing or to my friend's house	
Score	**/50**

1a. Translate the following sentences (worth two points each) into Indonesian

When the weather is nice	
When the weather is bad	
When the sky is clear/sunny	
When it is cold	
When it is hot	
I go skiing	
I play with my friends	
I go to the mall	
I go to the gym	
I go cycling	
Score	/20

1b. Translate the following sentences (worth four points each) into Indonesian

When the weather is nice, I go jogging	
When it rains, we go to the gym and do weights	
At the weekend, I do my homework and a bit of sport	
When it is hot, she goes to the beach or goes cycling	
When I have time, I go jogging with my father	
When there are thunderstorms, we stay at home and play cards	
When the sky is clear/sunny, they go to the park	
On Fridays and Saturdays, I go to parties with my girlfriend	
We never play sport. We play on the computer or on PlayStation	
When it snows, we go to the mountains and ski	
Score	/40

1a. Translate the following sentences/phrases (worth one point each) into Indonesian

I get up	
I have breakfast	
I eat	
I drink	
I go to bed	
Around six o' clock	
I relax	
At midday	
At midnight	
I do my homework	
Score	/10

1b. Translate the following sentences (worth three points each) into Indonesian

Around 7.00 in the morning I have breakfast	
I shower then I get dressed	
I eat then I brush my teeth	
Around 8 o'clock in the evening I have dinner	
I go to school by bus	
I watch television in my room	
I go back home at 4.30	
From 6 o'clock I play on the computer	
After that, around 11.30, I go to bed	
My daily routine is very simple	
Score	/30

1a. Translate the following phrases (worth one point each) into Indonesian

I live	
In a new house	
In an old house	
In a small house	
In a big house	
On the coast	
In the mountains	
In an ugly flat	
On the outskirts of town	
In the centre of town	
Score	**/10**

1b. Translate the following sentences (worth three points each) into Indonesian

In my house there are four bedrooms	
My favourite room is the kitchen	
I like relaxing in the living room	
In my apartment there are seven rooms	
My parents live in a big house	
My uncle lives in a small house	
We live on the coast	
My friend Sari lives in the countryside	
My cousins live in Singapore	
My parents and I live in a simple house	
Score	**/30**

1a. Translate the following sentences (worth one point each) into Indonesian

I chat with my mother	
I play on the PlayStation	
I read magazines	
I read comics	
I watch films	
I listen to music	
I rest	
I do my homework	
I go on a bike ride	
I leave the house	
Score	**/10**

1b. Translate the following sentences (worth three points each) into Indonesian

I never tidy up my room	
I rarely help my parents	
I brush my teeth three times every day	
I upload many photos onto Instagram	
Every day I watch a serial on Netflix	
I eat breakfast at around 7.30	
After school I relax in the garden	
When I have time, I play with my brother	
I usually leave home at 8 o'clock	
Sometimes I watch a movie	
Score	**/30**

1a. Translate the following sentences/phrases (worth two points each) into Indonesian

I am going to go to	
I am going to stay in	
I am going to play	
I am going to eat	
I would like to	
I am going to relax	
I am going to go sightseeing	
I am going to go to the beach	
I am going to play sport	
I am going to dance	
Score	**/20**

1b. Translate the following sentences (worth five points each) into Indonesian

We are going to buy souvenirs and clothes	
I am going to stay in a cheap hotel near the beach	
We are going to stay there for three weeks	
I am going to spend two weeks there with my family	
We are going to go on holiday to Bali tomorrow	
We will spend two weeks in Indonesia and we will travel by plane	
I would like to play sport, go to the beach and dance	
We are going to spend 3 weeks in Queensland and stay in a campsite	
We are going to go stay in a luxury hotel at the beach	
We are going to go sightseeing and shopping every day	
Score	**/50**

The End

We hope you have enjoyed using this workbook and found it useful!

As many of you will appreciate, the penguin is a fantastic animal. At Language Gym, we hold it as a symbol of resilience, bravery and good humour; able to thrive in the harshest possible environments, and with, arguably the best gait in the animal kingdom (black panther or penguin, you choose).

There are several hidden penguins (pictures) in this book, did you spot them all?

www.ingramcontent.com/pod-product-compliance
Lightning Source LLC
LaVergne TN
LVHW060405200726
843506LV00007B/368